HOW THE
EARTH
WORKS

Pushing up a fold in layers of "rock"

Making an orrery to show the motion of
the Earth, Sun, and Moon

Seeing how "magma" rises underground

How continents are moved apart
by pushing up new "ocean crust"

Making the sound of rain

HOW THE EARTH WORKS

John Farndon

Photography by

Michael Dunning

Demonstrating the Earth's magnetic field

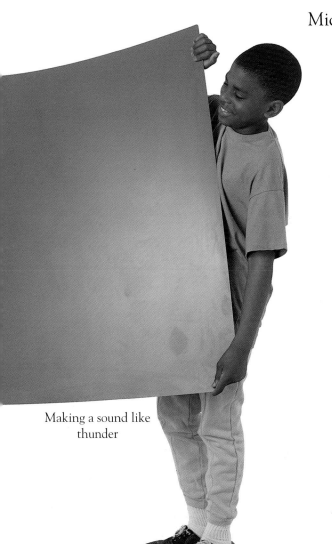
Making a sound like thunder

Creating patterned "cross-beds" with mud and sand

Dorling Kindersley
London • New York • Stuttgart

A DORLING KINDERSLEY BOOK

Senior Art Editor	Geoffrey Manders
Project Editor	Jonathan Metcalf
Designer	Alison Donovan
Editor	Susannah Steel
DTP Designer	Joanna Figg-Latham
Production	Vivienne Frow
Managing Editor	Josephine Buchanan
Deputy Art Director	Nick Harris

Special Contributor   David Burnie

This Eyewitness ®/™ Science Guide
first published in Great Britain in 1992
by Dorling Kindersley Limited,
9 Henrietta Street, London WC2E 8PS

Copyright © 1992 Dorling Kindersley Limited,
London

A CIP catalogue record for this book is available
from the British Library

ISBN 0 86318 831 1

Reproduced by Colourscan, Singapore and printed
by Tien Wah Press, Singapore

Contents

Introduction _____ 6
The home laboratory _____ 8

Planet Earth

What is the Earth? _____ 12
The Earth in space _____ 14
The spinning Earth _____ 16
Sun and Earth _____ 18
Our Moon _____ 20
The shape of the Earth _____ 22
Flat Earth? _____ 24
The globe _____ 26
Making the world flat _____ 28
How big is the Earth? _____ 30

The Earth's structure

Solid Earth? _____ 34
Inside the Earth _____ 36
Magnet Earth _____ 38
Moving mantle _____ 40
Tectonic plates _____ 42
Drifting continents _____ 44
Spreading oceans _____ 46
Moving plates _____ 48
Inside a continent _____ 50

The violent Earth

Volcanic activity _____ 54
Volcanic eruptions _____ 56
Molten rocks and fiery gases _____ 58

Volcanic intrusions —————— 60
Earthquakes —————————— 62
Mountain building —————— 64
Fold mountains ——————— 66
Folded landscapes ————— 68
Faults in the Earth ————— 70

Rocks and soil

Rocks ————————————— 74
Rocks and minerals 1 ——— 76
Rocks and minerals 2 ——— 78
Fiery rocks ——————————— 80
Rocks remade ————————— 82
Rocks from water ————— 84
Beds and joints ————— 86
Fossils ———————————— 88
Precious rocks ————— 90
The geological clock ——— 92
The geological map ——— 94
Soil ——————————— 96
What is soil? ——————— 98
Types of soil ————— 100

The changing landscape

Shaping the land ———— 104
Weathering —————————— 106
Shifting slopes ————— 108
Mass movement ————— 110
Changing slopes ———— 112
The evolving landscape —— 114
Rivers and streams —— 116
Water on the land ——— 118
Water underground ——— 120
Running water —————— 122
A river's burden ———— 124

Flowing streams ————— 126
Meandering ——————— 128
Ice and wind ———— 130
Erosion by ice —————— 132
Dropped by ice ———— 134
Wind in the desert ——— 136

The oceans

The open sea ————— 140
Oceans on the move ——— 142
Wave power ——————— 144
Shifting shores ———— 146

The atmosphere

Layers of the atmosphere —— 150
Up in the air ——————— 152
Heat from the Sun ———— 154
Air pressure ——————— 156
Wind and pressure ——— 158
Humidity ———————— 160
Clouds ——————————— 162
Sky colours —————— 164
Weather patterns —— 166
Wind ——————————— 168
Rain ——————————— 170
Global weather ———— 172
Fronts and lows ———— 174
Thunder and lightning —— 176
Hurricanes and whirlwinds —— 178
Weather forecasting —— 180

Glossary ——————————— 182
Index ——————————— 188
Acknowledgments ———— 192

INTRODUCTION

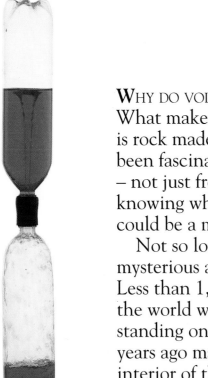

WHY DO VOLCANOES ERUPT?
What makes the wind blow? How
is rock made? People have always
been fascinated by questions like these
– not just from idle curiosity, but because
knowing when to expect an earthquake or a hurricane
could be a matter of life and death.

Not so long ago much of the world seemed as dark and
mysterious as the outer limits of space are to us today.
Less than 1,500 years ago some scholars believed
the world was supported by four elephants
standing on a giant turtle. Less than 300
years ago many scientists thought the
interior of the Earth was full of
water; others insisted that volcanoes
were just large coal fires.

Since then we have learned much
more about the Earth and how it
works. One important recent discovery
is that the Earth's surface is made from a
series of moving plates. This explains
how mountains are made, why some places
have earthquakes and others volcanoes,
and much more besides. Some
discoveries have been made only
by probing into barely accessible
places, such as the ocean deeps,
or by using sophisticated
equipment, such as lasers. But
many have come just from
simple experiments and careful

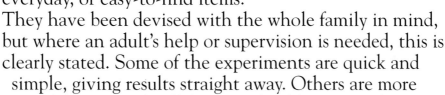

observation. The aim of this book is to help you find out about the world in the same way.

All the experiments featured here can be performed in and around the home with simple, everyday, or easy-to-find items. They have been devised with the whole family in mind, but where an adult's help or supervision is needed, this is clearly stated. Some of the experiments are quick and simple, giving results straight away. Others are more elaborate and call for considerable time and effort.

To get the best from a model stream, for example, you need to leave it running for several days, returning every now and then to check progress. If you can, get outside and see how your experiments and projects compare with the real thing. Once you know how ice shatters rocks, or why some clouds bring rain, you may begin to look at them in a different way and make your own discoveries.

There is one more thing you need to know about this book. Try flicking the tops of the pages from back to front. If you look at the little globe in the top corner of every left-hand page, you will see it spinning round, just as our Earth does.

The home laboratory

NEARLY ALL THE EXPERIMENTS in this book can be performed with simple, everyday materials, tools, and utensils. Most of the things you need can be found in and around the home, especially in the kitchen, or they can be acquired very easily from other sources. On these two pages, we show some of the items you may find useful in building your own earth sciences laboratory.

Plastic spoon *Plastic knife* *Stirrers*

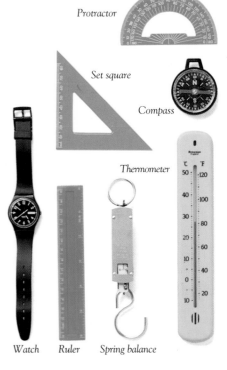

Protractor

Set square

Compass

Thermometer

Watch *Ruler* *Spring balance*

■ Mixers, measures, and fasteners

Here are some items you might find useful for mixing, fastening, and measuring. Your watch should show seconds, and the thermometer should indicate temperatures from −10°C (14°F) to 40°C (104°F).

Screws *String* *Wire*

Nails *Wood glue* *Paperclips* *All-purpose glue*

Measuring jug

■ Materials

For some of the experiments and projects, you need to buy basic materials, such as plywood, balsa wood, plasticine, card, food colouring, and so on. Sand and gravel you can find on the beach, or you may be able to buy small quantities from a builder's merchant or garden store.

Plasticine

Modelling clay

Plastic putty

Sand *Gravel* *Soil*

Coloured card

Food colouring

Plywood *Balsa wood*

Chisel

Drill bit

Tenon saw

Hacksaw

Pliers

Fretsaw

Screwdrivers

Hand-drill   Scissors   Hammer

▦ Tools

You will need scissors, a good craft knife, and pens, pencils, and paints for many experiments. For projects involving construction, ordinary tools such as a small hammer, tenon saw, hand-drill and bit, etc., are quite adequate. You should ask an adult to help with any project that involves the use of sharp tools or instruments.

Plastic tubing

Pencil   Craft knife   Pen   Marker pen   Torch

Adhesive tape

Protective goggles

Paintbrush

Paints

Nightlight candle

Plastic soft drinks bottle

▦ Useful items

All kinds of items from the kitchen – even old plastic bottles and food jars – may be used for experiments. But do not use them for food storage afterwards.

Large heatproof bowl

Saucepan

Sieve

Heatproof gloves

Small glass jar

Magnifying glass

PLANET EARTH

A sphere in space
There is no simpler or better way to study the world as a whole than with a globe. This one (above) dates from the 18th century. Yet the clearest view of Earth's round rim is now obtained from space (left).

PICTURES TAKEN FROM SPACE have finally shown with startling clarity what people had worked out long ago, yet never seen for themselves – that our Earth is just a tiny blue globe spinning around in the vast emptiness of space. Around us all is darkness, except for the fiery glow of a much larger globe, the Sun, and the pale light of distant stars.

WHAT IS THE EARTH?

OUR WORLD IS JUST A TINY BALL amongst countless billions scattered through the universe. Every day it spins around once on its axis. Every year it glides billions of kilometres around the Sun, along with the eight other planets that make up the solar system. Our nearest neighbour, Venus, is over 40 million km (25 million miles) away, our own Moon is 400,000 km (250,000 miles) away, and the nearest stars are so distant that light from them takes many years to reach us.

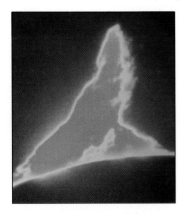

The enormous heat radiated by the Sun keeps our planet warm and gives us light.

We are so familiar with the idea of the Earth as a globe spinning in space that it is hard to imagine how people ever thought of it any other way. But if you had only your own eyes to go on, what would you think? The world certainly looks flat as far as you can see. It does not feel as if it is moving either – not like a moving train. All you see is that the Sun, Moon, and stars move. If you didn't know otherwise, you might believe you were at the centre of the universe, and that the Earth is flat and unmoving.

That was what many people thought until the end of the Middle Ages. Then, in the 1520s, two dramatic events in eight years shattered this cosy view forever. In 1522 Ferdinand Magellan's ship *Victoria* arrived back in Spain after sailing around the world – proving, once and for all, that the world is round. In 1530 Polish astronomer Nicolaus Copernicus (1473–1543) wrote his book *De revolutionibus orbium coelestium (On the revolutions of the heavenly spheres)*, in which he showed that the Earth is not fixed at the centre of the universe, but spins daily on its axis and journeys around the Sun every year with the other planets.

The Sun's path changes due to the Earth's tilt. It is highest in summer (top), lowest in winter (bottom).

Most people accepted the idea of the Earth being round. But the idea that it was just another planet was so shocking that the Catholic Church eventually banned Copernicus's book. It remained banned until 1830.

Copernicus showed that the Earth revolved around the Sun, not the Sun around the Earth.

■ Round world

Neither the idea of a round world nor Copernicus's view of the universe was entirely new. In fact, these ideas dated back to the days of Ancient Greece, more than 1,700 years before. Because early civilizations knew so little of the world, theories about its shape were not much more than myths. For all their brilliant astronomy, the Ancient Egyptians regarded the Earth as a flat square under a pyramid-shaped sky, while early Hindus believed that the world was a plate resting on the backs of four elephants standing on a giant

Sundial shadows move as the Earth spins around (p.18).

floating turtle. The Ancient Greeks, however, realized that even though they could see only a tiny fraction of the world, there were clues to its shape.

No-one knows who first suggested a round Earth, but it was in the school of Pythagoras (c.580–c.500 BC), in a Greek colony in Italy, that it became a firm belief. The Greeks could see how ships vanished over the horizon, and they heard from travellers how, as you went north, new stars rose in the sky to the north but dropped from sight in the south. What better explanation than that the Earth was round? The Pythagoreans developed the idea of a round Earth into a complete picture of the universe, with the Earth surrounded by transparent spheres, carrying around Sun, Moon, planets, and stars, all whirring in perfect harmony.

By the time of Aristotle (384–322 BC), Greek astronomers had an elaborate system of 55 spheres. They were sure the Earth was round. As Aristotle pointed out, the round shadow of the Earth on the Moon during eclipses (p.24) showed that. But they were convinced the Earth was at the centre of the universe. Why then, some asked, did the planets seem to travel slowly across the stars from west to east, while the star pattern as a whole moves through the sky from east to west? And wouldn't the spheres carrying the stars have to revolve at incredibly high speeds for the star pattern to be able to rotate once every day, as it does?

■ Central Sun

Greek astronomer Aristarchus of Samos had an answer. It is not the stars that spin every day but the Earth. The Earth also travels once a year in a huge circle around the Sun, which is why the star pattern changes through the year. The planets seem to move backwards simply because they are circling slightly slower than the Earth.

But there were few who agreed with Aristarchus, arguing that if the Earth orbited the Sun, you

The Sun drops below the horizon
in the west every day as the Earth
spins east, whipping us around out
of reach of the Sun's rays.

The problem with the spinning concentric spheres was that they did not quite fit observations, for the tracks of the Sun, the Moon, and the planets wobble a little. Astronomers such as Hipparchus (c.175–c.120 BC), at Alexandria in Egypt, suggested that the Sun, Moon, and planets rotate "eccentrically" (slightly off-centre). Ptolemy (AD c.90–c.170) introduced the idea of "epicycles" (circles within circles) to build a machine that seemed to fit perfectly the way the heavens moved – while still keeping the Earth at the centre. This system was widely accepted up until the time of Copernicus.

■ The Dark Ages

In the Dark Ages, many Greek ideas were forgotten in Europe. Some Christian scholars even insisted that the Earth was not round, scoffing at the idea that there were people on the other side of the world "standing on their heads", instead picturing the universe as a house roofed by heaven. In the sixth century AD, the Greek traveller Cosmas Indicopleustes saw the universe as a huge chest, with the heavens in the lid and the Earth on the bottom. *Mappa mundi* (world maps) of the Middle Ages

When astronauts
from the Apollo 8
spacecraft landed on
the Moon in 1968,
they saw the disc of
the Earth moving
through the sky, just
as we see the Moon
from the Earth.

showed the world as a flat disc in a circle of ocean.

Yet scholars in the Arabic world kept the ideas of the Greeks alive. As Europeans came into contact with Arabs from the thirteenth century onwards, and European merchants travelled further afield, the idea of a round world was gradually revived. The revival was further boosted by the rediscovery of Ptolemy's great book *Geography* in 1395, after 1,000 years of neglect.

■ Rediscovery

The great sea voyages of the 1400s expanded people's knowledge of the world enormously and, by the time Magellan's ship made its round-the-world voyage in 1522, few doubted the world was round.

A change in the Ptolemaic view of the universe, with the Earth at the centre, was much harder to accept. Yet, as Copernicus showed, all the motions of the Sun, the Moon, and the planets could be explained so much more simply if you placed the Sun at the centre. If the Earth spins around daily and orbits the Sun yearly, there was no need to look for complex epicycles and eccentrics. There was just the tiny Earth and the planets gliding through empty space around the Sun, with the stars far away in the distance.

Such a picture was too disturbing for most of Copernicus's contemporaries. Even today it can make the Earth seem a lonely and insignificant place.

The Earth takes a
year to orbit the Sun;
the Moon a month to
orbit the Earth.

Devices called "orreries" were
developed in the late seventeenth
century to help demonstrate how the
Earth moved around the Sun.
You can make this simple orrery
yourself (pp.14–15).

would see "parallax shifts" in the stars – that is, they should appear to shift relative to each other as the Earth moves past them. Aristarchus could only reply that the stars are so far away that any parallax shift is too small to see. In fact he was right, and with modern telescopes we *can* detect slight parallax shifts. But his ideas fell on deaf ears, and for many years the Greeks continued to place the Earth at the centre of the universe.

The Earth in space

As you sit safely reading this book, it is hard to imagine that the Earth is just a minute ball in the vastness of space. It is even harder to imagine that the Earth is also whirling you round like a top at over 800 kmh (500 mph), and hurtling through the dark at over 80,000 kmh (50,000 mph).

Our planet is just one of nine that make up the "solar system", the ring of planets forever circling around the Sun, and the Sun is just one of the 100 billion stars in our galaxy – a vast disc that light itself takes 80,000 years to cross. And our galaxy, the Milky Way, is just one of ten billion scattered through the universe.

EXPERIMENT
Making an orrery

Adult help is advised for this experiment

In the 1600s people at last became sure that the Earth is just a ball spinning around the Sun. Soon after, they began making devices called orreries to help demonstrate the movement of the Earth, the Moon, and the Sun.

You Will Need
● round tin ● thick card ● balsa pieces ● cotton reels ● dowel ● elastic band ● bead ● 2 washers ● ping-pong ball ● torch bulb & holder ● battery ● leads ● aluminium tube ● wire ● glue ● tape ● tools & instruments as shown

1 Tape a lead to each battery terminal. Slip the leads through an aluminium tube thin enough to slide into a cotton reel and 4½ reels long.

2 Drill a hole the size of the tube in a balsa block. Glue the block inside the tin, thread two reels on to the tube and slot the tube into the block.

3 Make a hole in a card disc cut to the size of the tin and slot it over the tube. Drill holes in each end of two balsa strips just longer than the tin's radius.

4 Fit one end of a balsa strip on to the tube; fix dowel into the other end. Slide a washer and reel on to both tube and dowel, then the second balsa strip.

5 Fix a ping-pong ball on to the table with a blob of plastic putty. Ask an adult to drill a hole the diameter of your wire in the ping-pong ball.

6 Bend 8 cm (3 in) of wire as shown in the diagram opposite, using a protractor for the exact angles. Drill a hole in the dowel and slot in the wire.

The Sun, the centre of our solar system

The Earth *The Moon*

8 STRETCH AN ELASTIC BAND over the reels and connect the leads to light the bulb. Push the handle gently round, so that the Earth moves around the Sun. Notice how, as the Earth turns, it always stays at the same angle.

7 FIT THE PING-PONG BALL over the wire. Twist a thinner wire around the thicker wire and attach a bead to the end. Connect the leads to the bulb holder and glue in place.

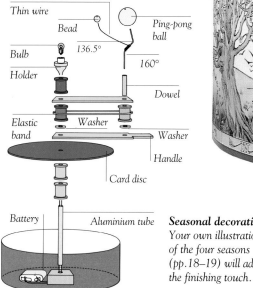

Thin wire
Bead
Ping-pong ball
136.5°
Bulb
160°
Holder
Dowel
Elastic band
Washer
Washer
Handle
Card disc
Battery
Aluminium tube

Seasonal decoration
Your own illustration of the four seasons (pp.18–19) will add the finishing touch.

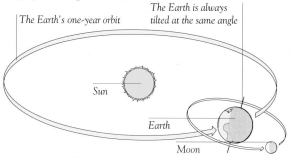

■ DISCOVERY ■
Nicolaus Copernicus

For thousands of years, most people believed that the Sun and all the planets revolved around the Earth, just as the Ancient Greek astronomer Ptolemy had suggested. Then in 1530 a Polish priest called Nicolaus Copernicus (1473–1543) showed that the Earth, along with the other planets, actually revolved around the Sun. Church leaders were outraged by his ideas, believing they would "overturn the whole art of astronomy", which they eventually did. However, it was another century before most people began to accept that Copernicus was right – and his book *De revolutionibus* stayed banned by the Church for 300 years!

■ Yearly journey

The Earth takes exactly a year to circle round the Sun – or, rather, it takes $365\frac{1}{4}$ days. This is why there are 365 days in a year. We make up the quarter by adding a day to February every fourth year, called a leap year. The Earth's orbit is not perfectly round but elliptical (oval), so the Earth is closer to the Sun at some times than others. It is closest, at 147,500,000 km (91,650,000 miles), on 3 January (the "perihelion"). It is furthest away, at 152,500,000 km (94,760,000 miles), on 4 July (the "aphelion").

The Earth's one-year orbit
The Earth is always tilted at the same angle

Sun

Earth

Moon

The spinning Earth

THE EARTH IS LIKE A VAST WHEEL with an axle (or axis) running from the North Pole to the South Pole. Once every 24 hours it spins right round on its axis, turning us towards the Sun and away again, thus giving us night and day. You are never aware of this movement because the speed is completely steady and because everything around moves with you, like everything inside a moving train. The Earth always spins the same way, turning eastwards all the time. If you could look down on the North Pole, you would see that it turns anti-clockwise. Because of this easterly rotation we see the Sun coming up in the east every day, and going down in the west.

Every place on Earth takes 24 hours to spin round, but different places spin at different speeds. Places near the poles barely move at all, while things at the equator have to whizz around at over 450 m (1500 ft) a second – almost 40,000 km (25,000 miles) every day.

Location lines
To pinpoint places better, globes are given lines of "latitude" running parallel from east to west, and lines of "longitude" radiating from the poles.

■ Night and day

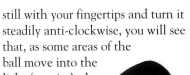

It is the Earth's rotation that gives us night and day – as you can show by shining a torch at a ball in a dark room. The torch represents the Sun and the ball the Earth. Notice that only half the ball is lit at any time – the other half is in shadow. If you hold the "poles" of the ball still with your fingertips and turn it steadily anti-clockwise, you will see that, as some areas of the ball move into the light (sunrise), the points on the far side of the ball move into the shadow (sunset).

Pendulum swings

A good way to show that the Earth spins is with a weight swinging on a very long wire. The direction of swing gradually seems to change. In fact, the swing stays the same but the Earth beneath is moving. This device is called Foucault's pendulum, after physicist Jean Foucault, who first demonstrated it in 1851.

YOU WILL NEED
● *large plastic soft drinks bottle* ● *sand* ● *hookeye* ● *ball of string* ● *card* ● *funnel or paper disc to fold into funnel* ● *plastic putty* ● *very short pencil* ● *hand-drill* ● *scissors*

1 ON A PIECE OF WOOD (or in a vice), drill a hole in the bottle cap, just smaller than the thread of the hookeye.

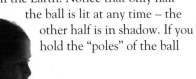

2 SCREW THE HOOKEYE firmly into the bottle cap with your fingers. Give it a tug to make sure it is perfectly secure.

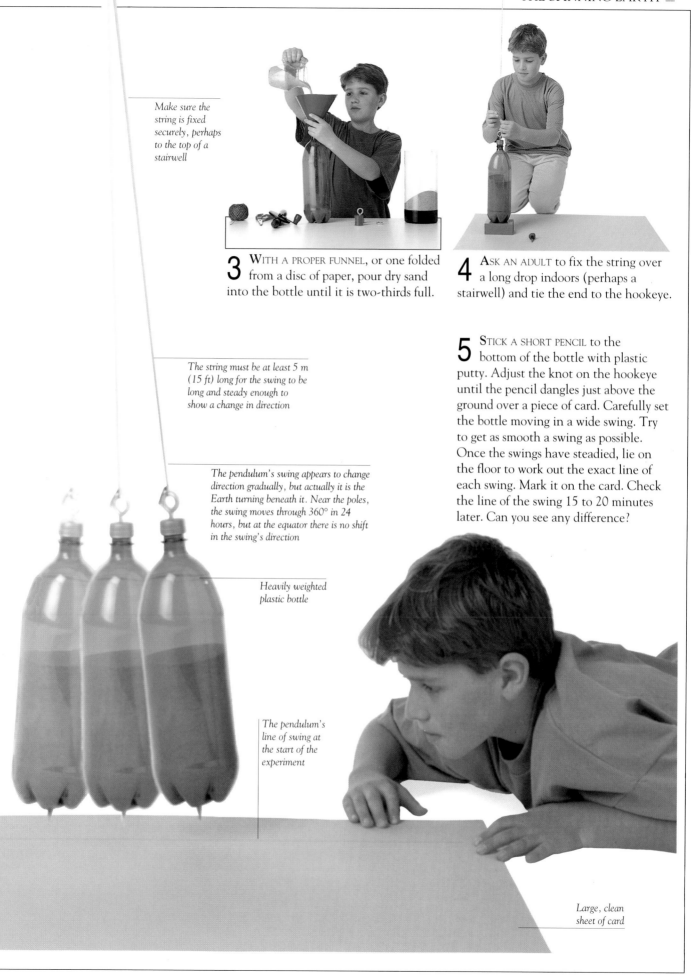

Make sure the string is fixed securely, perhaps to the top of a stairwell

3 WITH A PROPER FUNNEL, or one folded from a disc of paper, pour dry sand into the bottle until it is two-thirds full.

4 ASK AN ADULT to fix the string over a long drop indoors (perhaps a stairwell) and tie the end to the hookeye.

The string must be at least 5 m (15 ft) long for the swing to be long and steady enough to show a change in direction

5 STICK A SHORT PENCIL to the bottom of the bottle with plastic putty. Adjust the knot on the hookeye until the pencil dangles just above the ground over a piece of card. Carefully set the bottle moving in a wide swing. Try to get as smooth a swing as possible. Once the swings have steadied, lie on the floor to work out the exact line of each swing. Mark it on the card. Check the line of the swing 15 to 20 minutes later. Can you see any difference?

The pendulum's swing appears to change direction gradually, but actually it is the Earth turning beneath it. Near the poles, the swing moves through 360° in 24 hours, but at the equator there is no shift in the swing's direction

Heavily weighted plastic bottle

The pendulum's line of swing at the start of the experiment

Large, clean sheet of card

Sun and Earth

WHENEVER THE SUN SHINES BRIGHTLY you can see the strong shadows it casts. At noon, when the Sun is high in the sky, shadows are short. But as it sinks lower in the afternoon, shadows grow longer and longer. Shadows are long in the morning, too, when the Sun is equally low in the sky. In fact, the length of shadows is forever changing – not only during the course of each day but throughout the year, depending on the height of the Sun in the sky.

Of course, although the Sun appears to move through the sky, it is really the Earth and you that are moving around the Sun. The Sun appears to rise and fall as the Earth turns you around to face it more or less directly. Shadows are shortest at midday on midsummer's day, when the Earth turns you to face the Sun almost directly, and the Sun is at its "zenith" (highest point). Shadows are longest at sunrise and sunset, and in winter, when you are at such an angle to the Sun that it is nearly hidden behind the horizon. Night falls when the Earth spins around so far that you face away from the Sun.

EXPERIMENT
Sun and latitude

The height of the Sun in the sky varies not only with the time of day and year, but also with the distance from the equator. The Sun is at its highest in the tropics – which is why they are so hot (pp.154–155). But it drops lower and lower further away from the equator – the higher the latitude (p.16), the lower the Sun. This is why the North and South Poles are so cold. You can see for yourself the relationship between the height of the Sun and latitude with this simple experiment using a globe and a desk lamp. The length of shadow cast by the card on the globe shows how high the Sun is.

YOU WILL NEED

● globe ● lamp ● set square ● card ● ruler ● scissors ● glue ● plastic putty

EXPERIMENT
Making a sundial

YOU WILL NEED
● wooden board ● set square ● card ● saw ● pen & pencil ● ruler ● scissors ● protractor ● glue

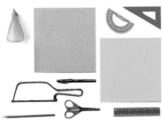

Shadows show clearly how the Sun moves, so you can use them to tell the time on a simple sundial. Time is indicated by where the shadow of an upright, or "gnomon", falls on a dial.

1 CUT A PIECE of board about 15 cm (6 in) square and cover it with card.

2 DRAW HOUR LINES (see right) and glue the gnomon (protractor) upright.

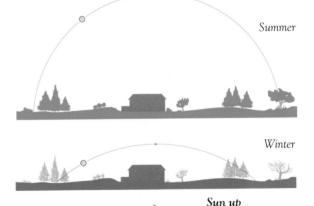

Summer

Winter

Sun up
The Sun follows a higher path through the sky in summer than in winter.

Reading the dial
The board should always be set up in exactly the same place, with the gnomon side directly facing the midday Sun. The time can then be read off from the shadow.

Hour marks can be calculated by a watch as the shadow moves round, or by the formula on p.185

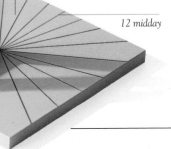

12 midday

Gnomon

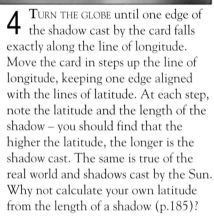

1 FROM THIN CARD OR PAPER, cut out the shape shown on the yellow square below left. Do not cut where lines are shown in dashes.

2 FOLD SHARPLY along the dashed lines to make a shape with two upright, right-angled triangles at 90° to each other. Stick down the small square flap.

3 FIX THE CARD SHAPE exactly along a longitude line, using plastic putty. Shine a desk lamp on the globe so that the shadow edge runs from pole to pole.

4 TURN THE GLOBE until one edge of the shadow cast by the card falls exactly along the line of longitude. Move the card in steps up the line of longitude, keeping one edge aligned with the lines of latitude. At each step, note the latitude and the length of the shadow – you should find that the higher the latitude, the longer is the shadow cast. The same is true of the real world and shadows cast by the Sun. Why not calculate your own latitude from the length of a shadow (p.185)?

■ The four seasons

Have you ever wondered why we have four seasons during the year – spring, summer, autumn, winter? It's because the Earth stays tilted at the same angle as it circles the Sun. So sometimes the northern half is tilted towards the Sun, giving the northern "hemisphere" the long, warm days of summer (left of picture on right), while the south has short, cool, winter days. Yet when the Earth travels round to the far side of the Sun, it is the south that is tilted sunwards, and the seasons reverse (right of picture).

A year in space
By turning the orrery (pp.14–15) you can see how the Sun's light creates the seasons on the tilted globe. The summer and winter "solstices" appear left and right; the autumn and spring "equinoxes" front and back.

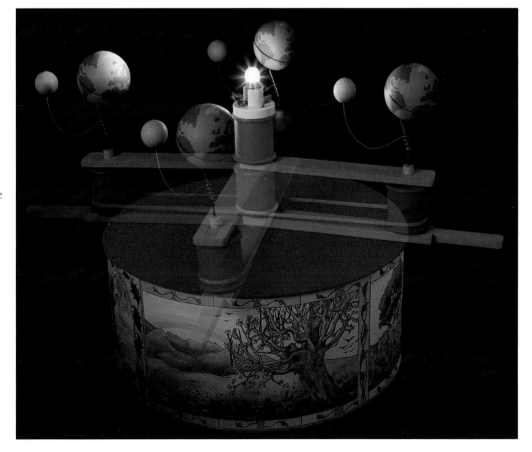

Our Moon

As it journeys through space our tiny planet is never quite alone, for it is kept constant company by the Moon. Other planets have moons whirling around them but ours is very large compared to its parent. In fact, by a strange coincidence, the Moon is the same size in the sky as the Sun, despite it being much closer to the Earth – about 385,000 km (240,000 miles). It has no light of its own, but reflects the light of the Sun so well that it is by far the brightest object in the night sky. Just like the Earth, the Moon has a day and a night side. Because we see these two sides from different angles, the Moon appears to change shape or "phase" – from a "new moon", when we catch only a glimpse of the day side, to a "full moon", when we see it all as a bright disc.

8 Old moon
Only a sliver of the day side is visible as the cycle ends.

1 New moon
In this position we catch barely a glimpse of the Moon's day side.

2 Crescent moon
As the Moon swings away from its position between the Sun and Earth we see more of its day side.

■ The Moon and tides

When the Sun and Moon are at right angles to the Earth, their pulls conflict, causing very small "neap" tides

Every 12 hours, all the sea on opposite sides of the world rises a little, then falls back. This is called a tide. The causes of tides are complicated, but one reason is that the weight of the Moon (its "gravity") pulls the sea towards it, creating a high tide on the side of the Earth nearest the Moon.

The sea away from the Moon is flung out by "centrifugal" force, like whirling a ball on a string

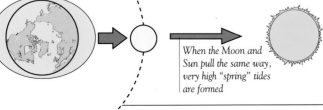
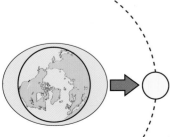

When the Moon and Sun pull the same way, very high "spring" tides are formed

EXPERIMENT
The spinning Moon

Like the Earth, the Moon is always spinning around. But while the Earth takes just a day to spin right round on its axis, the Moon takes over 27 days – exactly the same time that it takes to circle the Earth once. This is why we always see the Moon from the same side. To see how this works, follow the steps of this simple experiment (above right).

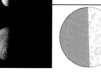
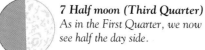

7 Half moon (Third Quarter)
As in the First Quarter, we now see half the day side.

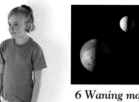

■ The lunar month

As the Moon slowly circles around the Earth, our view of its night and day sides constantly changes, giving the Moon's different phases. It takes 29 days altogether to go from one full moon to the next, even though it actually takes the Moon only 27.3 days to circle the Earth. This is because the Earth is moving as well as the Moon. This 29-day cycle is called a "lunar month".

6 Waning moon
As the Moon swings back towards the Sun, the day side gradually passes out of our sight.

1 Sit on a stool and ask a friend to circle slowly around, or "orbit", you. Although she is facing you all the time, her body will turn completely around once every orbit. In the same way, the Moon always keeps the same face towards the Earth as it orbits every 27.3 days – and still makes a complete turn of its own.

2 Just to be sure, ask your friend to orbit the stool again – but this time watch from the outside. You will see her front, side, back, side, and front – showing that she has spun around once while orbiting the stool, just like the Moon.

5 Full moon (Second Quarter)
We can see all the Moon's day side as a bright disc in the sky.

4 Gibbous moon
The Moon begins to "wax" fuller and we see more of its day side.

The phases of the Moon
Using the orrery in a darkened room (pp.14–15), it is easy to see why the Moon changes shape, or "phase". Looking at the Moon from eye level from the far side of the Earth ball, you can see the Moon bead much as we see the real Moon as it orbits the Earth. When we see more and more of the day side with each successive phase, the Moon is said to be "waxing" (2 to 4 opposite); when we see less and less, it is said to be "waning" (6 to 8 opposite).

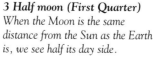

3 Half moon (First Quarter)
When the Moon is the same distance from the Sun as the Earth is, we see half its day side.

THE SHAPE OF THE EARTH

SATELLITE PHOTOGRAPHS OF THE EARTH show that it is an almost perfect sphere – but it is not quite perfect. Over the centuries people have measured and mapped the Earth with increasing accuracy. We can now pinpoint every place on Earth to within a few metres, and know its circumference to within a fraction of a kilometre. But as the measurements have become more accurate, so we have discovered that our planet is not as round as was once thought.

The world looks like an almost perfect sphere from space, but it bulges just enough at the equator to make it slightly harder to achieve high jump records there, because of the extra gravity.

Around 230 BC, Eratosthenes (c.270–c.194 BC), head of the great library in Alexandria in Egypt, made a remarkable calculation. At a time when most people still thought the Earth was flat, Eratosthenes worked out how big the Earth is to within one per cent of today's measurements. His method was ingeniously simple, depending on the difference in the angle of the Sun between two places at noon on midsummer's day (p.31). In this way he estimated that the circumference of the Earth was about 40,000 km (25,000 miles), compared with the figure of 40,024 km (24,870 miles) arrived at by modern measurements.

Sadly, Eratosthenes' work was forgotten over the centuries. When the Alexandrian scholar Ptolemy (AD c.90–c.170) wrote his famous *Geography* 400 years later, he based his estimate of the size of the Earth on guessing how far apart stars were and then measuring their height in the sky. Using this system, Posidonius (c.135–c.51 BC) had calculated that the Earth was no more than 28,970 km (18,000 miles) around, and this was the figure that Ptolemy gave.

So great was Ptolemy's authority that scholars tended to underestimate the size of the

Gerardus Mercator devised a way of projecting the Earth's curved surface on a map, allowing sailors to plot straight courses.

world for 1,300 years. When, in the 1490s, Christopher Columbus (1451–1506) decided he could reach Japan by sailing west across the Atlantic, he thought it was much nearer than it is. Columbus reckoned it was only 4,500 km (2,800 miles) from the Canary Islands to Japan. In fact it is four times as far – which is why Columbus thought he had reached Japan when he landed in the New World in 1492.

Thirty years later, when Ferdinand Magellan's ship *Victoria* made the first round-the-world voyage, it was clear that the world was much bigger than had been thought. In 1525 a young Frenchman named Jean Fernel (1497–1558) worked out a new size for the Earth. If you know how long a degree of latitude is, you can work out the Earth's circumference by multiplying this by 360. So, using a "quadrant" to sight stars, Fernel found two points a degree apart

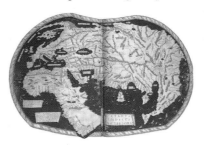

In the fifteenth century maps were still drawn as if the world was flat – 1,700 years after Eratosthenes.

between Paris and Amiens. He then worked out the distance between them by counting the turns of his coach wheels. Multiplying this by 360 then gave him a figure for the size of the Earth within 0.1 per cent of modern calculations.

■ Finding the bulge

Over the next 150 years, scientists achieved increasingly accurate figures for a degree of latitude – called a "meridional degree", since it was measured along a "meridian" or line of longitude. By the 1670s French survey teams led by the

To find the size of the Earth, measure the shadows of two poles a known distance apart (p.30).

Cassini family had measured the degree of latitude at 110.46 km (68.65 miles), very close to today's figures. Then the English scientist Isaac Newton (1642–1727) dropped a bombshell, suggesting that a degree might be shorter near the equator than near the poles.

Newton knew that the Earth spins faster at the equator than at the poles. It must, because the poles move no distance in a day, while points along the equator cover 40,000 km (25,000 miles). If so, Newton argued, centrifugal force must be greater at the equator than at the poles, making the Earth bulge out at the equator and flatten at the poles, so that it is a tangerine shape (or "oblate spheroid"), not a perfect sphere.

When close study of Jupiter and Saturn revealed slight flattening at the poles, it seemed as if Newton might be right. But the Cassinis were not convinced, for according to their measurements a degree got longer not shorter as you moved north. Determined to find out who was right, King Louis XV of France sent two teams of surveyors – one to Peru, near the equator, and one to Lapland, near the Arctic – to measure an "arc", or meridional

To make a globe, the Earth is divided into segments or "gores" along lines of longitude (pp.26–27).

degree. By 1743 each had their figure for the arc – 111.09 km (69.04 miles) for Lapland, and 109.92 km (68.32 miles) for Peru. Newton *was* right after all.

There was another surprise to come. The launching of satellites into space in the 1950s made it possible to achieve incredibly accurate measurements by taking readings from different satellites at precisely the same time. Satellite measurements confirmed that the Earth is 43 km (26.7 miles) fatter across the equator than between the poles. They also showed that the equatorial bulge is 8 m (26 ft) bigger in places south of the equator. So now the Earth is described as a "geoid" rather than an oblate spheroid.

■ Where on Earth?

At much the same time that Eratosthenes made his calculation of the Earth's size, he made a second important contribution. He realized that any place in the world can be pinpointed precisely with a basic grid of lines of "latitude" and "longitude". For longitude, he divided the world into 360 degrees like the segments of an orange. These lines of longitude, or "meridians", run from the North Pole to the South Pole, and are expressed in degrees east or west of a "prime" meridian. For latitude, he divided the world into 90 slices on either side of the equator. These lines of latitude stretch around the world parallel to the equator, and are expressed in degrees north or south of the equator.

■ Location

In practice, latitude was much easier to work out than longitude. In the time of Eratosthenes, people could work out their latitude during the day by measuring the length of a shadow cast by the Sun behind a pole or "gnomon". By the first century AD they could work it out at night, using an "astrolabe", an instrument for measuring the angle of particular stars above the horizon. But there was no easy way to find longitude. The Greeks knew that the key was time. Since the Sun swings around the world from east to west, you could find longitude

The only way to work out longitude for many centuries was to wait for an eclipse. Then you could find out the time in two different places.

from the direction of the Sun – but only if you knew the precise time at the prime meridian (at Greenwich, England). For centuries, the only way to find longitude was to measure the distance from the prime meridian on the ground – or wait for an eclipse. Ships navigated by "dead reckoning" – that is, calculating the distance travelled from their speed, timed with "logs" thrown overboard. This worked well in coastal waters, but was inadequate for vast ocean voyages in the 1500s. Navigators could find precise latitude with an astrolabe, but the vagaries of wind and weather meant they might be hundreds of kilometres out on longitude.

In 1616 the Italian scientist Galileo (1564–1642) realized

that time could be calculated by looking at the moons of Jupiter through a telescope. For 150 years this was the basis of working out longitude. But it was impossible to look for the moons of Jupiter from a tossing ship. Since the accuracy of longitude could be a matter of life and death, people came up with all kinds of bizarre and ingenious methods of calculation, but it wasn't until an accurate clock (or "chronometer") was invented by John Harrison (1693–1776) in the 1720s that longitude could be measured with some certainty. Nowadays the task is made simple by navigation satellites in the sky.

Sighting the stars was the best way of finding your location on Earth for thousands of years. In the days before magnetic compasses were used, looking for the pole star was the only way to find north. But because of the way the Earth moves, there is not always a pole star. There was no pole star in AD 1000, for instance, and this may have delayed the growth of navigation by sea.

The Earth is the fifth biggest planet in the solar system, between Venus, which is about 37,000 km (23,000 miles) in circumference, and Neptune, which is 155,000 km (96,000 miles) in circumference.

Flat Earth?

IT IS EASY TO SEE why people once thought the Earth was flat. Without being told, you'd never know you were walking around on a ball. From the ground, even the furthest horizon appears straight and level. But now that we can fly high in the sky we can see that the horizon is curved, and pictures from space prove beyond doubt that the Earth is round.

Yet there were always other clues. These were enough to convince some thinkers that the world was a globe long before intrepid explorers in the fifteenth and sixteenth centuries proved it by sailing right round. Why, for instance, did ships gradually disappear as they sailed beyond the horizon? Why did some stars drop below the horizon as people travelled north or south? And why was the shadow of the Earth on the Moon round, as the Greek thinker Aristotle (384–322 BC) pointed out? For all of these puzzling phenomena, a round Earth was gradually recognized as the best explanation.

*The edge of the world –
until Columbus discovered
the Americas in 1492*

■ The known limits

This fifteenth-century map shows all the world as it was known a few years before the time of Columbus (see opposite). The continents of Europe, Africa, and Asia are mis-shapen but clearly recognizable. What lay beyond the margins of the map, no-one knew. Could it be, as some believed, empty space? Or was the Earth round?

*In the fifteenth
century, voyages by
Portuguese sailors enabled the mapmaker
to show the west coast of Africa in detail*

■ Earth shadow

When the Earth passes directly between the Sun and the Moon, its shadow falls upon the Moon. This is an eclipse of the Moon. As Aristotle saw, the shadow is not oval, as it would be if the Earth was a flat disc, but round, the shadow of a ball.

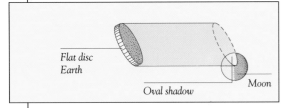

Flat disc
Earth

Oval shadow · Moon

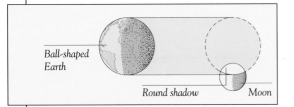

Ball-shaped
Earth

Round shadow · Moon

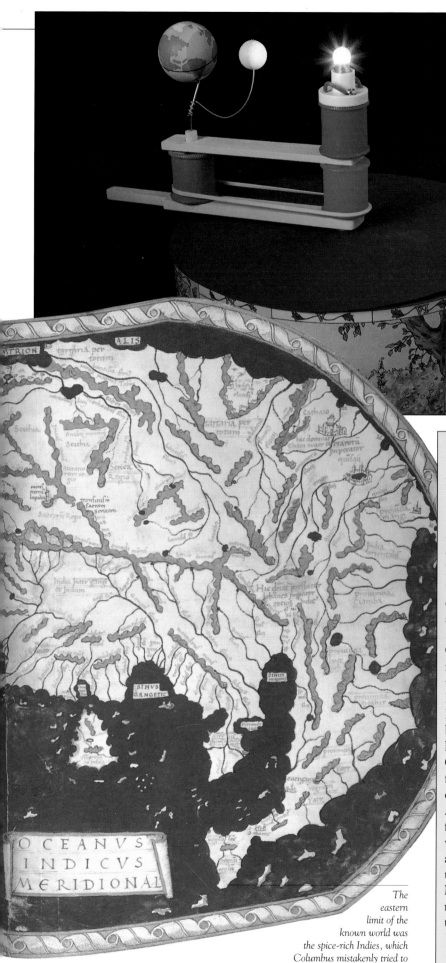

The eastern limit of the known world was the spice-rich Indies, which Columbus mistakenly tried to reach by sailing westwards

■ Eclipses

Up to three times a year, the Moon passes into the Earth's shadow, creating a "lunar" eclipse. Up to five times a year, the Moon's shadow falls on the Earth, creating a "solar" eclipse – or eclipse of the Sun. You can create a solar eclipse with the orrery (pp.14–15) by swinging the Moon bead between the Sun and Earth (left). The Moon's shadow can be seen on the Earth. To those in the shadow, the Sun is blotted out for a while. Because the Earth spins, the Moon's shadow sweeps across it during a solar eclipse in a line called the "path of totality". In a lunar eclipse, however, the entire Moon is in shadow because the Earth is so much bigger, but the Sun's rays, distorted by the Earth's atmosphere, turn it a deep red.

■ DISCOVERY ■
Christopher Columbus

Like many other explorers and thinkers of his time, Christopher Columbus (1451–1506) thought the Earth was round. But no-one knew for sure, and many still believed that if you sailed far enough you would fall off the edge of the Earth. To reach the Indies (Southeast Asia) and their rich spices, Europeans always travelled eastwards. But if the Earth is round, Columbus argued, it might be quicker to go west. To prove it, he set off west across the uncharted Atlantic Ocean, with just a few small ships. When he reached the far side in 1492, he thought he had reached the Indies and proved his point. In fact, the world was bigger than anyone had realized. Columbus had found an unknown continent, later called the Americas. The Indies lay far away across another vast ocean. It was to be another 30 years before the ship of Ferdinand Magellan would sail right around the world.

The globe

SINCE OUR WORLD IS ROUND, the best way to represent it is with a a globe. On a good globe you can see the location of every place, the correct size and shape of every continent, and the shortest route over vast distances. These features give the globe a great advantage over flat maps, all of which involve some distortion (see pp.28–29).

The problem with globes is that they are hard to make. You could make one simply by painting the details on a ball, but this is not very practical or reliable. The surface detail on most globes is created instead by printing shield-shaped segments called "gores". These must be made very accurately, and the flat paper placed carefully on to the globe.

EXPERIMENT
Make a globe

A good globe is very difficult to make, but one way to make your own is by wrapping paper gores around a football. You may not achieve a perfect fit, but the principle is the same as for professional globes.

YOU WILL NEED
● paper ● ball ● glue ● tape ● board
● baton ● pin ● wire ● 2 washers
● paints ● instruments as shown

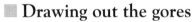

1 TO FIND HOW LONG the paper must be, tape it to the seam of the ball and roll it round, back to the taped edge.

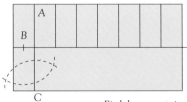

2 WORK OUT THE WIDTH by rolling the ball from the valve to a point directly opposite, marking each point.

■ Drawing out the gores

To draw out the gores you will need to attach additional sheets of paper to the original sheet and extend the equator line at both ends. Then make an extra-long compass arm from a balsa baton, fixing the radius (as calculated below) with a pencil and pin. The first curve can be drawn with the pin at D. Keep moving back a gore's width to draw the other curves, then reverse the compass and work back in the other direction.

3 DRAW A RECTANGLE on a large sheet of paper, using the measurements made in steps 1 and 2, and cut it out.

4 DIVIDE THE PAPER into eight by folding in half three times, or using a ruler. Draw a line down each fold.

5 BEGIN WORKING OUT the gore shapes by finding the bisector of line B to C (see top diagram on right).

6 FIND THE RADIUS for drawing the gores (see bottom diagram on right). Attach sheets of paper left and right to extend the equator line.

Find the centre point of the first eighth (B). Then find a line to bisect a line from B to C by drawing parts of circles with the point of the compass first on C, then on B

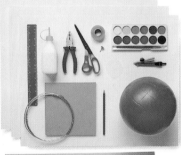

Draw a line through the crossing points of the two circles to the equator. The radius for all gores is then D to B. Now draw the first curve with the point of the compass at D

7 FIX THE PIN of your own compass arm at each circle's centre and draw out the gores, as described left.

8 CUT OUT THE GORES and draw a grid over them. Then draw out the features from the gore plan below.

9 MAKE A STAND by bending wire around half the ball and then over at the ends (see drawing below).

10 FIT THE WIRE into a soft wooden board and glue washers top and bottom to allow the ball to turn.

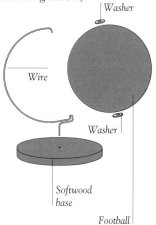

Washer

Wire

Washer

Softwood base

Football

11 TAPE ONE END of the gore strip to the ball at the seam, then roll it around the equator and join the ends.

12 FOLD THE POINTS of the gores in at each pole and stick down, taking care to fold opposite points together.

Round the world
Making a round globe from flat paper gores will help you to understand the equally complex task of the mapmaker (pp.28–29).

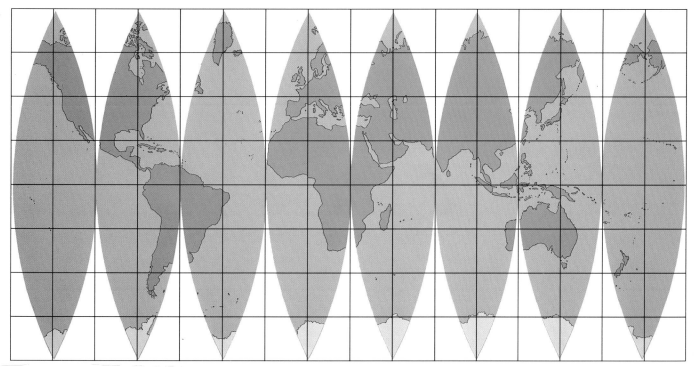

▨ Filling in the details

Globes can be made from different numbers of gores, but here we have used just eight for simplicity. To draw the continents and oceans on your gores, lightly pencil in a grid as above, but to the length and width of your own cut-out gores. Work through square by square, drawing lines for the coasts in exactly the same places on your gores. Then erase the grid and either colour or paint in the continents and oceans.

Making the world flat

THERE IS NO BETTER WAY to represent the world than with a globe. But globes are expensive to make and often impractical. You can hardly slip a globe into your pocket! And imagine how big it would have to be to show everything from footpaths to entire continents. This is why we need flat maps.

Yet how can the features of a round world be shown accurately on a flat map? In fact, they cannot: any method of showing the curved world on a flat map involves some distortion and inaccuracy, especially over large areas. But mapmakers have now evolved thousands of methods to represent the world, called "map projections". Each is a compromise: to show some features accurately, it allows others to be distorted.

All map projections work by using the criss-crossing lines of latitude and longitude (pp.16–17) in order to locate things in the right place, and no matter what type of projection is used, every place in the world must appear at the correct latitude and longitude.

■ DISCOVERY ■
Gerardus Mercator

Once people were sure their world was round, navigation at sea made startling progress. Maps improved as voyages of exploration brought new knowledge of the world, and map projections were devised to map a round world accurately. Yet early projections helped sailors little, for plotting even a straight course was a complicated business. Then in 1552 a Dutch mapmaker called Gerardus Mercator (1512–1594) invented a special kind of cylindrical projection (see right). Although it makes countries near the poles far too big, Mercator's projection has one unique quality – sailors can work out how to steer a steady course by compass simply by drawing a straight line on the map.

■ Pros and cons

Each kind of map projection has its good and bad points. Some distort size and distance in order to show shapes of features, such as continents, accurately. These are called "conformal" maps. Maps that show size well are "equal-area" maps; those showing distance well are called "equidistance" maps.

Direction is a particular problem for mapmakers – yet it is of vital importance for steering ships and planes. A map may show the location of your destination but not the "heading" – that is, the direction on a compass you need to steer by. Because the surface of the Earth is curved, a compass heading (a "rhumb line") that is straight in reality may be a curve on the map. Only on Mercator's projection are they straight.

EXPERIMENT
Map projections

This simple experiment shows how map projections work, by shining light through a half-globe to project the lines as shadows on paper. The lines represent longitude and latitude. Maps are not actually made in this way – the projection is really mathematical, and many projections are now produced by computer. Nevertheless, the principle is identical. Demonstrated here are the three basic kinds of map projection: planar, cylindrical, and conical.

YOU WILL NEED
● *plastic soft drinks bottle* ● *torch* ● *tracing paper* ● *scissors* ● *marker pen* ● *protractor*

1 MAKE A HALF-GLOBE by cutting the top neatly off a plastic soft drinks bottle. Then cut off the neck as cleanly as possible.

2 USING ROUND OBJECTS to guide you, draw circles inside the globe to act as lines of latitude, and radiating spokes to act as lines of longitude.

■ Planar projection

This is projection on to a flat surface. To see how it works, rest the plastic globe on a piece of tracing paper in the dark. Now hold the torch at the centre of the globe.

See how the shadows of the longitude lines radiate in the same direction on the globe. This is why this projection shows the true direction from one point on the map to another.

Plane view
Planar projections (sometimes known as azimuthal or zenithal projections) can show only half of the world at a time. They are basically circular (although they can be cut to make a rectangular map), with the centre directly beneath the light. Conventionally, they are centred on either the North or South Poles, but the centre, or "azimuth", can be anywhere. Here, it is directly over the equator.

■ Cylindrical projection

This popular method involves projecting the globe onto a cylinder, which is then rolled out flat to make the map. To see how it works, roll a tube of tracing paper around the globe. Now if you hold the torch in the middle, you can see how the longitude lines have straightened out.

Square world
Cylindrical projection can show the whole world on a single map. Lines of longitude and latitude cross at right angles just as they do on the globe. But the effect is to make polar countries, such as Greenland, far too large.

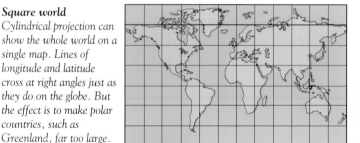

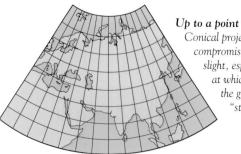

■ Conical projection

In conical projection, the globe is projected on to a cone, which is unrolled to make a flat map. To see how it works, rest a cone of tracing paper over the globe and hold the torch in the centre. See how the shadows of longitude lines radiate, just as on the globe.

Up to a point
Conical projection is a good compromise, and distortions are slight, especially near the line at which the cone rests on the globe, called the "standard parallel".

How big is the Earth?

PICTURES FROM SPACE seem to show the world as a perfectly round ball. But this is not strictly true. The force of the Earth's rotation actually makes the world bulge out a little at the equator and go a little flat at the poles. So rather than being a perfect sphere, the Earth is what is known as an "oblate spheroid". The difference between that and a perfect sphere is very, very tiny – but air and sea navigators and surveyors cannot afford to ignore it. The diameter of the Earth at the equator is 12,758 km (7,927 miles), while the distance from pole to pole is just 12,714 km (7,900 miles) – a difference barely thicker, relatively, than the paper on a model globe. Scientists can now measure this difference with satellites, but it has always been possible to calculate the size of the Earth more simply, as the experiment here shows. In fact, Eratosthenes worked it out over 2,200 years ago.

EXPERIMENT
Measuring the Earth

If you have a couple of friends living a few hundred kilometres due north or south of you, you don't have to take a scientist's word for the size of the Earth – you can work it out for yourself. You and your distant friends must both measure the length of the shadows cast by identical poles at midday on the same day. The slight difference enables you to calculate the Earth's size, provided you know how far away your friends live.

YOU WILL NEED

For each pair of experimenters:
● *pole or broom handles (these must be identical)* ● *tape measure* ● *string* ● *modelling clay to make a weight for the plumb line* ● *chalk* ● *large clip*

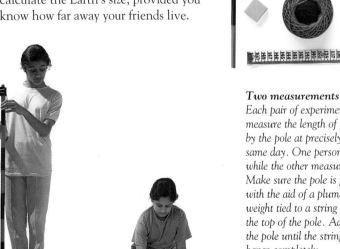

Two measurements
Each pair of experimenters must measure the length of the shadow cast by the pole at precisely midday on the same day. One person holds the pole while the other measures the shadow. Make sure the pole is perfectly upright with the aid of a plumb line – simply a weight tied to a string and hung from the top of the pole. Adjust the pole until the string hangs completely parallel to it.

∎ Calculations

To find out the size of the Earth, follow the steps below:

1 Work out the angle of the Sun in each place. The box below right shows how.

2 Work out the difference in angles in each place by taking one from the other.

3 Divide 360 by the difference in angles, then multiply by the distance between the two places, giving the circumference of the world. So if your friends were 223 km away, and the difference in angles 2°, the sum would be:

$$(360 \div 2) \times 223 = 40,140$$

4 To find the diameter from your own figures, divide your answer by 3.143.

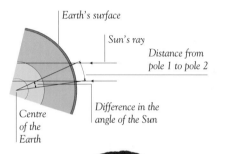

Earth's surface

Sun's ray

Distance from pole 1 to pole 2

Centre of the Earth

Difference in the angle of the Sun

∎ DISCOVERY ∎
Eratosthenes

The Greek astronomer Eratosthenes (c.270–c.194 BC) devised an ingeniously simple method of working out the size of the Earth. He was the chief librarian at the great museum in Alexandria, on the Egyptian coast, and he had learnt from his books of a peculiar phenomenon. At midday on Midsummer's Day, the Sun's reflection could be seen on the water at the bottom of a well at Syene, 800 km (500 miles) to the south of Alexandria. This meant that the Sun was exactly overhead there at this time. Eratosthenes also knew that at the same time in Alexandria an obelisk cast a short shadow. By measuring the angle of this shadow (about 7°), he worked out that Alexandria was roughly one-fiftieth of the way around the world from Syene (360° divided by 7°). Since he knew Syene was 800 km (500 miles) away, he was able to estimate that the Earth's circumference was about 50 x 800 km (500 miles) – that is, about 40,000 km (25,000 miles). Modern measurements put the average figure at 40,024 km (24,870 miles).

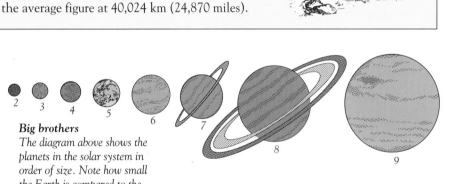

Big brothers
The diagram above shows the planets in the solar system in order of size. Note how small the Earth is compared to the four largest planets – Uranus, Neptune, Saturn, and Jupiter. But even Jupiter is tiny compared to the Sun. In fact, you could get more than a million Earths inside the Sun!

1 Pluto
2 Mercury
3 Mars
4 Venus
5 Earth
6 Neptune
7 Uranus
8 Saturn
9 Jupiter

∎ The angle of the Sun

To work out the Sun's angle from the pole's shadow, divide the length of the shadow by the length of the pole. This gives the tangent (*tan*) of the angle (A). To find the angle from the tangent, use a calculator with a *tan* function, or tangent tables.

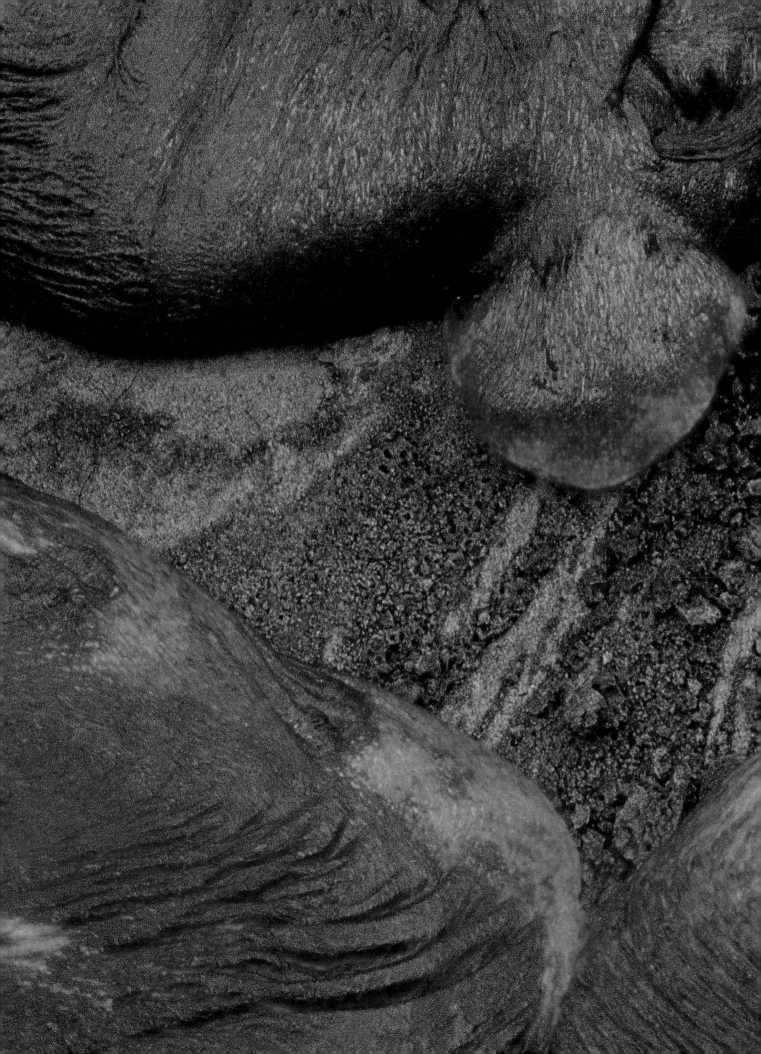

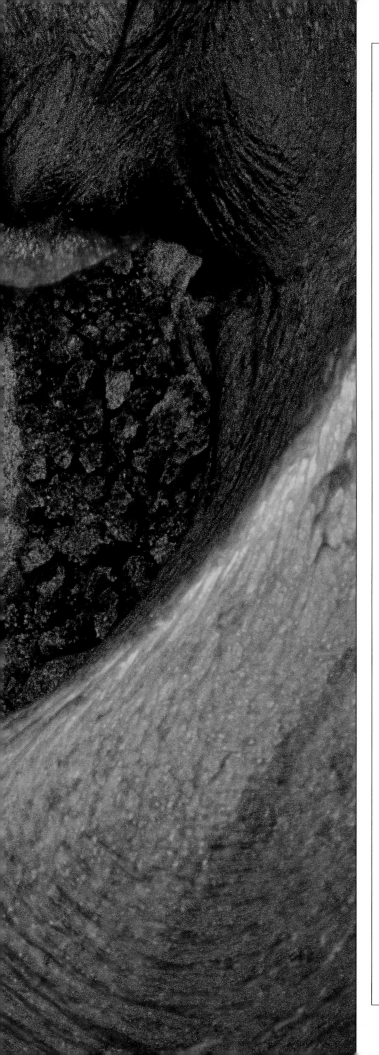

The Earth's STRUCTURE

A world built on sand
Nearly three-quarters of the Earth's crust is made from silicates like sand and quartz (shown above in crystal form). New crustal rock is formed from material melted by the heat of the Earth's interior and forced to the surface (left).

THE CENTRE OF THE EARTH IS a fiery furnace, hot enough to melt rock. All the time, beneath our feet, the insides of our planet are churning with an awesome power that can make the ground tremble, throw up mountains and volcanoes, and force continents to collide or split apart as they ride on the giant conveyor belts of molten rock circulating beneath the Earth's crust.

SOLID EARTH?

PEOPLE ONCE THOUGHT the Earth was just a simple solid ball. But skilled scientific interpretation of vibrations from earthquakes and explosions has revealed a far more complex structure – ranging from a twisted, crumpled, and broken solid shell, down to a dense, metallic core some 4,000 km (2,500 miles) below the surface of the Earth. Here pressures are immense and temperatures reach as high as 5,000°C (9,000°F), hot enough to melt just about any known substance.

Attempts to find out more about the Earth's interior by drilling and mining have not been very successful. The world's deepest borehole, on the Kola peninsula in Siberia, goes down only 12 km (7 miles), which is barely halfway through the crust.

The Earth's interior was such a mystery that, even in the late nineteenth century, authors invented stories of underground fantasy worlds with vast caverns such as this.

For thousands of years, the problem with understanding the Earth was finding out what it was like inside. Scientists could peer far into space, but could not study the world beneath their feet to a depth of more than 200 m (660 ft) or so, the depth of the deepest mines until recently. So most of the early theories about the Earth's internal structure were simply speculation.

The Ancient Greek thinker Aristotle (384–322 BC) thought the Earth was a solid ball and, for almost 2,000 years, few disagreed with him. But by 1600, some people began to wonder if the shape of the Earth's surface had anything to do with the workings of the Earth as a whole. One puzzling aspect was the shape of the oceans. New maps showing the discoveries of the 1500s revealed a startling similarity between the coasts of Africa and South America. According to the English philosopher Francis Bacon (1561–1626), this could be "no mere accidental occurrence". Many people guessed they had once been joined together.

At the time, most Europeans were still guided by the Bible, and the split between Africa and South America was easily explained by Noah's flood. Known as the Deluge, the flood became a part of most of the "theories of the Earth" that were developed over the next 150 years. Yet if there had been such a flood, scientists asked, where had all the water come from? Could it be that the Earth had just a thin solid crust enclosing a watery interior?

■ Water v. fire

By the late eighteenth century there were two opposing theories. One was the "Neptunist" idea that the Earth once had a solid core, surrounded by water thick with chemicals that slowly settled out to make the rocks we see today. The other was the "Plutonist" idea that the Earth had a hot interior of molten rock, which erupted on to the surface through volcanoes. Early geologists did not think volcanoes were very important, as few are active at any one time. But by 1820 it was shown that, over billions of years, volcanoes have played a huge role in shaping the landscape (p.54).

By the 1870s most geologists agreed that the Earth probably had a solid central core, which was surrounded by a "mantle" of liquid rock, around which there was a solid outer crust. But there was no proof of this until the "seismograph" was developed in 1880 by English engineer John Milne (1850–1913).

Magnetic lodestones were used in the first compasses, and gave early evidence of the Earth's iron centre.

■ Vibrations

Seismographs detect vibrations in the Earth made by earthquakes and let geologists "see" inside the Earth by comparing the vibrations (called "waves") at seismograph stations around the world. Earthquakes send out two types of wave: "surface waves", which shudder around the outside of the world; and "body waves", which run through the interior. It is the body waves that reveal the structure of the Earth.

Two kinds of body wave have proved to be especially useful. These are fast-moving primary

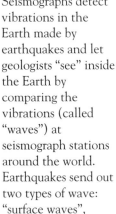

Compasses respond to the electromagnetic effect created by the motion of the Earth's outer core (p.38).

(P) waves and slower-moving secondary (S) waves (pp.62–63). Because P waves arrive before S waves, seismologists can work out where they originated by comparing the time lag at various seismograph stations.

However, the real value of body waves for probing the Earth's interior comes from the way their speed is affected by the nature of the material they pass

The Earth's dense metallic core creates a "magnetic field" that extends far out into space (p.39).

through. Just as light is refracted (bent) by glass, so earthquake waves are refracted when they pass through different materials, because they move at different speeds. By studying such refractions, seismologists have learned a great deal about the Earth's interior.

By 1900 seismologists found that the Earth's mantle was solid, not liquid – although we now know that it behaves as both solid and liquid (p.48). Six years later, British seismologist Richard Oldham (1858–1936) showed that the Earth had a liquid core, because there was a zone where P waves bent strikingly, and S waves stopped altogether.

Then, in 1909, Croatian seismologist Andrija Mohorovicic (1857–1936) discovered a sharp increase in the speed at which waves travelled when 20 km (12 miles) below the Earth's surface. This suggested that there must be an abrupt change in material here. We call this the "Mohorovicic discontinuity" and it marks the boundary between the Earth's crust and its mantle. In fact, the change is less abrupt than Mohorovicic first thought, for the crust merges into the mantle in places over a depth of 60 km (37 miles). In 1914 the German seismologist Beno Gutenberg (1889–1960) detected the boundary between the mantle and the core – the "Gutenberg discontinuity".

▪ Solid centre?

More discoveries were to come. When P waves are bent through the Earth's core, it seemed at first that they could not emerge at certain angles, creating a "shadow zone". Then faint waves were detected even in the shadow zone. In 1936, the Danish geophysicist Inge Lehmann (born 1888) proposed that the inner part of the Earth's core is not liquid at all, but solid. This was confirmed in 1970 when more sensitive seismographs

Scientists now believe the Earth's mantle is not still, but is constantly churning, for the heat of the planet's interior creates convection currents like those in liquid over a candle (p.41).

The alignment of the Earth's magnetic field is slightly offset from the axis on which it spins. No-one knows why.

detected refractions from this solid core.

From the way waves are refracted, it is possible to work out the density of each layer of the Earth's interior. Knowing the density, geologists can guess what the layer is made of. Their findings suggest that the core is mostly iron and nickel, while much of the mantle is made of a special silicate called "olivine".

▪ New details

For many years, the picture seemed complete – upper and lower crust, upper and lower mantle, outer and inner core. Then in the late 1970s a new technique called "seismic reflection profiling" revealed that the continental crust was far more complicated than anyone had imagined. Just as crust is twisted and broken at the surface, so it is deep down. Moreover, the upper mantle also seems much more complex. Once earth scientists started looking at the way the different layers behaved, they realized the brittle topmost part of the mantle had more in common with the crust than with the treacly upper mantle just below. So they referred to the crust and topmost mantle as the "lithosphere", and the treacly layer as the "asthenosphere". Yet it seems that there are even more variations within the upper mantle – not only with depth, but around the world, too. It is clear there is still a great deal to learn.

New discoveries in geology excited many nineteenth century thinkers to speculate about what lay inside the Earth. In his book Journey to the Centre of the Earth, *published in 1864, the French author Jules Verne (1828–1905) let his imagination run wild. This forest of giant mushrooms far below ground is just one of the many strange sights encountered by his heroes as they travelled down into the Earth.*

Inside the Earth

PEOPLE HAVE ALWAYS WONDERED what lay at the heart of the Earth. The Ancient Greeks thought it was Hades, the mythical underworld where the dead go. Others have imagined fantastic caverns and hidden cities. The truth is that no-one really knows for certain. The world's deepest mine is less than 4 km (2.5 miles) deep, and no drill has ever bored down more than 15 km (9 miles). Yet the total distance from the surface to the centre of the Earth is 6,370 km (3,958 miles).

However, there are indirect ways of finding out what lies at the heart of our planet. The most important of these is the vibrations from earthquakes. Study of earthquake waves has revealed three main elements to the Earth's interior: the crust, the mantle, and the core. The crust is the thin outer layer that covers the world like a skin, barely 10 km (6 miles) thick in places. The mantle beneath is 3,000 km (1,864 miles) thick and made of extremely hot rock – often so hot that the rock flows around like treacle. The core, the metallic centre of the Earth, is even hotter than the mantle. It is thought to be liquid on the outside and solid on the inside.

■ Shaky knowledge

Almost all we know about the Earth's interior is based on earthquake vibrations – called "seismic waves" – which can be detected worldwide. By timing how long waves take to reach different places, scientists can work out whether waves have travelled directly there, or have been bent by passing through dense material.

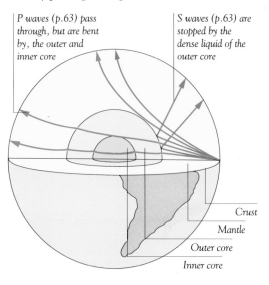

P waves (p.63) pass through, but are bent by, the outer and inner core

S waves (p.63) are stopped by the dense liquid of the outer core

Crust

Mantle

Outer core

Inner core

Crust to core
In this model, all the layers of the Earth's interior are revealed: the crust, the three layers of the mantle, and the inner and outer core. People often talk of the crust and mantle as if they are two distinct things, separated by the "Moho". Yet the base of the crust is very like the top of the mantle, so many scientists talk about the "lithosphere" instead. This extends 100 km (60 miles) below the surface and includes all the crust plus a bit of the upper mantle. It sits on top of a layer of slowly circulating rock called the "asthenosphere", which goes down a further 200 km (125 miles). Then comes the rest of the mantle, called the "mesosphere", followed by the molten outer core and solid inner core.

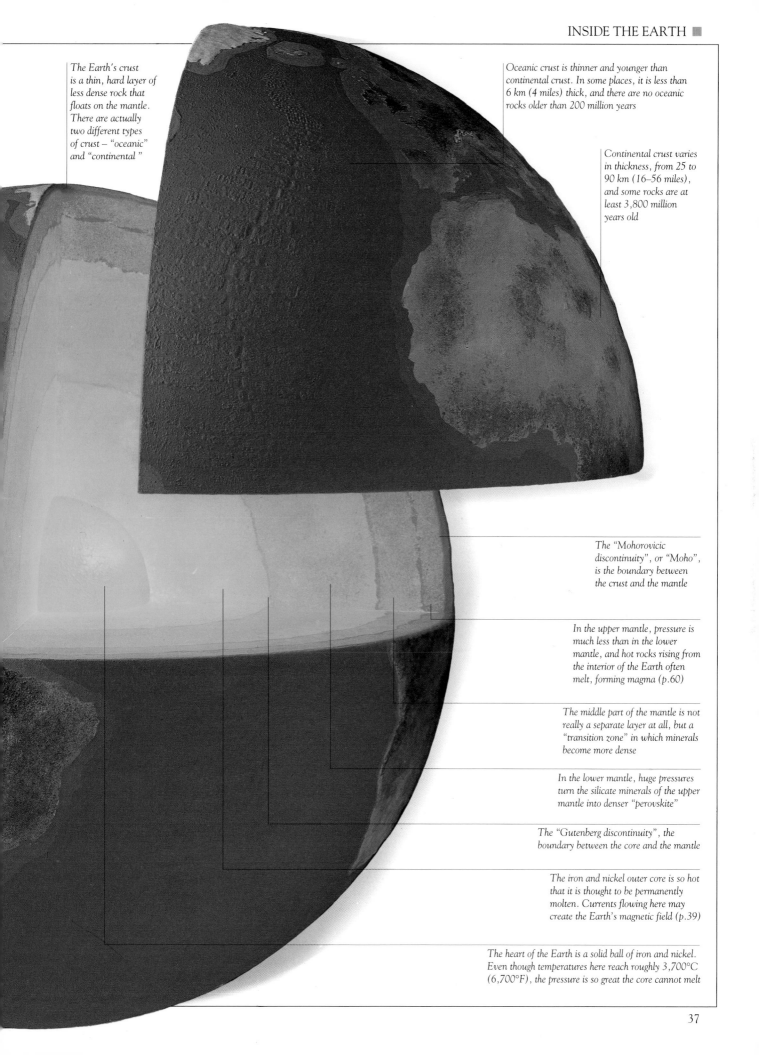

The Earth's crust is a thin, hard layer of less dense rock that floats on the mantle. There are actually two different types of crust – "oceanic" and "continental"

Oceanic crust is thinner and younger than continental crust. In some places, it is less than 6 km (4 miles) thick, and there are no oceanic rocks older than 200 million years

Continental crust varies in thickness, from 25 to 90 km (16–56 miles), and some rocks are at least 3,800 million years old

The "Mohorovicic discontinuity", or "Moho", is the boundary between the crust and the mantle

In the upper mantle, pressure is much less than in the lower mantle, and hot rocks rising from the interior of the Earth often melt, forming magma (p.60)

The middle part of the mantle is not really a separate layer at all, but a "transition zone" in which minerals become more dense

In the lower mantle, huge pressures turn the silicate minerals of the upper mantle into denser "perovskite"

The "Gutenberg discontinuity", the boundary between the core and the mantle

The iron and nickel outer core is so hot that it is thought to be permanently molten. Currents flowing here may create the Earth's magnetic field (p.39)

The heart of the Earth is a solid ball of iron and nickel. Even though temperatures here reach roughly 3,700°C (6,700°F), the pressure is so great the core cannot melt

Magnet Earth

JUST LIKE THE LITTLE MAGNETS often used to stick notes on freezer doors, the Earth is a magnet too. But it is so large that every magnet on Earth is affected by it. If you suspend a long magnet by a thread so that it can rotate freely, one end will always swing round to point to the North Pole and the other to the South Pole. Compass needles are simply tiny magnets, and so work in exactly the same way.

No-one knows quite why the Earth is magnetic. Most magnets stop working when they get hot – yet the centre of the Earth is hot enough to melt any metal. Most scientists now believe that the magnetism comes from the way the heat keeps the Earth's fluid outer core moving round and round (p.37). The core is rich in magnetic material and this circulation generates electricity – just like a dynamo on a bicycle or in a power station. It is these electric currents that turn the Earth into a giant magnet.

■ DISCOVERY ■
William Gilbert

It was William Gilbert (1544–1603), physician to Queen Elizabeth I of England, who first showed that the Earth is a giant magnet. Before 1600 no-one knew why compasses pointed north. In his book *De Magnete*, Gilbert described how he mounted a magnetic needle so that it could pivot freely – up and down as well as side to side. This is called a "dip" needle because it not only points north, but also dips down, at different angles, according to how far it is from the poles. Gilbert tried one next to a globe-shaped magnet and saw that the needle dipped in the same way, proving that the Earth acts just like a magnet.

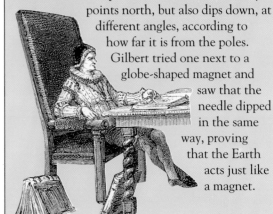

EXPERIMENT
Making a compass

If you like to be sure just where north and south are, why not make your own compass? You can turn a sewing needle into a magnet by stroking it repeatedly with another magnet. Then if it is mounted and allowed to float freely on water it will always swing round to point north.

YOU WILL NEED
● needle ● magnet ● polystyrene tile
● plastic pot ● cocktail stick
● plastic putty ● craft knife ● tape

1 DRAW A CIRCLE on to a polystyrene tile. Then cut out a disc very carefully with a craft knife.

2 STICK A BLOB of plastic putty on the bottom of the pot and push a cocktail stick upright into the middle.

3 MAGNETIZE THE NEEDLE by repeatedly drawing a magnet in the same direction along it for half a minute.

4 TAPE THE NEEDLE to the disc, centre it on the stick, and fill the pot with water until the disc just floats.

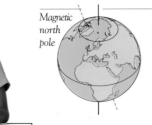

Magnetic north
Compasses do not point to the Earth's true North Pole, but at an angle to it. This is called the "magnetic declination".

EXPERIMENT
Magnetic field

A magnetic field is the area around every magnet where the magnetism exerts its force. Every magnet, from a tiny bar magnet to the Earth, has a field. In fact, the Earth's field is so similar to that of a simple bar magnet that people once thought there must be a giant core of solid iron inside the Earth. You can see the field around a bar magnet by doing this simple experiment with iron filings. It works because whenever an unmagnetized magnetic material such as iron comes near a magnet it becomes magnetized for a while. So each tiny filing acts like a compass, turning to line up with the magnetic field. The ball is included simply to represent the Earth.

1 CUT THE BALL in half and place it on the card. Tap the iron filings very gently from a bowl to sprinkle as thin and even a layer of filings as you can.

2 NOW CAREFULLY LOWER the card over the magnet so that the ball is right on top of it. Tap the edge of the card until the filings form a pattern.

YOU WILL NEED
● *magnet* ● *plastic ball* ● *card* ● *iron filings*

Iron filings are available from hardware shops, chemists, or perhaps from your school

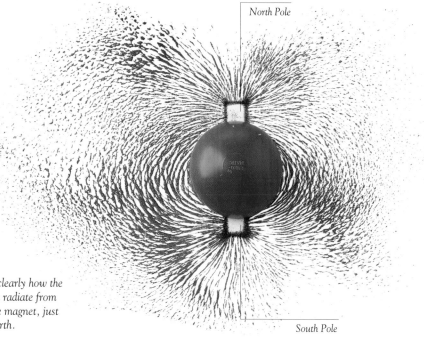

North Pole

South Pole

Force field
The iron filings show clearly how the lines of magnetic force radiate from each of the poles of the magnet, just as they do with the Earth.

■ The magnetosphere

The Earth's magnetic field is called the "magnetosphere" and stretches over 60,000 km (37,000 miles) into space. But it is not quite the same shape as that produced by a simple bar magnet, since it is blown out of shape by the "solar wind" – the stream of electrically-charged particles always rushing from the Sun. Some particles get into the Earth's atmosphere through clefts in the magnetosphere above the poles and create *aurora* – spectacular coloured lights sometimes seen in the night sky over the poles.

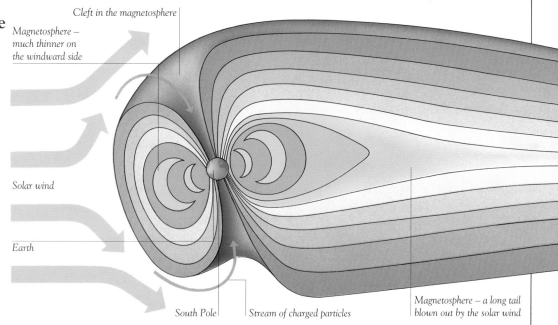

Cleft in the magnetosphere

Magnetosphere – much thinner on the windward side

Solar wind

Earth

South Pole

Stream of charged particles

Magnetosphere – a long tail blown out by the solar wind

Moving mantle

YOU MAY THINK THE EARTH beneath your feet is solid and unchanging. In fact, it is always moving. It is as if the ground you are standing on is a chunk of bread floating on thick, boiling soup. Inside the Earth's mantle, some scientists believe material is bubbling and churning – driven to the surface by the enormous temperatures in the Earth's interior, then cooling and sinking back again. This circular flow of material is known as convection, and you can observe "convection currents" in any liquid when heat is applied to it. But because the Earth's mantle is solid rock, this up and down flow of material is incredibly slow – 10,000 times slower than the hour hand on a clock. Some scientists estimate that it takes a piece of rock many millions of years to rise through the mantle. Of course, in geological terms this is a very rapid rate of movement.

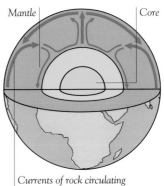

Mantle | *Core*

Currents of rock circulating throughout the mantle layer

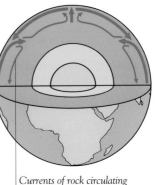

Currents of rock circulating in the upper mantle

■ Currents in the mantle

Deep heat
Some scientists think that convection currents extend throughout the Earth's mantle right down to the core.

Skin deep
Other scientists believe that convection occurs in the upper layers of the mantle only, down to about 700 km (435 miles).

■ The rock cycle

While convection currents are circulating material deep within the Earth's mantle, material is being circulated in the crust as well. This is called the "rock cycle". New hot rock is continually brought to the surface through volcanoes and other igneous processes (pp.56–61). There it cools and is slowly broken up by the weather (pp.106–107), then carried back to the sea in rivers. There it settles as sediment, some of which solidifies and is thrust back into the mantle by subduction (p.49), or exposed as surface rock again.

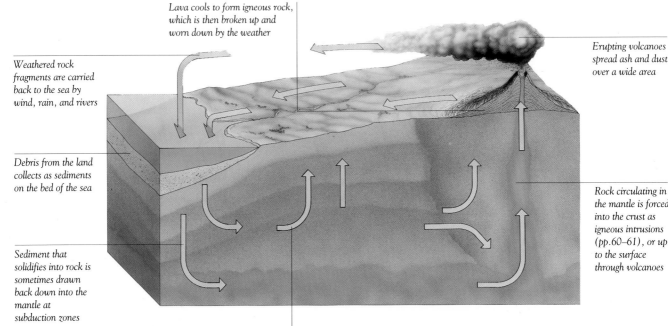

Lava cools to form igneous rock, which is then broken up and worn down by the weather

Weathered rock fragments are carried back to the sea by wind, rain, and rivers

Erupting volcanoes spread ash and dust over a wide area

Debris from the land collects as sediments on the bed of the sea

Sediment that solidifies into rock is sometimes drawn back down into the mantle at subduction zones

Rock circulating in the mantle is forced into the crust as igneous intrusions (pp.60–61), or up to the surface through volcanoes

Layers of sedimentary rock can eventually reach the surface again as sea levels change, or as plates collide

EXPERIMENT
Convection

Adult help is advised for this experiment

Convection currents similar to those found in the Earth's mantle circulate in all liquids and gases when heat is applied to them – the problem is being able to see the movement clearly. Here we have used food colouring to show the way convection currents move in cooking oil. Convection occurs because, as the oil is warmed, it expands and becomes less dense (lighter) than the oil around it. Since it is lighter, it drifts upwards through the cooler, denser oil around. Eventually it cools down, gets heavier again, and begins to sink. In this way, a continuous circulation is created.

YOU WILL NEED
● *heatproof glass dish* ● *nightlight candle*
● *food colouring (try different colours, some work better than others)* ● *cooking oil* ● *wooden blocks* ● *dropper*

1 PLACE TWO WOODEN BLOCKS on a level surface, a little way apart. Put a nightlight candle between them and ask an adult to light it.

2 HALF-FILL A HEATPROOF DISH with cooking oil and position firmly on the blocks. Squeeze a little food dye from a dropper into the bottom of the dish.

World circulation
Convection currents like those demonstrated here occur not only in the Earth's mantle, but also in the oceans and in the atmosphere, where they create winds (p.158 and p.178).

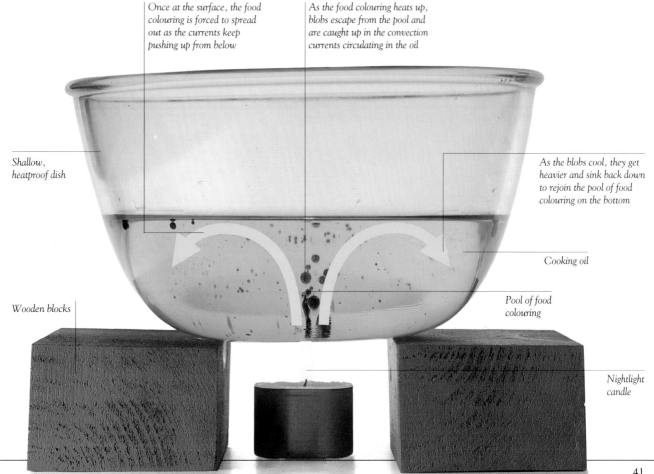

Once at the surface, the food colouring is forced to spread out as the currents keep pushing up from below

As the food colouring heats up, blobs escape from the pool and are caught up in the convection currents circulating in the oil

Shallow, heatproof dish

As the blobs cool, they get heavier and sink back down to rejoin the pool of food colouring on the bottom

Cooking oil

Pool of food colouring

Wooden blocks

Nightlight candle

TECTONIC PLATES

IT IS HARD TO BELIEVE THAT THE LAND BENEATH OUR FEET has ever moved, yet it is moving even now. Geologists believe that the Earth's surface is fragmented into 20 or so "tectonic plates". For millions of years the continents have drifted around the world on top of these plates as they jostle this way and that. The continual movement of the plates makes the earth quake and volcanoes erupt, builds and destroys mountains, and makes and breaks whole continents.

Long arcs of islands are created by the clash of two tectonic plates. The islands are formed by the volcanoes that erupt beside the deep ocean trench as one plate is forced down into the Earth's hot mantle.

When the young meteorologist Alfred Wegener (1880–1930) addressed a meeting of the American Philosophical Society in Philadelphia in 1923, he was not well received. "Utter, damned rot!" snorted the Society's president. Nor were his ideas any more popular elsewhere. "Ludicrous!" sneered Professor Chamberlin of the University of Chicago. "Wegener . . . is blind to every fact and every argument," another geologist blustered. In fact, Wegener met with extraordinary hostility from geologists everywhere he went.

What incensed them was Wegener's conviction that the world's continents were not fixed in one place, but had drifted around over the Earth's surface – and were still doing so. Such a notion seemed not only bizarre but flatly contradicted every current theory in geology. Yet it was not an entirely new idea.

Almost as soon as the first maps of the Atlantic were drawn in the sixteenth century, people noticed the remarkable way the coast of South America mirrored that of Africa. Then in the early nineteenth century, the German explorer Alexander von Humboldt (1769–1859) noticed striking similarities between the rocks of Brazil and those of the

Fossils of tropical plants are sometimes found far from the tropics. Could this be explained by the drifting of continents?

Congo. But no-one thought much about this until naturalists returned from their travels abroad with some strange findings. Not only did they find identical species of turtles, snakes, and lizards in both South America and Africa, they also found fossils of the extinct *Glossopteris* fern in India and Australia, and fossils of the reptile *Mesosaurus* in Brazil and South Africa.

■ Land bridges

To explain these strange coincidences, some naturalists suggested that continents had once been joined by land bridges long since drowned by oceans. At the time, most geologists believed the world was cooling and contracting; they assumed these land bridges had collapsed as the planet had shrunk.

There were flaws in the shrinking Earth and land bridge theory. But by the time Wegener dropped his bombshell in the 1920s, it was so firmly established that it was widely seen as all but fact. What Wegener suggested was that all continents had once been joined together in one vast land mass, which he called "Pangaea". But Pangaea split apart 300 million years ago, he said,

Tectonic plates slide around on material that flows like custard-powder paste (p.48).

and its fragments (our modern continents) have been drifting ever since. Fitting together Africa and South America, he found that the rock types seemed to match in numerous places. "It is just as if we were to refit the torn pieces of a newspaper by their matching edges," he wrote. But his ideas were still being ridiculed long after his tragic death in the Arctic in 1930.

■ Ocean proof

It was only when geologists began to explore the ocean floor in the 1950s that things began to change in favour of Wegener's theory. First of all, American geophysicist Maurice Ewing (1906–1974) discovered that the ocean floor was made of very young volcanic rocks. Then Ewing enlisted two young colleagues, Bruce Heezen and Marie Tharp, to make a map of the ocean floor. To their surprise, they found a deep canyon running right down the

The fact that rocks were lined up magnetically in matching stripes on either side of the mid-ocean ridge (p.47) convinced geologists that ocean floors spread.

middle of the Mid-Atlantic Ridge, the vast ridge in the middle of the Atlantic Ocean floor. What's more, when they plotted the location of recent earthquakes, they found that they all fell within this deep rift.

Within a few years, it was clear that the ridge was a feature not just of the Atlantic, but was part of a long submarine mountain range 60,000 km (37,000 miles) long, winding through all the

A polystyrene block sinks lower in water when it is loaded with sand, as continents may sink into the Earth's mantle when mountains are formed.

oceans of the world like the seam on a baseball. And everywhere along the ridge there was the same central rift.

■ Spreading oceans

Then in 1960 American geologist Harry Hess (1906–1969) made a startling suggestion. What if ocean floors are not permanent, but are spreading rapidly out from the mid-ocean ridge? As hot material wells up from the Earth's mantle through the central rift, Hess suggested, it pushes the two halves of the ocean apart.

This does not make the Earth's crust bigger, because as quickly as new ocean crust is created along the ridge, old ocean crust is dragged down into the mantle and destroyed along the deep trenches at the ocean's edge – a process that became known as "subduction". The continents are simply passengers on this ever-moving conveyor belt.

Many scientists were sceptical at first. Then Frederick Vine (born 1939) and Drummond Matthews (born 1931) identified

zebra stripes of strong and weak magnetism in the rocks on either side of the ridge – stripes that they realized indicated ancient switches in the Earth's magnetic field, recording the spreading of the ocean floor like the rings in a tree (p.47). A few years later, scientists on the research ship *Glomar Challenger* extracted a series of rock samples in a line away from the ridge – and it was discovered that the rocks became older on either side of the ridge.

■ Final proof

There was now no doubt that the ocean floor was spreading. At the same time, geologists confirmed that rock strata in Brazil matched those in Africa exactly, and a fossil of *Lystrosaurus*, a reptile known to have lived in Africa, India, and China 200 million years ago, was found in Antarctica. Geologists were now convinced that the continents were once joined, as Wegener had suggested 50 years earlier.

The new theory, known as "plate tectonics", developed

Today's continents can be fitted together like a jigsaw (p.45) to make one supercontinent – as geologists now believe they once were.

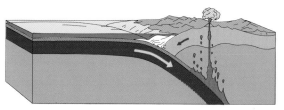

As fast as new crust is being created at the mid-ocean ridges, it is being destroyed at the margins, where one plate is forced down into the Earth's mantle beneath another – a process called "subduction".

rapidly during the 1970s and 1980s. Geologists suggested that the world's rigid outer shell, called the "lithosphere" (p.185), was split into nine large plates and a dozen smaller ones on which the continents ride. All but the large ocean plates – the Pacific, Nazca, and Cocos – are named after the continents that are embedded in them (p.186).

Tectonic plates are constantly being renewed along the mid-ocean ridges and destroyed by subduction. But no-one is quite sure what drives the plates. It may be caused by the heat circulating in the Earth's mantle (pp.40–41) or it may be simply because the plates slope away from the ocean ridges.

■ Implications

It soon became clear that plate tectonics explained much more than the coincidences of rocks and fossils. Earthquakes happen where plates shudder past each other. Volcanoes erupt where plates split asunder or dive into the mantle. Mountain ranges are thrown up where plates collide, buckling the edges of continents. It might even be that past changes in the world's climate occurred because the continents drifted to warmer or colder places. Geologists are only just beginning to appreciate the significance of this revolution in the way we look at the world.

High mountain ranges may have been thrown up where two tectonic plates have crashed together, crumpling rock strata and causing volcanoes to erupt.

Drifting continents

HAVE YOU EVER LOOKED at a map of the world and noticed how closely the west coast of Africa mirrors the east coast of South America? In fact, if you cut them out and push them together, their coasts fit as snugly as the pieces of a jigsaw – especially if you cut around their continental shelves (the bands of shallow water just next to the coast). And it is not only the coasts that match. So, too, do rocks, landscapes, and even ancient fossils. The coincidences are so many that scientists are now convinced the two continents were once joined together. Indeed, they now believe that all of today's continents, not just South America and Africa, were once joined together in one vast continent which they call Pangaea. About 200 million years ago, Pangaea began to break up, and the various bits – our modern continents – have been drifting apart ever since. Europe and North America are estimated to be moving 7 cm (3 in) further apart every year.

■ A world in motion

Pangaea
250 million years ago the continents were joined in one huge land mass (Pangaea) set in one ocean (Panthalassa).

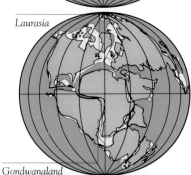

Laurasia

Split in the middle
200 million years ago Pangaea began to break up. A long arm of ocean split the continent almost in two bits, with Gondwanaland in the south, Laurasia in the north.

Gondwanaland

India
Atlantic Ocean
South America
Africa

The big break-up
135 million years ago Gondwanaland began to split into Africa and South America, creating the Atlantic, and India broke off and began to move north towards Asia.

Greenland

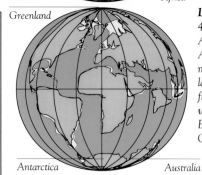

Antarctica
Australia

Lost continents
40 million years ago Australia and Antarctica began to move apart. A little later North America finally lost touch with northern Europe, leaving Greenland an island.

■ DISCOVERY ■

Alfred Wegener

As long ago as 1620, the English thinker Francis Bacon noticed how alike the coasts of South America and Africa are. But it was not until the twentieth century that scientists finally accepted the idea that continents drift about over the Earth. The man who pioneered the idea was a German meteorologist named Alfred Wegener (1880–1930). Wegener showed that bands of rock matched in continents divided by oceans, and so too did climates. On the Arctic island of Spitsbergen he found ancient traces of tropical ferns, and suggested that the best explanation for the presence of these tropical fossils in the Arctic was that Spitsbergen itself had moved there from the tropics. Wegener had no idea what made continents move, and at first geologists, especially in the United States, dismissed his ideas. What convinced most scientists was the discovery that magnetic rocks of different ages pointed in different directions, not just towards the magnetic north pole. The best explanation for these variations was that the continents themselves had swung round.

■ Shifting lands

One of the remarkable things about the idea of continental drift is that it explains many things besides the near-perfect fit of the South American and African coasts. It explains why fossils of the fern *Glossopteris* are found on every continent, and why fossils of the reptile *Lystrosaurus* are found in both South Africa and Antarctica. It also explains why continents have, in the past, experienced dramatically different climates. Northern Europe once had a tropical climate – simply because it was once in the tropics!

EXPERIMENT
Continental jigsaw

To see just how well the continents do fit together, why not try making this jigsaw? The shapes are based on the continental shelves of the continents – not the coast – because this is where they seem to have split apart. You can take the shapes of the continents from any map, but they will only fit together really well if you use a map which shows shapes accurately, such as a Mercator projection (p.28) or the one shown here. Notice how snugly Africa fits around South America, and the Great Australian Bight locks neatly around Antarctica. But continents join as well as split: India moved from Africa to collide with Asia, forming the Himalayan mountain range.

YOU WILL NEED
● *board* ● *card* ● *tracing paper*
● *pencil* ● *ruler* ● *scissors*

2 DRAW AN IDENTICAL but much larger grid and copy the shapes of the continents on, square by square. Then trace the shapes on to coloured card.

3 USING STRONG SCISSORS, cut out the shapes of the continents, and then the continental shelves, from the card. Be careful not to bend them.

4 ONCE YOU HAVE CUT OUT all the shapes, stick the continents on to the appropriate continental shelves and lay them on a piece of blue card (to represent Panthalassa, the world ocean). Now move them around until you can join them together perfectly as shown in the picture on the left. This is Pangaea.

North America
Panthalassa
South America
Asia
India
Great Australian Bight
Africa
Antarctica
Continental shelf

1 DRAW A SMALL GRID on tracing paper and tape it over the picture of the finished jigsaw (p.7 or above). Trace on the continents and continental shelves.

Spreading oceans

IT IS NOT ONLY THE CONTINENTS that move, but oceans too. In fact, the continents move because they are carried along on top of the moving oceanic crust, a bit like passengers on an escalator. The oceanic crust is made of rocks that are much, much younger than those often found in continents. Indeed, scientists now know that there are ridges underneath the oceans where new rock is being created all the time. These mid-ocean ridges are located where rising heat currents in the Earth's mantle (pp.40–41) hit the underside of the ocean crust. The currents are so powerful that they split the ocean floor, letting molten rock from the mantle come spilling out. Every time this happens, the ridge gets wider and wider, often forcing the edges of the ocean further and further apart.

The ocean floor
This model shows many features found by underwater exploration. Note that, for the depth shown, the sea bed should really be much wider.

At the edge of every ocean is a shallow sloping rim called the continental shelf

Running down from the shelf into the deep ocean is the very steep continental slope

Submarine canyons are cut through the continental slope by rivers flowing out to the sea

The vast abyssal plain makes up much of the ocean floor, and is covered in a thin layer of ooze formed from the remains of sea creatures

Submarine volcanoes and flat-topped "guyots", 1,000 m (3,300 ft) or more high, are dotted over the abyssal plain

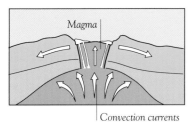

A ridge forms
As convection currents in the mantle rise towards the ocean floor, molten rock forces its way up, cracking the floor and opening a ridge. Magma gushes up through the cracks.

Magma

Convection currents

The ridge widens
As the ocean bed is pushed apart, some material sinks back toward the mantle. Rising magma freezes solid at the surface and is forced apart by new material coming up.

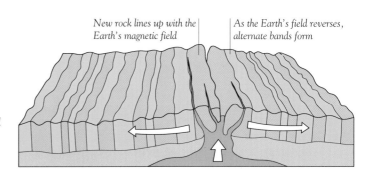

New rock lines up with the Earth's magnetic field

As the Earth's field reverses, alternate bands form

■ Bar code

As molten rock wells up from the ridge and freezes, magnetic material in the rocks sets in a certain way, lining up with the Earth's magnetic field. Because the field reverses every now and then, bands of new material set in alternate directions, creating a sort of "bar code" containing the history of sea floor spreading.

The top of the ocean crust is made from rock frozen as it wells from the mid-ocean ridge into rounded lumps of "pillow lava", set in ridges

Just beneath the pillow lava are sheets of volcanic rock that froze before they could pour out as lava

Beneath the layer of sheeted rock is another layer, formed by the settling of crystals from above

Molten rock, or "magma", wells up from the mantle, gathering in the "magma chamber" before forcing its way up through the mid-ocean ridge

Mantle

An ocean trench is formed when spreading oceanic crust meets a continental plate (pp.48–49) and plunges below it

Moving plates

IT MAY BE HARD TO BELIEVE, but there is almost no part of the Earth's surface that is fixed. Instead, it is made up of 20 or so "tectonic" plates that slip this way and that, jostling each other back and forth. Seven of the plates, like the vast Pacific Ocean Plate and the Eurasian Continental Plate, are huge, taking in almost entire oceans or continents. The rest are much smaller (p.186).

In some places, called "divergence zones", the plates are pulling apart, often because the sea floor is spreading (pp.46–47). But in "convergence zones", plates are pushing against each other, crumpling the crust or forcing one plate down into the mantle. In a few places, plates simply slide past each other.

■ Plastic rock

Earthquake vibrations show that the Earth's mantle is solid rock (p.40). But if it is solid, how do tectonic plates slide down into it (see right) as easily as if it were mud? The answer is that rock can be both fluid and rigid. When gradual pressure is applied (like the slow movement of tectonic plates), the mantle flows like mud. But if it gets a sharp shock, it turns solid. If this sounds odd, try mixing a teaspoon of custard powder with a teaspoon of water . Drag a spoon gently through the paste and it flows like liquid. Push sharply and it goes hard.

■ How do plates move?

No-one knows quite what moves the plates around on the Earth. Some believe the driving force is convection in the Earth's mantle (p.40), which pushes the plates around like scum on boiling jam. Scientists once thought that all convection currents moved in vast "cells" as big as the plates. Now it seems that blobs bubble up here and there in hot-spots, or "plumes", lifting the plates like piecrust in an oven.

Others believe the driving force is not convection but the weight of the oceanic plates alone. Mid-ocean ridges (p.46) are 2–3 km (1–2 miles) higher than the ocean rims, so plates could simply be sliding downhill. Another idea is that plates are like a cloth sliding off a table. Hot new rock forming at mid-ocean ridges cools down as it is pushed towards the ocean rim. As it cools, it gets heavier and sinks into the "asthenosphere" (p.36). Its weight then pulls the rest of the plate down with it – just as a cloth pulls itself off a table once enough is hanging over the edge.

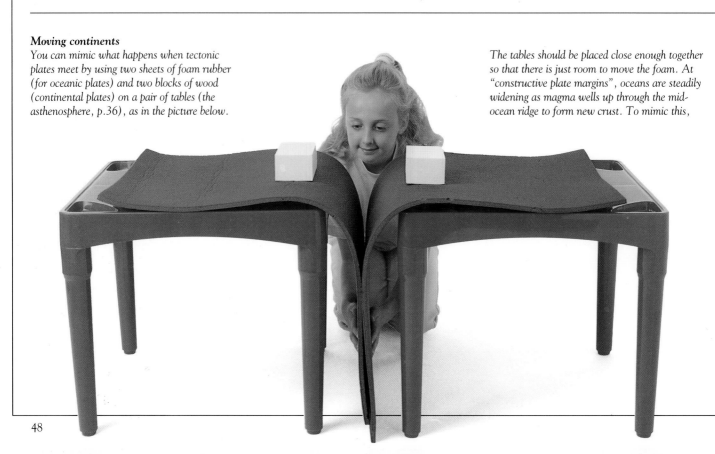

Moving continents
You can mimic what happens when tectonic plates meet by using two sheets of foam rubber (for oceanic plates) and two blocks of wood (continental plates) on a pair of tables (the asthenosphere, p.36), as in the picture below.

The tables should be placed close enough together so that there is just room to move the foam. At "constructive plate margins", oceans are steadily widening as magma wells up through the mid-ocean ridge to form new crust. To mimic this,

Subduction zones

In some places, and particularly at the edges of oceans, plates may collide with such force that one plate rides right over the other, forcing it down below the surface – a process called "subduction". Deep ocean trenches open up where the descending plate plunges into the asthenosphere. As it is thrust down, the plate starts to melt. Plumes of molten rock often rise up through the shattered edge of the overlying plate, and may even burst through to make huge volcanoes, such as Cotopaxi in the Andes. As the plate shudders down, the vibration can create earthquakes along what are called "Benioff zones", after the seismologist Hugo Benioff, who first associated earthquakes with subduction. Subduction usually occurs where thin oceanic plate is thrust beneath thick continental plate, or beneath another ocean plate; but even continents may be subducted in places.

Rock sponge

If the Earth's mantle is made of solid rock (see opposite), how do vast amounts of molten rock get to the surface to create new crust at the ocean ridges? The answer is that mantle rock is full of tiny holes through which the molten rock flows, just as oil flows through and out of a sponge when it is squeezed.

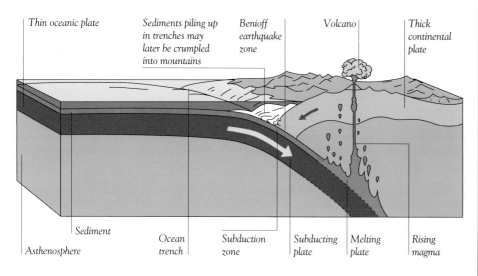

Thin oceanic plate — Sediments piling up in trenches may later be crumpled into mountains — Benioff earthquake zone — Volcano — Thick continental plate

Asthenosphere — Sediment — Ocean trench — Subduction zone — Subducting plate — Melting plate — Rising magma

simply push the two sheets of rubber up through the gap between the tables. You will see that, as the new "crust" is formed, the "continents" are gradually forced to move further apart, as demonstrated below. At "destructive plate margins", however, an oceanic plate may be sliding under a continental plate, or under another oceanic plate. As an oceanic plate is destroyed, continents may collide, just as the blocks will if you pull the rubber sheets down.

Inside a continent

As you read this, you are sitting on a vast slab of rock some 35–40 km (22–25 miles) thick, riding on the Earth's mantle. This slab – the continental crust – is much thicker and much older than the oceanic crust. And millions of years of being shoved around, bent, split, added to, and worn away have made the structure of continents varied and complicated. Geologists have a good idea of the nature of the material in the top half of the slab, down to a line called the "Conrad discontinuity". But their ideas about what lies below are vague. On the surface, continents seem to be essentially flat slabs of ancient crystalline rock, exposed at the surface as "shields" or concealed as platforms carpeted with sediments. Mountain ranges pile up at the margins, as rock is crumpled by the huge forces that move continents. But ongoing research paints an ever more complex picture.

Slice through a continent
No-one really knows what lies inside a continent, but this model of an imaginary continent, based on South America, has been constructed from what most geologists believe lies beneath our feet.

In parts of the mountain belt, vast blobs of igneous rock, called "batholiths" (p.60), form in the crust

The continental crust is at its thickest beneath mountain ranges

The Moho (p.37) marks the boundary between crust and mantle

Where the old crystalline basement rocks reach the surface, they form vast tablelands or high plateaux, known as "shields", such as the Canadian Shield

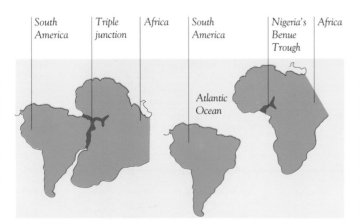

| South America | Triple junction | Africa | South America | Nigeria's Benue Trough | Africa |

Atlantic Ocean

■ Evolving continents

Geologists are now able to read the history of rocks in a continent, rather like reading tree rings. Continents seem to have a core of very ancient rock, forming "microcontinents", on to which younger rocks have been welded at various intervals ever since. Continents, though, are not fixed. They can move, merge, and split. At times, molten rock from the Earth's mantle bursts through the continental crust to split it apart in a triple junction (right). Africa and South America were formed when just such a junction slowly widened (left).

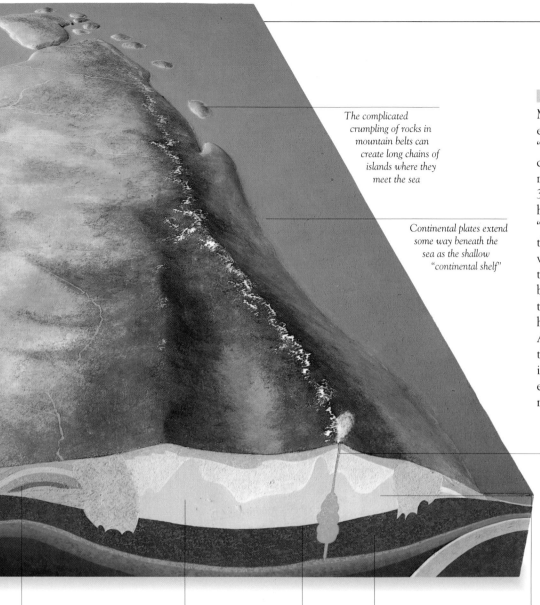

The complicated crumpling of rocks in mountain belts can create long chains of islands where they meet the sea

Continental plates extend some way beneath the sea as the shallow "continental shelf"

The constant movement of rocks in the mountain belts allows plumes of molten rock to shoot up from the mantle to form volcanoes

Basement rock

More than 80 per cent of every continent is an ancient "basement" of very, very old crystalline rock. These rocks may date back more than 3,800 million years, but they have been so distorted and "metamorphosed" over time that dating them accurately is very difficult. Geologists once thought that basement rocks, because they are worn flat on top, had not changed for hundreds of millions of years. And yet we now know that they contain folds and intrusions even more elaborate than those found in mountain belts.

Beneath many of the world's plains are stable platforms made from vast layers of sediment, undisturbed since they were laid down in shallow seas which once flooded the continents

The bulk of the crust is a "basement" of ancient crystalline rock, the upper half of which is mostly granite-like rocks, schists, and gneisses (p.83)

The Conrad discontinuity marks the bottom of the upper layer of the continental crust

The lower half of the basement is a mystery: in some places it seems to be basalt, like ocean crust; in other places, it may be a special kind of rock called "amphibolite"

Many continental plates are bordered or crossed by "orogenic belts", where shifting tectonic plates (p.48) have crumpled and distorted the rock, throwing up huge new mountain ranges such as the Alps and the Himalayas

Triple junction

A plume of hot rock doming up beneath the thick continental crust can split it apart. Typically, it will split three ways as cracks spread out from the centre of the bulging dome, creating huge "rift" valleys, such as the Great Rift Valley in East Africa. As the rupture spreads the valley gets bigger and may become partly inundated by ocean water.

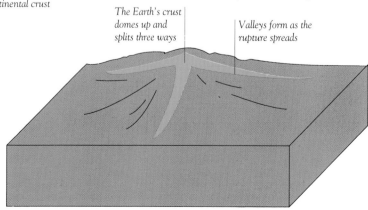

The Earth's crust domes up and splits three ways

Valleys form as the rupture spreads

The VIOLENT EARTH

Clouds of ash, streams of fire
*When a volcano erupts it can shower the land
around with volcanic ash. In Pompeii in Italy,
2,000 people were buried alive after the eruption
of Mount Vesuvius in AD 79 (above). Anyone
living close to an active volcano is in constant
danger from the rivers of molten rock spilling
from the Earth's fiery interior (left).*

MOST OF THE PROCESSES
shaping our planet are so
slow and gentle that we
barely notice them. But
there are times when the
Earth reveals its true power
suddenly and terrifyingly –
in massive earthquakes,
when the ground shudders
enough to bring down the
strongest building; or in
volcanic eruptions, when
gigantic explosions expel
devastating streams of
molten rock, showers of
red-hot cinders, and vast
clouds of gas and ash.

VOLCANIC ACTIVITY

WE OFTEN THINK OF THE EARTH'S SURFACE as solid and stable. Yet it shakes continually as the plates that make continents and ocean floors grind together; we feel these shakes as earthquakes. And every now and then the crust cracks to let hot magma and gases from inside the Earth burst on to the surface in a volcanic eruption. Some earthquakes and eruptions are scarcely noticeable; others are events of such vast power that they can create mountains and islands – or destroy them.

In a geyser, *underground water comes into contact with hot rocks. When the water reaches boiling point, steam forms, forcing water to surface above ground.*

Until this century, people had little idea what caused volcanic eruptions or earthquakes, and many ancient myths arose to explain these frightening and often dangerous events. In Europe, the Romans believed that volcanic eruptions were caused by Vulcan, the god of fire. According to Roman mythology, Vulcan lived beneath Mount Etna, a large volcano on the island of Sicily, where he made thunderbolts for the god Jupiter.

On the other side of the world, the Japanese had their own explanation for why earthquakes occurred. According to Japanese folklore, they were caused by a giant catfish, called the *namazu*, which lived beneath the ground, where it set off earthquakes by shaking its huge body.

The Ancient Greeks were the first people to suggest a "scientific" explanation for earthquakes. Aristotle, a philosopher who lived from 384 to 322 BC, thought that earthquakes might be caused by winds that fanned flames beneath the ground. Underground fires also seemed to explain the occurrence of volcanoes, and for centuries people believed that volcanoes burned like giant bonfires deep in the ground.

Seismometers were *invented in ancient China. They point to that part of the Earth where an earthquake has occurred.*

■ The tectonic link

Since the dawn of history, people have observed that eruptions and earthquakes frequently occur in the same places – often close to the sea. Volcanoes appeared on many early maps of the world, but it was not until the last century that an Irish engineer, Robert Mallet (1810–1881), drew up a detailed map that pinpointed where earthquakes occurred. He confirmed that they did not happen at random all over the world. Instead, they were concentrated in quite narrow zones – the same zones in which most volcanoes are found.

Mallet did not know why this was, and it was not until late in the twentieth century that the puzzle was solved. The answer was provided by the theory of plate tectonics. If you look at the map of the Earth's crustal plates on p.186, and then compare it with the map on p.62, you will see the connection for yourself. The great majority of volcanic eruptions and earthquakes take place along the boundaries of crustal ("tectonic") plates, and they are caused by the way plates grind together and pull apart.

■ Eruptions

There are about 500 active volcanoes on Earth, and the most powerful eruptions take place where plates collide. Here, enormous amounts of

energy build up in quite small regions of the Earth's crust. This energy is enough to melt rock, which comes to the surface as fiery liquid "magma". This pours over the ground as lava, or explodes into clouds of dust and lava "bombs".

In AD 79 an eruption of this type completely destroyed the

Magma rises through *the Earth's crust because it is less dense than the material around it (p.61).*

Roman city of Pompeii, engulfing it in a thick blanket of ash. The eruption, which is still famous over 1,900 years later, was described in vivid detail by a 17-year-old eyewitness, Pliny the Younger (AD c.61–c.113). Pliny's uncle, a famous naturalist, was one of the 2,000 people who died in the eruption, and Pliny the Younger was lucky to escape alive. Today, the term "Plinian" is applied to some of the greatest eruptions.

There have been several huge eruptions in recent years. In 1980 Mount Saint Helens in northwest USA

In the largest volcanic eruptions, *the crater of the volcano may collapse to form a circular caldera, which may often fill with water.*

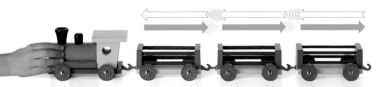

In an earthquake, "primary"
shock waves travel through the
ground, creating a pulse of movement
forwards and then backwards (p.63).

devastated over 600 square
kilometres (230 square miles) of
forest. In 1991 Mount Pinatubo
in the Philippine Islands woke up
from a "sleep" that had lasted 600
years to blow itself apart in a
gigantic eruption.

Volcanoes also erupt where the
crustal plates are separating.
These eruptions are much gentler
than those where plates collide.
As the plates pull apart, magma
wells up through vents to
seal the gap between the
plates, and sometimes spill
out to form a wide dome.
Because plates usually
separate under the sea,
magma sometimes emerges
underwater. In recent
years, remote-
controlled
cameras have
shown how the
red-hot liquid
rock cools and
solidifies only
seconds after emerging on to the
bed of the ocean.

Not all volcanoes occur near
tectonic plate margins. A few are
associated with "mantle plumes",
where magma rises beneath the
Earth's crust at permanent "hot
spots", well away from plate
margins. In oceanic areas, the
magma may punch through the
crust again and again to form a
succession of volcanic islands as
the plate drifts over the hot spot.
The Hawaiian island chain in the
Pacific formed in this way.

Where mantle plumes occur
beneath continents, the magma

Magma explodes because
it contains dissolved gases.
When the pressure falls, the
gases bubble out (p.57).

tends to stay trapped in the thick
crust. Occasionally, though, it
may break through to form vast
plateaux of basalt, called "flood
basalts", of which the most
spectacular example is possibly
the Deccan plateau in India.

■ Plates and quakes
When the Earth's crustal plates
collide, they do not slide
smoothly past each other.
Instead, they move in sudden
jolts. In a small earthquake, the
plates move less than a hair's
breadth. But a large earthquake
can make great changes to the
landscape. In 1835 the great
naturalist Charles Darwin
(1809–1892) reported how,
after an earthquake in
South America, the shore
rose, hoisting mussels and
other sea animals high into
the air. In an Alaskan
earthquake in 1899, huge
sections of the coast were
lifted up about 14 m (46 ft).
Blocks can also shift
sideways, leaving a tell-tale
scar, or "slip fault".

Some cities, such as San
Francisco and Tokyo, are
especially at risk because they are
close to where two plates are
colliding. The greatest hazard to
the people in these cities is not
the movement of the
ground itself, but
falling buildings and
fire. In 1906 San
Francisco was shaken
by a severe earthquake,
and then devastated as
fire swept through its
buildings, many of
which were made of
wood. Tokyo shared the

same fate in 1923, when an
earthquake struck at lunchtime,
upsetting cooking stoves and
setting houses alight all over the
city. Today, both cities have
strict regulations to ensure that
buildings are fireproof and that
they can withstand an intense
shaking of the ground.

■ Making predictions
The Ancient Chinese were the
first to use devices to register
earthquakes. Their instruments
were the forerunners of modern
seismographs and seismometers,
which register vibrations
and measure
earthquakes with
great precision. It
is with the help of such
sophisticated instruments
that vulcanologists (who study
volcanoes) and seismologists
(who study earthquakes) can
warn of danger ahead.

Devices have also been created
for measuring the size and effect
of earthquakes. In 1935 Charles
F. Richter (1900–1985) devised a
scale for measuring the energy
released during earthquakes. He
worked it out so that each
earthquake has just one
magnitude, and that each value
on the scale is 30 times greater
than the previous one. So, an
earthquake of magnitude 7 is 30
times more powerful than one of
magnitude 6. The Mercalli Scale,
on the other hand, measures the
effects of an earthquake, and its
12-point scale describes the
different levels of damage (p.62).

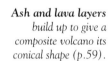

Ash and lava layers
build up to give a
composite volcano its
conical shape (p.59).

By comparing flow rates in a variety of
everyday liquids, you can see how different
kinds of lava can create many different kinds
of landscapes (p.59).

Volcanic eruptions

FEW SIGHTS ARE MORE AWESOME than a volcano erupting in a huge explosion of gas, ash, and lava (molten rock). But not all eruptions are so dramatic – many volcanoes gently ooze lava without blowing up. Sudden eruptions occur when rising hot rock (magma) is trapped underground. Gases slowly swell within the rock until the pressure forces the magma to the surface. Every year, there are 25 or so major eruptions on land, and many more under the sea. Some volcanoes are very "active", erupting year after year. Others are "dormant" (sleeping) and may become "extinct" (stop erupting altogether).

■ Inside a volcano

Deep beneath a volcano is a chamber of magma. Pressure builds up here until the magma escapes through narrow pipes and bursts out on the surface.

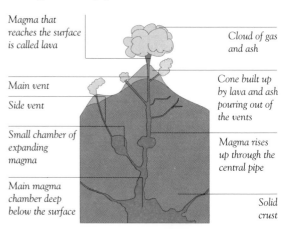

Magma that reaches the surface is called lava

Cloud of gas and ash

Main vent

Side vent

Cone built up by lava and ash pouring out of the vents

Small chamber of expanding magma

Magma rises up through the central pipe

Main magma chamber deep below the surface

Solid crust

EXPERIMENT
Baking a volcano

 Adult help is advised for this experiment

You can mimic a volcanic eruption by baking jam tarts. The tart's lid is the Earth's crust, and jam is magma. A small hole in the lid is like a weak point in the crust. As the tarts heat up, air inside forces the jam upwards. The "volcanoes" erupt, and lava flows out.

YOU WILL NEED
● shortcrust pastry
● jam ● rolling pin
● tray ● oven gloves
● knife & spoon
● pastry cutters

2 PUT A CIRCLE OF PASTRY in each bowl of the tart tray. Add a teaspoonful of jam to each one.

3 PUT A PASTRY LID on each tart, and press down the edges to seal them. Make a small hole in the centre of each.

Jam erupts from the tarts, like magma from a volcano

4 WHEN THE TARTS are cooked, the jam "magma" will have erupted. Your volcanoes are now ready to eat!

1 ROLL OUT SOME shortcrust pastry (not puff pastry), then cut out discs for the base and lid of each tart.

EXPERIMENT
Exploding gas

Adult help is advised for this experiment

Fizzy drinks contain a gas – carbon dioxide – which is invisible as long as the bottle is sealed. No bubbles form, because pressure inside the bottle keeps the carbon dioxide dissolved. The same is true of magma below the Earth's crust. Enormous pressure keeps huge amounts of carbon dioxide and other gases dissolved in the molten rock. With a *plastic* bottle of fizzy drink, you can find out what happens when magma rises and pressure falls.

You Will Need
- *plastic (not glass) bottle of fizzy drink*
- *food colouring*

Gas and magma

Nearer the surface, various gases form ever-larger bubbles

Bubbles continue to expand as magma rises and pressure falls

Tiny bubbles form in magma as it rises through the chamber

The amount of dissolved gas that magma can hold depends mainly on pressure. As magma rises towards the surface, the pressure falls and it can hold less gas. The gas released forms bubbles. At first these are tiny, as the pressure is still high. But as pressure falls further, the bubbles expand, giving magma its explosive power.

1 IF YOU UNSCREW THE CAP a little to reduce the pressure, bubbles appear. Tighten the cap, and they vanish.

2 TAKE OFF THE CAP AGAIN, and add some food colouring to the drink. This makes it easier to see the bubbles.

3 SCREW THE CAP ON TIGHTLY, and give the bottle a gentle shake. This ensures that lots of gas is dissolved.

4 UNSCREW THE CAP A LITTLE, holding the bottle away from your face. The fizzy "magma" will erupt from the bottle as the pressure suddenly drops.

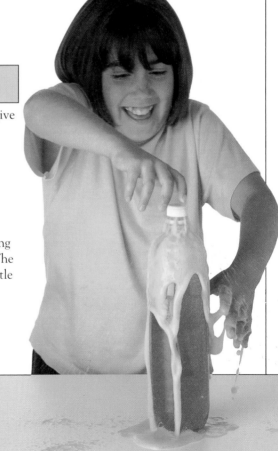

Molten rocks and fiery gases

WHEN A VOLCANO ERUPTS, a terrifying mixture of red hot lava, cinders, and gases bursts on to the Earth's surface. Some volcanoes spew runny lava that flows freely over wide areas. Others ooze sticky lava that piles up in a cone and may plug the vent. When this happens, pressure built up beneath the plug can blow it out in a jet of gas, steam, lava drops, and cinders that shoots high into the air, or roars down the volcano as a "nuée ardente" (glowing cloud), burning all in its path. How far the "pyroclastic" (solid) material is flung depends on its size. Lava drops fall close to the vent as solid volcanic "bombs"; cinders blanket a vast area in ash; while winds high in the air can carry fine dust right around the world.

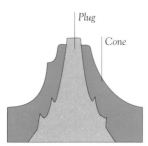

Ropy lava
Runny lava quickly cools to form a skin that is wrinkled by the lava still flowing beneath. In Hawaii, this is called "pahoehoe" lava.

■ Formation of a caldera

Magma chamber

Active volcano
In an active volcano, the magma chamber beneath the volcano is full of magma.

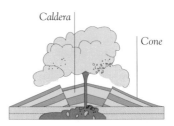

Caldera   *Cone*

The cone slips
If the magma level drops, the top of the cone may collapse, forming a giant crater, called a "caldera".

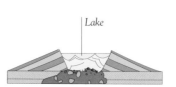

Lake

A lake forms
As the volcano dies down, the cone collapses and the caldera fills with water

■ Volcanic plugs

When the vent of a volcano is plugged by thick lava, it may explode – or die out altogether. If it dies out, the rest of the volcano may be slowly worn away to leave nothing but the hard plug, standing tall and sheer above the surrounding country. Sugar Loaf Mountain, in Rio de Janeiro, is a plug, as is the Devil's Tower in Wyoming.

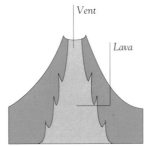

Vent

Lava

Plugged volcano
When the lava is very thick and sticky, a volcano's vent may become completely clogged up.

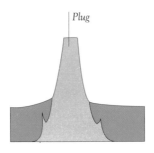

Plug

Cone

Eroded cone
As the volcano becomes inactive, weathering slowly strips away the soft ash and lava cone, but has little effect on the hard plug in the vent.

Plug

Surviving plug
Eventually, all that is left of the volcano is the plug, standing tall and isolated. There are whole landscapes full of such plugs.

■ DISCOVERY ■
Volcanoes and rocks

In the early days of geology, volcanoes were a puzzle. One important group of geologists, the "Neptunists", thought all rocks were created by sedimentation – in other words, from fragments of material laid down by water. They believed that volcanoes burned fuel, like coal, which was itself created by sedimentation. Leopold Buch (1774–1853), a German geologist and great traveller, was at first convinced by the theories of the Neptunists. But after studying Vesuvius, a volcano in Italy, and the Auvergne, a volcanic landscape in France, he began to have doubts. He found no trace of any fuel which the volcanoes might have burned.

His studies also showed that, in some places, basalt (p.81) must have formed volcanically. Buch did not completely reject the ideas of Neptunism, but his work helped make it clear that volcanoes play an important part in the rock cycle (p.40). He also coined the word "andesite" for the volcanic rock found in the Andes and in other subduction zones.

EXPERIMENT
Lava flows

There are many different types of lava. Some are so sticky they hardly flow at all. Others are so runny that they flow a great distance at speeds up to 100 kmh (60 mph). Lavas rich in silica (acid lava) are much stickier than the non-acid lavas, such as pahoehoe lava, that cool to form basalt rock. In this experiment, you can see how different liquids, or "lavas", flow. To do this, hold each liquid about 10 cm (4 in) above the plate, gently pour it out, and see how freely it spreads across the bottom of the plate. Heating the liquids with warm water shows how the flow changes with temperature too. Finally, you can see what happens to the rate of flow when liquid "lava" contains particles of a solid.

YOU WILL NEED
● *jar* ● *water* ● *sand* ● *spoon* ● *watch* ● *tray* ● *notepad* ● *pencil* ● *dish* ● *sticky liquids*

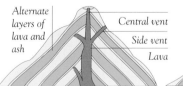

Home-made lava
This experiment uses everyday liquids, such as treacle, honey, washing-up liquid, and shampoo.

Like different lavas, they each have a different thickness, which can change with temperature.

1 TIME THE SPREADING of the thinnest liquids first. Then heat them in a dish of warm water and compare times.

2 REPEAT THE EXPERIMENT with a very sticky liquid, such as treacle. This liquid has a high viscosity.

3 MIX SOME SAND into the treacle. This makes the treacle so sticky that it will hardly flow at all.

4 POUR OUT THE MIXTURE, and time how long it takes to spread. Does its shape differ from the thinnest liquids?

■ Types of volcano

A volcano's shape depends on the kind of lava or ash that it produces. Where tectonic plates are colliding (p.48), the lava is very thick and sticky. It cools to form tall, cone-shaped volcanoes, like Mount Fuji in Japan. Where plates pull apart, the lava is runnier, and spreads out to form huge, flat volcanoes.

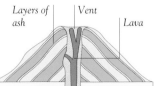
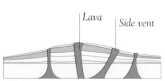
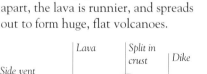

Composite volcano
Many of the world's tallest volcanoes are built of alternating layers of lava and volcanic ash. The lava is quite sticky, so does not flow far before it solidifies.

Cinder cone
A cinder volcano also has a steep conical shape, but is made mostly of volcanic ash, or "scoria". Each time the volcano erupts, more layers of ash are added.

Shield volcano
This kind of volcano forms where eruptions give runny lava that flows out across a wide area instead of making a cone. Shield volcanoes often have many side vents.

Fissure (flood basalt)
Sometimes runny lava floods out over vast areas from widening splits in the Earth's crust. It cools to form giant basalt plateaux, such as India's Deccan.

Volcanic intrusions

ERUPTING VOLCANOES LOOK DRAMATIC, but they are only a small part of the Earth's volcanic activity. Much of the molten rock (magma) rising from the Earth's mantle never reaches the surface, especially when it rises beneath continents. Instead it cools slowly and hardens underground, forming many different kinds of "igneous intrusion". These include: almost vertical walls of rock called "dikes", formed when magma is forced into cracks opened up in the crust; horizontal sheets called "sills", formed where magma seeps along existing cracks; and vast domes called "batholiths", formed where sticky magma wells up beneath the surface. Although they form underground, intrusions can often be seen on the surface. This occurs when the overlying rock is worn away, exposing the harder igneous rock underneath.

■ Hot rock from below

Volcanic activity tends to occur along the edges of tectonic plates (p.48), or where isolated plumes of hot rock bubble up beneath the surface. Where adjacent plates are moving apart, magma rises to

the surface to form ridges of new crust. When plates collide, one is forced under the other and melts into magma, which then rises through the adjacent plate, and may burst on to the surface to form a chain of volcanoes (p.67).

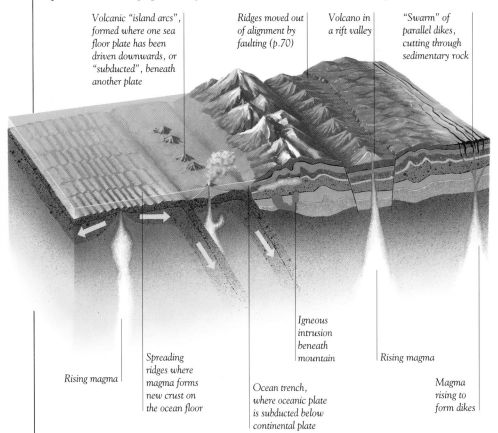

Volcanic "island arcs", formed where one sea floor plate has been driven downwards, or "subducted", beneath another plate

Ridges moved out of alignment by faulting (p.70)

Volcano in a rift valley

"Swarm" of parallel dikes, cutting through sedimentary rock

Rising magma

Spreading ridges where magma forms new crust on the ocean floor

Ocean trench, where oceanic plate is subducted below continental plate

Igneous intrusion beneath mountain

Rising magma

Magma rising to form dikes

■ How dikes form

Dikes usually cut right across existing rock formations. In some places, many dikes lie side by side, making a "swarm".

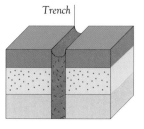

Protruding dike

Hard dike
Where a dike is harder than the rock around it, erosion leaves the dike protruding.

Trench

Soft dike
Where the dike is softer than the surrounding rock, it will wear away to form a trench.

Magma on the move

Magma rises to the surface because it is less dense than the rock around it, and mixes very little with the surrounding rock. In this experiment, you can use oil and water to see how this happens. The oil forms bubbles that float to the surface, where they may join to form an "intrusion". Each rising bubble represents a "pluton", a giant globule of igneous rock. Just like bubbles, plutons often join together to make even bigger masses of rock.

YOU WILL NEED
● cooking oil ● food colouring ● funnel
● washing-up liquid bottle ● tank or deep dish

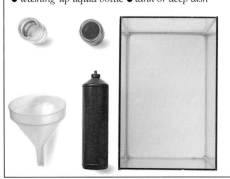

Yellowstone geyser
Geysers form when groundwater is boiled by hot rocks and explodes into the air.

■ Igneous intrusions

When molten rock rises up from the mantle, it can squeeze between the existing layers of rock, or break across them, forming intrusions. A sill is an example of a "concordant" intrusion, because it fits in with the shape of the surrounding rock. A dike is "discordant", because it cuts through the rock around it. When magma arches up into the rock, squeezing into existing cracks, it cools to form domes called "laccoliths".

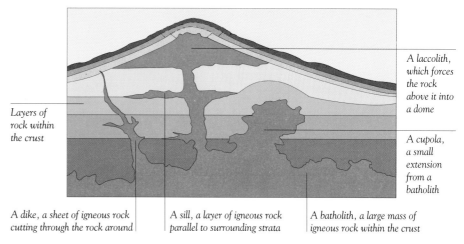

A laccolith, which forces the rock above it into a dome

A cupola, a small extension from a batholith

Layers of rock within the crust

A dike, a sheet of igneous rock cutting through the rock around

A sill, a layer of igneous rock parallel to surrounding strata

A batholith, a large mass of igneous rock within the crust

1 PARTLY FILL the washing-up bottle with oil, using a funnel, and replace the cap on the bottle.

2 FILL THE TANK WITH WATER, and add colouring. Put your finger over the bottle's spout, and lower into the water.

3 TAKE YOUR FINGER OFF the cap, and give the bottle a gentle squeeze. The "magma" will rise to the surface.

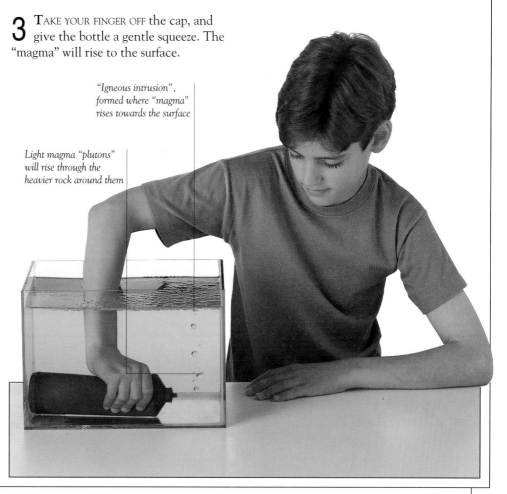

"Igneous intrusion", formed where "magma" rises towards the surface

Light magma "plutons" will rise through the heavier rock around them

Earthquakes

WHERE THE EARTH'S tectonic plates collide, huge amounts of energy push rock against rock. In some places, the plates slide over each other little by little. But in other places they get stuck. For years, and even decades, the forces pushing the plates build up. Then, quite suddenly, the pent-up energy is released. The plates slip over each other, sending shock waves of energy in all directions. When these waves reach the surface, they are felt as earthquakes.

An earthquake produces two kinds of shock waves. "Body" waves, which include P waves and S waves, travel through the rock itself. "Surface" waves travel only on the Earth's skin, just like waves in water (p.144).

■ Earthquakes and volcanoes

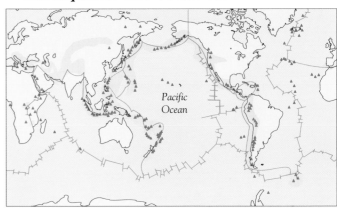

Pacific Ocean

▲ *Volcanoes*   *Earthquake zone*

Your chances of actually experiencing an earthquake, or of seeing an active volcano, are greatest if you live near a "subduction zone", where one plate is being forced under another. On the map above you can see that earthquake zones and volcanoes closely follow the Earth's plate boundaries (blue lines). In fact, the "Ring of Fire" that almost encircles the Pacific Ocean has more earthquakes and eruptions than anywhere else on Earth.

■ Measuring earthquakes

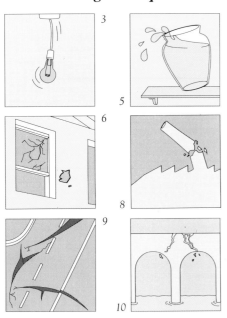

Earthquakes are measured by the Richter Scale for overall power, or "magnitude", but by the Mercalli Scale for their effect. Six points on the 12-point Mercalli Scale are shown above, from intensity 3, which is a light vibration felt indoors, through intensity 8, in which vulnerable structures are damaged, to intensity 10, which includes major structural damage.

EXPERIMENT
Shock waves

The energy of an earthquake's shock waves is greatest near the earthquake's "focus", the point underground where the plate movement takes place. The focus can be up to 600 km (370 miles) deep. The ground directly above the focus is called the "epicentre". This is usually (but not always) where most damage occurs. The waves' power decreases as they move further from the epicentre. In this experiment, you can see the effect of a shock wave near its focus, and how it fades as it spreads.

Spreading shock
Scatter some sand over a table and then tap the table with a rubber hammer. The shock wave will make the sand jump into the air. Move the sand further away from where the hammer strikes the table, and then tap the table again.

A shock wave from the hammer makes the sand jump

▪ DISCOVERY ▪
The seismometer

A seismometer is a device that registers an earthquake. One of the earliest was designed by the Chinese scholar Chang Heng during the second century AD. It was built around a heavy pendulum attached to several dragons' heads, each of which held a metal ball. When an earthquake took place, it set the pendulum in motion. As the pendulum swung, it opened a dragon's mouth, letting a ball drop down into a metal frog below. The location of the earthquake could then be worked out by observing which ball had fallen.

EXPERIMENT
Up and down waves

People who witness earthquakes sometimes describe how the ground ripples up and down like water. This is caused mainly by Secondary, or S, waves. S waves get their name because they are the second pulse of waves to be felt after an earthquake. Unlike P waves (see below left), they can only pass through solid rock.

Wave direction

Height of S wave

Making S waves
You can see the effect of S waves by snaking a wave along a rope. Like the ground in an earthquake, the rope rises and falls as a wave of energy passes along it.

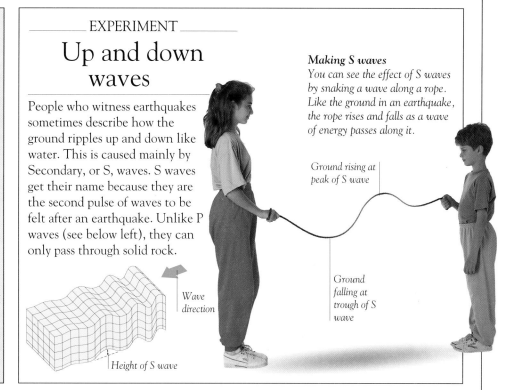

Ground rising at peak of S wave

Ground falling at trough of S wave

EXPERIMENT
Push and pull waves

At a seismographic recording station, the first sign of an earthquake is a burst of Primary, or P, waves. These shock waves travel in the same way as sound waves, alternately compressing and expanding the material that they travel through. Also, like sound, they can move through liquids as well as solids, although they move more slowly in liquids. P waves can pass directly through the Earth's molten core, so that they can be felt on the opposite side of the world. A toy train gives a good idea of how P waves are transmitted. If you quickly push and pull, a wave of movement runs forward and back along the wagons.

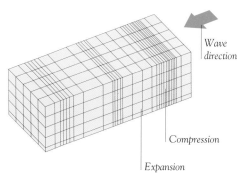

Wave direction

Compression

Expansion

As a P wave travels outwards, the wagons are pushed together, or "compressed"

Each "compression" is followed by "expansion", as the wagons pull apart

MOUNTAIN BUILDING

A FEW OF THE WORLD'S HIGHEST MOUNTAINS are isolated volcanoes, such as the lofty peaks of Mount Kilimanjaro in Africa and Mount Fuji in Japan, built up higher and higher by successive eruptions. But most mountains occur in huge ranges that stretch for hundreds or even thousands of kilometres – like the Asian Himalayas and the South American Andes. Ranges like these have been thrown up by the enormous power of the Earth's crust in motion. Many are still growing.

The titanic force of tectonic plates coming together can create enormous fractures in the rock, as in the case of California's San Andreas fault.

Earth scientists are now fairly certain that most of the world's high mountain ranges were created by the crumpling of thick layers of rock between the edges of two colliding tectonic plates (p.48). But the huge forces needed to warp, tear, and fracture so much rock are so hard to imagine that it is only fairly recently that geologists have begun to understand the process of mountain building.

In the seventeenth century, when people like Isaac Newton (1642–1727) were starting to lay the foundations of modern science, the English cleric Thomas Burnet (1635–1715) suggested that mountains were the ruins of the Earth's crust left after the biblical flood. He thought that the Earth once had a smooth shell, from which the flood waters gushed when God cracked it to create the Deluge. Mountains were the tilted fragments of this shell.

One hundred years later, many people still insisted that only such

Rocks can be fractured in many ways by tectonic processes, from simple tear faults (below left) to vast rift valleys (far right), which are formed where continents pull apart. Fault types are described in detail on pp.70–71.

an extraordinary catastrophe could have had the force to build mountains. But some geologists thought mountains were built much more gradually. The Scottish geologist James Hutton (1726–1797), for instance, argued that the Earth is reshaped by gentler forces working steadily over millions of years in an endlessly repeated sequence – the wearing down of rocks by water and weather, the accumulation of eroded material as sediments, the solidifying of sediments into rock, their uplift as the Earth's hot interior expands, and, finally, their folding into mountains.

■ Shrinking?

Yet while the science of geology advanced, there was little real understanding of how mountains came to be. By the mid-nineteenth century, geologists agreed they were made of folded rock strata – the crumpled, twisted, and fractured rocks of ranges like the Himalayas made it only too clear. They also agreed that mountains were built up

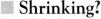

during distinct "orogenic" (mountain-building) phases when rocks were uplifted and folded, the phases being separated by periods of inactivity. But there was no agreement on just how mountains were built. The catastrophe idea was still popular, as was another idea – the shrinking Earth theory. Behind this theory was James Dwight Dana (1813–1895), Professor of Geology at Yale University. Dana argued that the Earth was once a red-hot ball of semi-molten rock. Mountains were formed by the way the Earth cooled as it shrank – just as the skin of an apple wrinkles as it dries. The idea was taken up enthusiastically.

But if the shrinking Earth theory was right, why didn't the Earth wrinkle evenly all over, rather than forming a few long mountain chains? And why does mountain building occur in distinct orogenic phases rather than all the time?

Peaks like these in the European Alps have been thrown up in the last 40 million years.

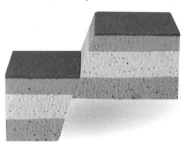

In 1859, American geologist James Hall (1811–1898) had an alternative idea. He suggested that mountain building began with the steady accumulation of sediments. As they built up, the Earth's crust gradually bent under their weight, creating huge troughs called "geosynclines". Eventually, after 100 million years or so, the crust was so

A simple demonstration of the way mountain ranges are built up by the crumpling of layers of rock as two continents crash together (p.67).

warped that the edges of the trough began to move together, crumpling the sediments and squeezing them up as ranges of folded mountain. Since sediments accumulate mostly on the sea bed, Hall argued, such structures would occur along the edges of continents – which is precisely where mountain ranges do occur.

■ Mountain roots

Meanwhile, fieldwork was beginning to undermine the shrinking Earth theory. At that time, surveyors always used a plumb-bob (a weighted string) to find a vertical line. Since a lead plumb responds to gravity, surveyors expected the line to be pulled slightly towards mountain ranges by their great mass – yet it seemed barely affected even by the biggest mountain ranges, as if mountains were hollow.

The answer to this mystery was supplied by British geophysicist George Airy (1801–1892). He suggested that mountains were not hollow, but simply made of less dense rock than the rock of the Earth's mantle beneath. If mountains had deep roots, as he believed, the plumb would be pulled as much towards the dense mantle rock beneath the plains as towards the mountains.

■ Isostasy

Airy also argued that mountains floated on the Earth's mantle like icebergs in the sea. As they were gradually worn away by water and weather, they slowly bobbed up, just as a boat does when it is unloaded. The American geologist Clarence Dutton (1841–1912) developed this idea, arguing that the Earth's crust is in a permanent state of floating balance, called "isostasy", with lighter rocks rising to form continents and denser rocks sinking to form the sea floor. His theory provoked great controversy. If it was right, then continents could not be sinking, as the shrinking Earth theory insisted.

■ Colliding continents

As support for the shrinking Earth theory dwindled, another American geologist, Frank Taylor (1860–1939), suggested that the Earth's crust was wrinkled into mountains not by continents sinking, but by continents colliding. His ideas were soon

forgotten, but a few years later the German meteorologist Alfred Wegener (1880–1930) became convinced of the reality of "continental drift" (pp.42–43). The concept, however, was so extraordinary that Wegener found few supporters.

It was another 50 years before scientists were finally convinced of the essential truth of Wegener's ideas. Now geologists believe that ranges like the Alps and Himalayas were thrown up by the collision of two continents, while mountains like the Andes and Rockies rose where the ocean plunged beneath a continent, releasing volcanic activity and crumpling rock strata.

It seems that most mountain ranges are created in short phases, rarely lasting more than 50 to 100 million years. Most of today's

The tight folding of thick layers of rock is evidence of the massive forces involved in mountain building.

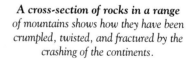

A cross-section of rocks in a range of mountains shows how they have been crumpled, twisted, and fractured by the crashing of the continents.

major mountain ranges have been created within the last 250 million years, as remnants of the supercontinent Pangaea (p.44) crashed together. But mountain building has probably been going on throughout the Earth's history as plates moved to and fro, and continents may be full of the remnants of old mountain ranges.

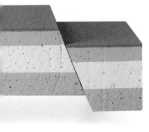
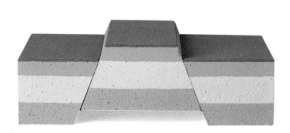

Fold mountains

THE SIGHT OF A RANGE of icy mountain peaks rearing into the sky can be awe-inspiring. But how did the mountains get there? Geologists realized long ago that mountain ranges are born when layer upon layer of rock is crumpled and thrust upwards by enormous forces. But what folds the rock? The answer only became clear when geologists understood how tectonic plates (pp.42–43) moved about on the surface of the Earth. Mountains are built where one plate collides with another. The Andes, for example, were thrown up where the Pacific plate crashed into South America; the Himalayas where India ran up against Asia.

Tilted rock
You can see evidence of folding all around, particularly along coastlines. Strata (layers of rock) like this were originally horizontal, but they have been tilted and twisted by the force of continents and oceans colliding.

EXPERIMENT
Folding up

Most rocks originally form in flat layers called "strata". Some are sedimentary, which means they are created from sand and mud settling on the sea bed. Some are volcanic, such as the vast tracts of basalt plateaux in continental shields (pp.50–51). But they all tend to be flat. Mountains are formed where the Earth's crust is unstable and the strata are tilted, crumpled, squeezed, broken, and lifted between the shifting plates. If you find it hard to believe that folding layers of rock can build a mountain, try this simple experiment with a few sheets of foam rubber or some old magazines. It shows a simple upfold, which geologists call an "anticline". But you can make a downfold, called a "syncline", just as easily, by creating a series of folds.

1 GRASP ONE END of the foam rubber sheets in each hand and bring your hands slowly together.

■ DISCOVERY ■
Grove Karl Gilbert

Only towards the end of the nineteenth century did geologists begin to see the importance of folding in the creation of mountain ranges. One of the first to realize this was the American, Grove Karl Gilbert (1843–1918), who coined the word "orogeny" to describe the process of mountain building. Mountain ranges soon became known as "orogenic belts", because they were zones where only the massive uplift and crumpling of rock strata could create a spectacular range of peaks. Experiments with models similar to ours (above right) confirmed the idea. But still no-one understood what force crumpled the rocks.

2 AS YOUR HANDS move, the foam bows up. Folds can be this small or hundreds of kilometres across.

Anticline

Pushing up mountains

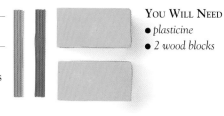

YOU WILL NEED
- *plasticine*
- *2 wood blocks*

With a little plasticine and a pair of wood blocks, you can mimic the way colliding continental plates fold and crumple rock strata. The picture shows just a simple fold, but with much longer strips of plasticine you can create a series of folds as complex as the real mountain chain illustrated below.

1 LAY THREE OR FOUR STRIPS of plasticine on top of each other as rock strata. Set the blocks at each end as the colliding continental plates. Enlist the help of a friend.

2 WHEN YOU BOTH PUSH at the same time, it is as if the two continents are coming together. The harder you push, the more the layers of plasticine are crumpled.

■ Shattered peak

Mountain rocks are often so distorted and fractured by the collision of tectonic plates that they are prone to attack by the frost and ice that form on the highest mountains, and that create the shattered peaks and ridges found in the Alps and Himalayas.

The rock in belts of upright folds like these is often formed into fine layers, making slate

Here the rock has been folded over so much that the strata have fractured altogether. This is called a "thrust fault" (p.71)

Bands of harder rock stand up to erosion better and are left as high peaks

The ancient crystalline basement of the continental crust is sometimes unaffected by folding

The overlying layers of sediment are pushed and crumpled into upright folds

■ Mountain belts

When two continents collide, the results can be spectacular. Where Europe crashed into the northern edge of the Africa plate (northern Italy), the Alps were thrown up – and the Alps are still growing, for in the last 40 million years Africa has moved 400 km (250 miles) closer to Europe. In some places, the impact seems only to have rumpled the layers of overlying sediment, without affecting the crystalline rock basement (p.50) – a bit like pushing a tablecloth into folds over a table. This happened in the Alpine Jura Mountains, shown in cross-section above. Sometimes, however, the force of the collision may be enough to crumple the table – that is, the basement – as well. In places, both basement and overlying sediments are folded right over on top of each other in vast complex structures called "nappes". There are structures like this under Mont Blanc in the Alps.

Folded landscapes

WHEN LAYERS OF ROCK are crumpled and distorted by the collision of continental plates, they rarely stay in their new shape for long. Indeed, even as the rocks are being folded, rain, snow, ice, and running water are busy at work, wearing some parts of the landscape away and building up others. These "erosive agents" exploit any weaknesses in the rock, opening up fractures created as the rock crumbles, or cutting quickly into softer rocks to form valleys, leaving ridges of harder rock. In this way, distinctive and complex landscapes are formed from folded layers of rock.

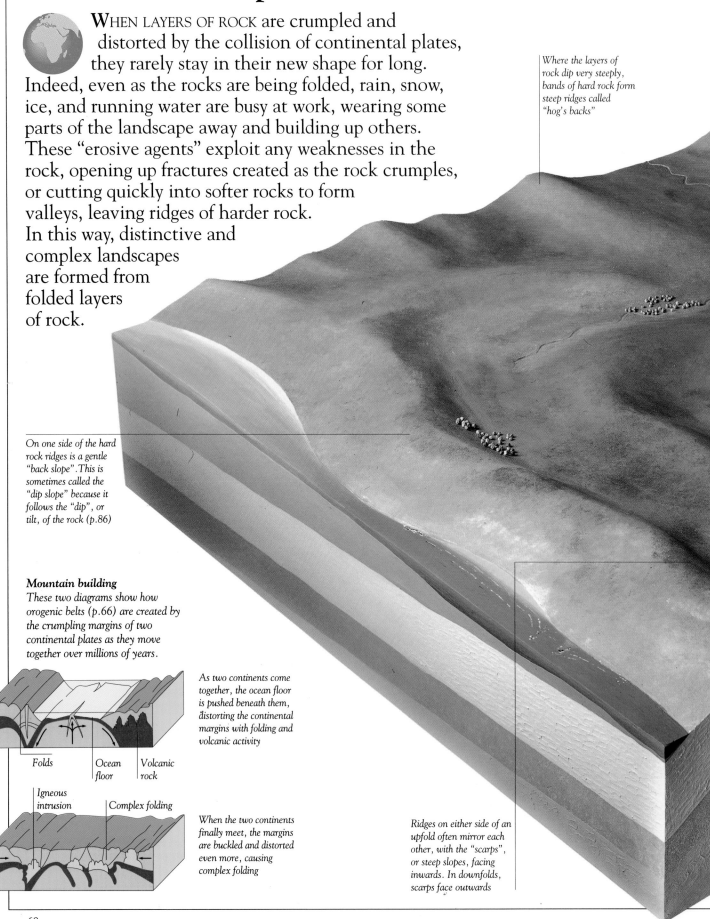

Where the layers of rock dip very steeply, bands of hard rock form steep ridges called "hog's backs"

On one side of the hard rock ridges is a gentle "back slope". This is sometimes called the "dip slope" because it follows the "dip", or tilt, of the rock (p.86)

Mountain building
These two diagrams show how orogenic belts (p.66) are created by the crumpling margins of two continental plates as they move together over millions of years.

Folds | Ocean floor | Volcanic rock

As two continents come together, the ocean floor is pushed beneath them, distorting the continental margins with folding and volcanic activity

Igneous intrusion | Complex folding

When the two continents finally meet, the margins are buckled and distorted even more, causing complex folding

Ridges on either side of an upfold often mirror each other, with the "scarps", or steep slopes, facing inwards. In downfolds, scarps face outwards

Belted landscape

Where sedimentary rocks are gently folded, the steady erosion of each band of rock creates a "belted landscape", with long lines of ridges and valleys following the alignment of the folds. In this model the main upfold of rock is not an arch but a long "dome", in which rock dips away from the centre. At each end, "scarps" (steep ridges) and "vales" (valley bottoms) loop round, showing how rock on opposite sides of the fold was once part of a continuous layer.

Cross-section

Geological cross-sections often reveal just how closely the surface landscape reflects the arrangement of the rocks beneath. Harder, more resistant rocks form ridges and steeper slopes, while beneath valleys and gentler slopes lie softer, less resistant rocks.

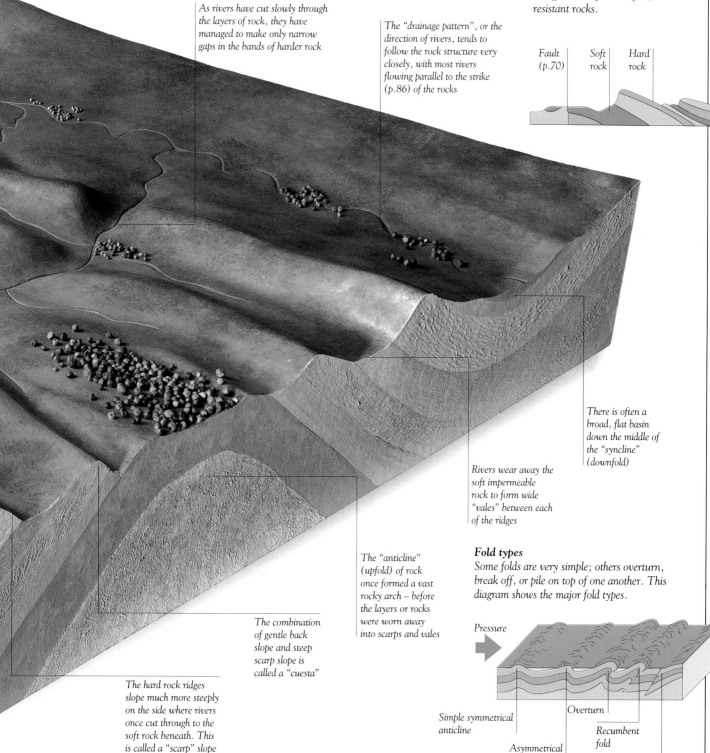

As rivers have cut slowly through the layers of rock, they have managed to make only narrow gaps in the bands of harder rock

The "drainage pattern", or the direction of rivers, tends to follow the rock structure very closely, with most rivers flowing parallel to the strike (p.86) of the rocks

Fault (p.70) Soft rock Hard rock

There is often a broad, flat basin down the middle of the "syncline" (downfold)

Rivers wear away the soft impermeable rock to form wide "vales" between each of the ridges

The "anticline" (upfold) of rock once formed a vast rocky arch – before the layers or rocks were worn away into scarps and vales

Fold types

Some folds are very simple; others overturn, break off, or pile on top of one another. This diagram shows the major fold types.

The combination of gentle back slope and steep scarp slope is called a "cuesta"

The hard rock ridges slope much more steeply on the side where rivers once cut through to the soft rock beneath. This is called a "scarp" slope

Pressure

Simple symmetrical anticline

Overturn

Recumbent fold

Asymmetrical anticline

Overthrust

Faults in the Earth

CONTINENTS AND OCEANS SLIDING and juddering past each other can make the ground tremble or crumple layers of rock – or make rocks snap altogether, so that whole blocks slip this way or that along a "fault" line. Sometimes an earthquake moves the blocks just a fraction of a centimetre apart along this fault; sometimes it moves them several metres. In the 1906 earthquake in San Francisco the land beside the San Andreas Fault moved 6 m (20 ft). Most faults involve fairly small movements, but the effect of earthquake after earthquake over millions of years can throw faulted rock 30 km (19 miles) up or down, and even further sideways. In the Sierra Nevada in California faulting has created a steep "scarp" slope, 3,350 m (11,000 ft) high and 645 km (400 miles) long. In Africa it has produced the Great Rift Valley, a huge trough stretching thousands of kilometres from Turkey to Mozambique.

The San Andreas Fault
On either side of California's San Andreas Fault, the land is moving along the fault at 5 cm (2 in) every year, as the Pacific Ocean Plate and the North American Plate move past each other along a vast "strike-slip" fault.

■ Cutting polystyrene

To cut polystyrene for your fault blocks, use a craft knife or a hot wire cutter. In either case, you must ask an adult to help. To make the cutter, cut a wooden handle as below. Stretch fuse wire between screws on each prong. Connect wires from a battery to each screw via a switch. Switch on and the fuse wire will heat up just enough to melt the polystyrene.

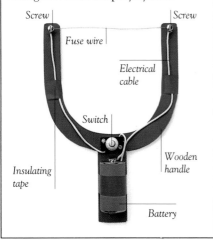

Screw
Screw
Fuse wire
Electrical cable
Switch
Wooden handle
Insulating tape
Battery

EXPERIMENT
Modelling faults

Adult help is advised for cutting polystyrene blocks

If you want to appreciate the different ways in which blocks can be faulted, or demonstrate it to others, you can make simple models from polystyrene. You can then experiment with different ways of moving the blocks apart. See if you can relate them to features in the landscape. On maps, try spotting faults by looking for unusually straight valleys or slopes.

YOU WILL NEED
● *polystyrene block or tiles* ● *paints & paintbrush* ● *glue*
● *ruler* ● *pencil*
● *craft knife, or, for the cutter:*
● *fuse wire & screws*
● *electrical cable*
● *battery* ● *switch*
● *insulating tape*
● *wooden handle*

1 TO MAKE THE BLOCKS, cut through the polystyrene with a craft knife, or draw the cutter through as shown. Be careful not to touch the wire. Cut out the shapes shown on pp.64–65.

2 IF YOU ARE USING polystyrene tiles, glue three together in a single block. When they are stuck firmly, cut through them with the knife or hot wire cutter to make the fault block shapes.

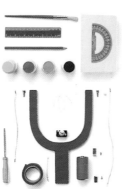

■ Fault types

Each picture on this page shows a different kind of fault. Some are caused by "compression" – that is, the squeezing of the Earth's crust, which often happens when two plates are moving together. Other faults are caused by "tension", which occurs when two plates are pulling apart. Some fault structures may be the result of both tension and compression.

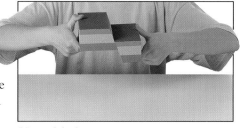

Normal fault
If you relax your hands and allow one block to slip down a little way, you are mimicking a normal fault, created by tension in the crust.

■ Fault features

When rocks fracture along a fault, the surface along which they slip is called the "fault plane", and the angle of the fault plane is called the "dip". Typically, normal faults dip at around 65–90°, so they are all fairly steep. Reverse faults, however, have more varied angles, and may even be less than 45°, in which case they are called "thrust" faults. In the Himalayas, the largest thrust faults may be more than 30 km (19 miles) deep.

Overall movement

Dip or "hade", the angle of the fault plane

Fault

"Throw", the vertical shift

"Heave", the sideways shift

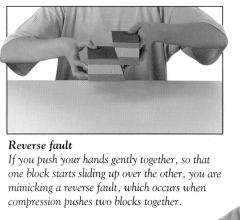

Reverse fault
If you push your hands gently together, so that one block starts sliding up over the other, you are mimicking a reverse fault, which occurs when compression pushes two blocks together.

Complex faults
Not all faults happen neatly at right angles; they can tilt in all directions. Vast areas may be shattered by complex tilted blocks, as in the Basin-and-Range country of the southwestern USA, and the Brazilian plateau.

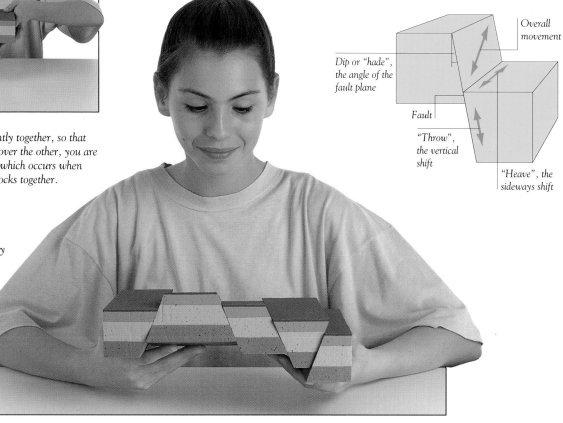

Tear, or strike-slip
By making a diagonal cut down through the block, and then sliding one block towards you and the other one away from you, you are mimicking a tear or strike-slip fault. This occurs when blocks slip sideways past each other, as in California's San Andreas Fault. Transform faults (p.187) are a massive kind of tear fault.

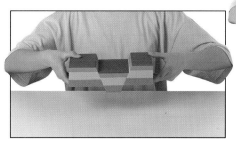

Rift valley, or graben
Pulling the outer blocks apart to let the middle drop mimics the formation of a rift, or graben.

Horst
Relaxing your grip on the outer blocks and pushing the middle block up with your fingers mimics the formation of a horst, a block uplifted between two normal faults. The Sinai Desert, the Ruwenzori mountain range in East Africa, and the Black Forest in Germany are all examples of horst blocks.

ROCKS and SOIL

Rock of ages
Rocks can tell geologists a great deal about the Earth's past – whether they are looking at a lump of granite crystallized from once-molten rock (above), or layers of sediments laid down over millions of years (left).

ROCKS AND SOIL ARE THE raw material of the landscape. Every valley, hill, and mountain is made of rocks and soil, and their nature controls the shape of the landscape. But every rock is also a clue to the Earth's history, for the characteristics of a rock depend on how and where it was formed – whether it was forged in the heat of the Earth's interior, transformed by volcanic activity or the impact of continents, or laid down in gently settling layers on the sea bed.

ROCKS

ROCKS COME IN A HUGE VARIETY of shapes, textures, and colours. But they are all made in one of just three ways. Some are cooled from molten magma from the Earth's hot interior, which erupts on to the surface in volcanoes or intrudes into the overlying rock. Some are made when sediments settle out of water, and are then squeezed and cemented until solid. And some are remade from other rocks by the tremendous heat of molten magma or the crushing forces that build mountains.

In the seventeenth century, many European scholars thought that fractured rock structures like this were the aftermath of the great Deluge of the Bible.

It seems so obvious today that many rocks are very, very old that it is hard to imagine people did not always believe this. Yet in 1650, the Irish Archbishop, James Ussher (1581–1656), concluded after detailed study of the Bible that the world began on Sunday 23 October, 4004 BC – and has barely changed since, except during the time of the Deluge, the biblical flood, which he dated to 2349 BC.

Ussher took the Bible more literally than most, but he was expressing a view widely held in Europe at the time – that the world was made as it is today during the Creation, a few thousand years ago. Of course, non-Christian countries had always looked at things differently. The Ancient Greeks, for instance, saw fossil shells in mountains as evidence that sea levels had changed, while the Arabian scholar Avicenna (AD 980–1037) described in his *Book of Minerals* how rivers eroded valleys and sea laid down sediments. But such ideas only began to capture the attention of Europeans in the 1600s. It was at about this time that some scholars began to question whether the Earth really was quite as the Church insisted. They could see that many rocks were formed from sediments, for

Many rocks are formed from compacted sediments, as geologists soon realized (p.85).

they were full of fossils of sea creatures. Yet if the world was so young, how could such thick sediments have piled up? And how could mountain ranges have risen and valleys been eroded so quickly by just the gentle flow of water?

■ Catastrophes

The only plausible explanation seemed to be that the Earth had been shaped not by the slow processes operating today but by a series of huge catastrophes – volcanoes, earthquakes, and floods. Of course, the Deluge was the obvious catastrophe, and it figures largely in most of the "theories of the Earth" developed in the seventeenth century to explain the nature of rocks and the landscape. In fact people were still talking about the Earth's early history as "ante-diluvian" (before the Deluge) in the nineteenth century.

The Deluge was the main process in the Earth theories of Danish geologist Nicolaus Steno (1638–1686), but he realized that all rocks were originally laid down in horizontal beds, even if they have been tilted, broken, and twisted since. He also realized that layers of sediment were laid down one on top of another, so the oldest beds are always at the bottom and the youngest at the

top, which he called "the principle of superposition". For many "cosmogonists" (those who query the origin of the universe), catastrophes explained how the Earth could be shaped so quickly.

But what if the world was much, much older? If so, there could have been time for gentler forces to have shaped the land.

It was with this in mind that the flamboyant French naturalist, the Comte de Buffon (1707–1788), timed how long two dozen white-hot metal balls took to cool. From this, he estimated that it must have taken at least 75,000 years for the Earth to cool to its present state from its origin as a white-hot ball. Cosmogonists soon began to discuss the age of the Earth, not in thousands of years but in millions. If the Earth was this old, its surface may have been shaped entirely by the same

Many sedimentary rocks form when salty water evaporates (p.84). The Neptunists of the seventeenth century believed (wrongly) that such rocks were formed in a middle era of the Earth's history.

Fossils buried deep down in sediments hinted that the world might be much older than was widely believed in the seventeenth century.

slow processes operating today, without the intervention of catastrophes. This idea later became known as "uniformitarianism", and the debate between catastrophists and uniformitarians raged well into the nineteenth century – and is still going on today.

■ Hot debate

Another crucial battle in the eighteenth century was between the "Neptunists" and the "Plutonists". The Neptunists were led by the German geologist Abraham Werner (1750–1817). He insisted that all types of rock originally settled out from water. Rocks like granite and quartzite that had no fossils must be "primitive" rocks, laid down before life began. It was a persuasive theory, and seemed to explain the order in which rock beds appeared in the landscape.

The Plutonists argued that rocks were formed by processes

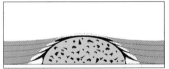

The existence of haloes of changed rock around granite domes indicate granite's igneous origin.

driven by the heat of the Earth's interior. They also thought many rocks were volcanic, a view later shown to be an understatement, since geologists now believe that 90 per cent of the Earth's crust is "igneous" rock (p.80).

The leading Plutonist was the Scottish geologist James Hutton (1726–1797), often regarded as the father of modern geology. Hutton was a uniformitarian as well as a Plutonist, and his crucial insight was to unite the two ideas by seeing geological history as a series of endlessly repeated cycles of erosion, sedimentation, and uplift. Rocks are slowly eroded,

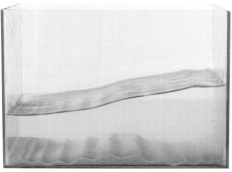

Ripples that are formed as waves roll over sand in shallow water are preserved as bedding marks in sedimentary rocks hundreds of thousands of years later (p.86).

mainly by running water, over many thousands of years. The material worn away is washed into the oceans where it settles to form sedimentary rock. Then the sediments are uplifted and distorted by the heat of the Earth's interior. Rocks such as granite, Hutton argued, were not ancient "primitive" rocks, but comparatively young rocks made by the cooling of molten material from the Earth's interior as it pushed up under the sediments.

■ Rock study

As geologists ventured out into the field more and looked at rocks in detail, Hutton's ideas seemed vindicated. Hutton himself pointed out "unconformities" (breaks in the sequence of rock beds) – clear signs that sedimentation was forever stopping and starting again. He also pointed out granite "dikes" – fingers of igneous rock that could only have been injected into the overlying sediments long after they had formed. After Hutton's death, his friend John Playfair (1748–1819) promoted his ideas, stressing the

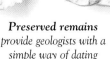

Preserved remains provide geologists with a simple way of dating rocks (pp.88–89).

vastness of geological time, but many scientists remained unconvinced.

At the same time, an English engineer named William Smith (1769–1839) was studying rock strata as he surveyed the ground for new canals. He saw that each layer of rock in a sequence contained a particular range of fossils, and that the same ranges of fossils were repeated in different rocks. He rightly concluded that if two layers of rock had the same set of fossils, they must be the same age, even if one was sandstone and the other clay. In this way he was able to date every rock he came across simply by looking at the fossils it contained. By 1815, he had made the first real geological map. Soon similar surveys were being made all over the world.

Using new knowledge from the surveys, British geologist Charles Lyell (1797–1875) wrote his *Principles of Geology* (1830), in which he examined the entire geological history of the Earth. Like Hutton, Lyell stressed how the world was shaped gradually over the vastness of geological time by the same slow forces operating today. So persuasive was he that his book became geologists' standard text for more than a century, and much of what he wrote is still relevant today. It is only recently, with the tectonic plate revolution (pp.42–43), that his ideas have really seemed inadequate.

Once geologists learned how to date rocks with sets of fossils in the early nineteenth century, and understood how layers of sedimentary rock were laid down and uplifted, they could construct complete cross-sections of rock strata.

Rocks and minerals 1

LOOK AT ANY PIECE OF ROCK closely and you will see that it is rarely completely smooth like plastic or metal. Instead, it is made up of grains or crystals, like a sugar cube. These crystals, which are sometimes minute and sometimes quite large, are called "minerals". All the different rocks in the world are made up from minerals. A mineral is simply a chemical that forms naturally in the Earth. There are several thousand different kinds, but only 30 or so common ones. Some rocks contain just one mineral, while others contain six or more – it all depends on how the rock is formed. You may be able to identify some of the more common minerals contained in rocks by carrying out the experiments on the following four pages.

■ Mineral tests

Feldspar
Haematite
Quartzite
Slate
Shelly limestone
Marble
Granite
Sandstone
Basalt
Clay
Chalk
Gabbro

All rocks are made up of minerals. If you make a sample collection like the one above, you can identify the minerals with the following tests.

EXPERIMENT
Colour and lustre

Simply looking at a rock gives you a good clue as to its identity. Colour can be misleading because the same mineral can come in many colours. But looking at lustre (the way the mineral reflects light) can be more useful. Is it metallic (shining like metal), vitreous (glistening like broken glass), or dull? Can you see any light through the rock or is it completely "opaque" (meaning that you cannot see anything at all through it).

1 EXAMINING A ROCK with a magnifying glass is the best way to see the mineral content. Sketch what you see.

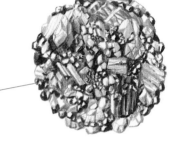

Close-up view
Minerals in a rock vary in colour, and they may be different sizes and textures, too.

■ Glass-like rock

Some minerals are almost transparent, like glass. Others are "translucent" – which means you can see a vague light through them. When you look through calcite (below), you see two of everything – the green here is modelling clay.

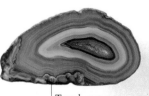

Translucent agate

Double-vision calcite

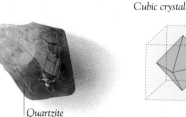

Quartzite

■ Shape

Mineral crystals come in an enormous variety of shapes, but they are all basically regular. Crystals based on two kinds of shape – cubic and hexagonal (six-sided) – are shown below.

Simple cube

Cubic crystal

Hexagon

Hexagonal crystal

EXPERIMENT
Streak test

A "streak" is the colour of a mineral when it is ground down to powder. While the colour of a mineral may change, its streak will usually stay the same. You can show the streak of many minerals simply by rubbing the mineral on the back of a porcelain tile. The mark on the tile is the streak. If the mineral is harder than the tile and leaves no mark, scratch the mineral carefully with a knife. Look at the colour of the scratch.

1 RUB THE MINERAL across the back of a porcelain tile, noting the colour the scratch produces.

Red streak
The iron-rich mineral haematite gives a very distinctive red streak.

EXPERIMENT
Hardness test

Another clue to a mineral's identity is its hardness – that is, what will scratch it and what will not. In 1812, the German mineralogist Friedrich Mohs set a scale of hardness, from talc (1) to diamond (10), on which every mineral can be placed. A mineral can scratch any other mineral lower on the scale. Try scratching a mineral with one of the equivalent objects listed below to see where it lies on the hardness scale.

Mohs' standard minerals	Equivalent
1 Talc	(no everyday equivalent)
2 Gypsum	Fingernail
3 Calcite	Bronze coin
4 Fluorite	Iron nail
5 Apatite	Glass
6 Feldspar	Penknife blade
7 Quartz	Steel file
8 Topaz	Sandpaper
9 Corundum	(no everyday equivalent)
10 Diamond	(no everyday equivalent)

YOU WILL NEED
● *bronze coin* ● *iron nail* ● *glass tumbler*
● *penknife* ● *steel file* ● *sandpaper*

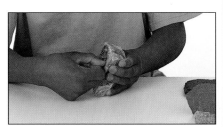

1 TO FIND THE HARDNESS of a mineral, scratch it with each tester to find out which will scratch and which will not. Start by using your fingernail; then work through the harder objects.

2 IF YOUR FINGERNAIL does not leave a scratch, try a bronze coin. If a bronze coin leaves no scratch, you know the mineral must be 4 or harder on the hardness scale.

3 BE VERY CAREFUL when trying to scratch with a penknife. If it is the softest object to leave a scratch, the mineral has a hardness of 6. Now try the tests on other minerals.

■ Cleavage

Many minerals break apart in certain directions more easily than in others; some break in several directions. This is called "cleavage", and different minerals have different cleavage patterns. You may be able to identify a mineral simply by the way it has broken.

Flaky cleavage
Minerals such as mica, graphite, and selenite gypsum tend to flake apart along one plane only.

Two-way break
Minerals such as orthoclase feldspar break apart in two directions.

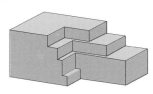

Block break
Minerals such as galena and halite break into cubic blocks along three planes at right angles.

Rhombic
Calcite breaks along three planes, but not at right angles. This cleavage is called "rhombic".

Rocks and minerals 2

LIKE ALL SUBSTANCES, minerals are made up of a few basic chemicals called "elements". For geologists, there are two kinds of element – the few "major" elements found in large quantities in the Earth's crust, and many more, rarer, "minor" elements. Just two of the major elements – silicon and oxygen – make up more than 75 per cent of the Earth's crust and join together to form the commonest of all mineral groups – the "silicates". Indeed, silicates are so common that minerals are usually divided into silicates and non-silicates. Silicates, such as all the minerals in granite, make up 98 per cent of all the rocks of the Earth's crust.

EXPERIMENT
Acid test

There is an important group of minerals called "carbonates", which contain carbon and oxygen. Most tend to be fairly soft and whitish in appearance, like calcite (calcium carbonate), which is the commonest of all carbonates. It is from calcite that limestones and marble are made. All carbonates can be identified by the fact that they dissolve in acid – although some dissolve only in very strong acids. Acid makes carbonates fizz and bubble. The fizzing is the carbon dioxide gas that is released by the carbonate as it dissolves. Sulphides, such as galena, also dissolve in acid, but they give such a strong smell of rotten eggs that they cannot be mistaken for carbonates. Geologists use dilute hydrochloric acid when they perform an acid test, but you can use strong vinegar (acetic acid) to test the softer calcium carbonates, such as chalk. Remember, even dilute acids can be dangerous, so do not use any without adult supervision.

YOU WILL NEED
● dropper ● vinegar
● magnifying lens
● plate

1 DROP A LITTLE VINEGAR on to your sample through a dropper. If it is a soft carbonate, such as chalk, it will begin to fizz straight away.

2 WITH VINEGAR, which is a very weak acid, you may have to examine the rock with a magnifying glass to see any sign of a reaction.

■ Stronger acid
An adult can conduct the acid test using dilute hydrochloric acid.

Limestone fizzes dramatically with dilute hydrochloric acid

Protective glove

Apply dilute acid with a dropper

Shelly fossils also fizz when tested with dilute hydrochloric acid

EXPERIMENT
Density

Metals are usually much more "dense" (heavier for their size) than non-metals, so there is often a clear difference in density between metallic and non-metallic minerals. But how can you gauge the density of a rather irregular lump of rock? These two methods show you how to work out a rock's "specific gravity" (SG), which is its density relative to water. One uses a spring balance, the other a plastic bottle.

You Will Need
● spring balance
● thread ● scissors
● bowl of water
● notebook

■ Eureka can

Make a hole in a plastic bottle and fix a tube with plasticine. Fill with water. Weigh, then immerse the rock. Weigh the spilled water and divide this into the rock's weight to give the SG.

■ Shapes of minerals

When a mineral forms, it usually grows by adding more and more layers to the outside. The resulting shape is often formless, or "massive". How a mineral adds its extra layers often depends on the circumstances in which it forms. If a mineral can grow freely – such as in a vein or cavity – the result may be a very clearly shaped crystal. However, some minerals, such as haematite and malachite, form special non-crystalline shapes. Haematite, for example, comes in bulbous, kidney-shaped lumps.

1 TIE A THREAD round your rock and hang it from the spring balance to weigh it. Note the weight. Call this weight 1.

2 IMMERSE THE ROCK in a bowl of water and weigh it again. Call this weight 2. Subtract weight 2 from weight 1, and divide weight 1 by the result. This gives the SG of the rock. You can now compare the SGs of different rocks.

Suspend the rock just above the bottom of the bowl

MINERAL PROPERTIES

Mineral	Colour	Lustre	Streak	SG	Hardness	Special Properties
Calcite	White	Glassy	White	2.7	3	Fizzes with acid
Feldspar	White-pink	Glassy	White-pink	2.7	6	Good cleavage
Fluorite	Pale purple	Glassy	White	3.1	4	Cubic crystals
Galena	Lead-grey	Metallic	Lead-grey	7.5	2.5	Bad egg smell in acid
Gypsum	White-yellow	Variable	White	2.3	2	Powdery
Haematite	Grey-red	Dull	Dark red	5.2	6	Kidney-shaped lump
Halite	Colourless	Glassy	White	2.2	2.5	Salty taste
Hornblende	Dark green	Glassy	Pale grey	3.2	5.5	Rhombic cleavage
Magnetite	Iron-black	Metallic	Black	5.2	6	Magnetic
Malachite	Bright green	Dull	Pale green	4	3.5	Distinctive colour
Mica	Silvery black	Glassy	White	3	2.5	Flaky
Olivine	Olive-green	Glassy	White-grey	3.8	6.5	Looks like hornblende
Pyrite	Gold	Metallic	Green-black	5	6.5	Looks like gold
Quartz	Milky	Glassy	White	2.7	7	Looks like glass
Sphalerite	Dark brown	Resinous	Pale brown	4	4	Shiny

Fiery rocks

MOLTEN MAGMA is ferociously hot when it explodes from volcanoes as lava, or forces its way into surface rocks as an "intrusion", but it soon starts to cool. As it does so, crystals begin to appear. The more it cools, the more crystals grow, until all the magma becomes a solid mass of hard, crystalline rock, called "igneous" (fiery) rock.

There are many different types of igneous rock, each with a slightly different crystal structure and mineral composition, depending on how and where it cooled. You can usually identify igneous rocks by their hard, mottled, crystal look – although the crystals in rocks such as basalt are so fine you can barely see them.

■ Collecting rocks

YOU WILL NEED
● *small hammer* ● *goggles* ● *felt pen*
● *magnifying lens* ● *bubble sheet to protect samples* ● *compass for identifying dip and strike (p.86)*
● *notebook and pencils for sketching*
● *local map* ● *backpack*

Collecting rocks can be fun, provided you take basic safety precautions and cause no damage to the environment. Always collect your samples from loose stones (hammering at a cliff may bring down loose rock). Obey local safety notices and stay away from dangerous sites like old quarries. Wear goggles when breaking up rocks. Number each specimen, sketch it, and note where you found it.

EXPERIMENT
Rock display

If you plan to build up a rock collection, don't just put the rocks away in a drawer. Organize and store your specimens carefully. Enter the number of each rock in a record book, along with information about the specimen, such as its name and where and when you found it. You can buy special storage cabinets for your rocks, but it is easy to make your own from a shallow box, as shown here, with dividers to ensure that rock samples do not scratch each other.

YOU WILL NEED
● *shoe box* ● *card* ● *cellophane* ● *adhesive tape*
● *scissors* ● *ruler* ● *pencil*

1 MEASURE THE BOX and cut out dividers from the card, leaving tabs on the dividers as shown below left. Now tape the tabs to the box base and sides.

3 MAKE A LABEL for each rock, showing the same information as in your notebook. Put this under the appropriate rock in each section of the cabinet.

2 CUT A LARGE WINDOW FRAME in the lid of the box. Cut a piece of cellophane to fit the lid, stretch it taut over the frame, and tape it in place.

Organizing your collection
You can organize your specimens according to type. But it may be better to arrange them according to where you found them – just in case your identification is inaccurate.

EXPERIMENT
Rock breaking

This is an adult demonstration and should not be attempted by children

If you want to study the grains and minerals in granite and other coarse-grained igneous rocks, you cannot simply smash them up with a hammer – they are much too hard. But an adult may be able to weaken the rock by rapidly heating and then cooling it, before hammering.

YOU WILL NEED
● *heatproof gloves* ● *tongs* ● *saucepan of cold water* ● *thick cloth* ● *board* ● *hammer* ● *gas burner or ring* ● *tweezers* ● *magnifying glass*

■ Texture and origin
The longer it takes igneous rock to cool down, the bigger the crystals or grains tend to be. There are three main types: fine-grained rocks, such as basalt, which are formed by lava spewed on to the surface by volcanoes and cooled quickly; medium-grained rocks, such as dolerite, which are formed in small intrusions; and coarse-grained rocks, such as gabbro, which cool slowly in massive intrusions deep underground.

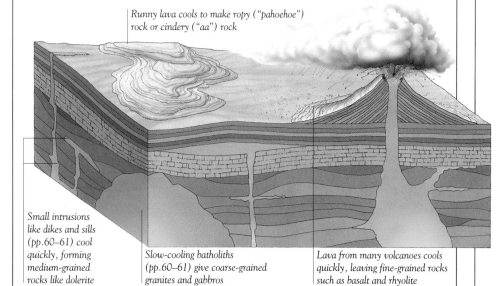

Runny lava cools to make ropy ("pahoehoe") rock or cindery ("aa") rock

Small intrusions like dikes and sills (pp.60–61) cool quickly, forming medium-grained rocks like dolerite

Slow-cooling batholiths (pp.60–61) give coarse-grained granites and gabbros

Lava from many volcanoes cools quickly, leaving fine-grained rocks such as basalt and rhyolite

1 WEARING HEATPROOF GLOVES, hold the rock over a gas flame with tongs. Keep children well back all the time.

2 WHEN THE ROCK IS VERY HOT, plunge it into a pan of cold water. Then heat and plunge into cold water again.

3 WRAP THE ROCK in a thick cloth, place it on a board, and hit it with a hammer to break it up.

4 TIP THE FRAGMENTS on to a clean surface. Using a magnifying glass, try to separate the different types of grain.

Three minerals
Once broken down, the granite can be sorted into three groups of minerals.

Large pinky or pearly grains are feldspar

Small shiny black flakes are mica

Medium-sized glassy grey grains are quartz

Rocks remade

WHEN THEY GET IN THE WAY of the searing heat of a volcano, or are crushed by the forces that build mountains (pp.66–67), rocks are changed – so dramatically that they become a new kind of rock, known as "metamorphic" rock. Igneous rocks, sedimentary rocks, and even metamorphic rocks themselves can be scorched and squeezed to make new rocks in this way. Look at the panel on the right to find out more about metamorphic rocks.

On these two pages we show how to begin the process of identifying a particular rock. Starting at step 1, work through each step as instructed.

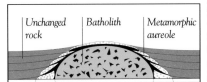

Halo of heat
Heat from molten rock creates a halo of metamorphosed rock – an "aureole" – around a batholith (p.60).

■ Identification

By following a series of simple procedures, all of them described in detail on pp.76–79, you can identify many different kinds of rock.

1 Is it limestone?
*If the rock fizzes when tested with acid (p.78), it is likely to be a kind of limestone. G*O TO STEP *2 (left) to find out which. It could also be marble,* *however, so check the panel on the right. If the rock does not fizz, even in stronger acid applied by an adult (p.78),* GO TO STEP *3 (below).*

2 What kind of limestone?
If limestone crumbles to a white powder, it is chalk. If it has tiny grains, it is oolitic limestone. If hard and mottled, it may be shelly limestone.

Chalk

Shelly limestone

Oolitic limestone

4 What kind of rudite?
Rocks that are embedded with large stones are sedimentary rocks known as rudites (p.84). If the embedded stones are round, the rudite is known as a conglomerate. If they are angular, it is known as breccia.

Breccia

Conglomerate

3 Studying the grains
Now look at the grains in the rock. If it has stones as big as your fingernail, GO TO STEP *4 (left). If it consists of fairly coarse grains, like those in* *demerara sugar,* GO TO STEP *6 (middle right). If you can only see the grains under a magnifying glass, then* GO TO STEP *5 (top right).*

5 Testing soft rocks

If you can scratch it with a nail or copper coin, the rock may be sedimentary (p.85). Coal is black; fine bands suggest shale; or it could be mudstone or clay. If it is too hard to scratch, GO TO STEP 8 *(above right).*

6 Testing hard rocks

If a knife can scrape grains off, GO TO STEP 7 *(below). Otherwise, if whitish in colour, it is quartzite. If banded, it is gneiss or schist. If neither, it may be gabbro, granite, or dolerite (*STEP 9*, above).*

7 What is the relative density?

Try measuring the relative density as shown on p.79. If your measurement is greater than 3, it is probably ironstone; otherwise it is a sandstone.

8 What kind of hard rock?

Fine-grained igneous rocks and metamorphic rocks (see below), are hard to break (p.81) and hard to identify. A very dark rock could be basalt or hornfels. Hornfels is often almost black; rhyolite and andesite are a little lighter.

9 Coarse-grained rocks

Coarse-grained igneous rocks are hard to tell apart. Granite is lighter overall than gabbro. Dolerite has a slightly finer grain. Pegmatite always contains very large crystals.

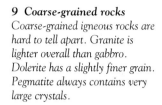

Basalt

Rhyolite

■ Metamorphic rocks

Metamorphism makes rocks tough and crystalline, but there are two different types of metamorphism: "contact" and "regional". Contact metamorphism occurs when rocks are remade by the heat of a volcanic intrusion, like the aureole around a batholith. Just how much they are changed depends on how big the intrusion is, and how far they are from the hot magma. Sandstone changes to hard, close-grained metaquartzite; pure limestone becomes brilliant white marble; and mudstone and shale turn into dark hornfels close to the intrusion, while further away they may become spotted rocks.

Regional metamorphism occurs when rock is crushed beneath a range of mountains that develop between colliding continental plates. The enormous pressure can give the rock a very distinctive "foliated" (banded) texture. Sandstone is turned to metaquartzite, and limestone to marble. Mudstone and shale are turned to slate near the edge of the range, schist a little further in, and gneiss deep beneath the mountain roots where both pressure and temperature are immense.

Nodular grey marble

Quartzite

Slate

Gneiss

Spotted hornfels

Mica schist

Eclogite

Migmatite

Rocks from water

MUCH OF THE EARTH'S CRUST is igneous rock (pp.80–81), but three-quarters of this rock lies hidden beneath thin layers made from the debris that settles on the beds of oceans, lakes, and rivers. Over millions of years, this debris is squeezed together to form "sedimentary" rocks. Some, like limestones, are made mainly from plant and animal remains, or from chemicals that settle out of water. But most, like sandstone, are "clastic"; this means they are made from fragments of rock that are worn away by the weather and washed into the sea by rivers.

Salt deposited when salt solution evaporates

No deposit when distilled water evaporates

■ Salt rocks

If you dissolve a lot of table salt in water, then pour it on to a saucer and leave it in a warm place, you will find that the water evaporates quickly, leaving a crust of salt on the saucer. (Try this with a saucer of distilled water, and compare the result.) In the same way, salty lakes and seas must once have evaporated in very dry climates to leave behind the vast deposits of salts, such as rock salt, anhydrite, and gypsum, that are now mined industrially.

EXPERIMENT
Graded grains

Moving water is like a natural sieve, sorting rock fragments into little and large by carrying smaller grains further and faster (pp.124–125). As a result, the grains in many clastic sedimentary rocks are all much the same size. Sedimentary rock can be split into three different groups, according to grain size: large-grained "rudites" such as conglomerates and breccias; medium-grained "arenites" such as sandstones; and fine-grained "lutites" such as shale and clay.

In some rocks, such as greywackes, there is a mixture of grain sizes, but the rock is banded into layers in which grains are graded in size from top to bottom. This is called "graded bedding". It is caused by the grains settling out of water at slightly different rates, as this simple experiment shows.

YOU WILL NEED
● plastic bottle ● funnel ● trowel ● range of mud, sand, shingle, and gravel ● jug

1 PUT A SMALL AMOUNT of each of the muds, sands, and so on into the bottle. Then fill it up with water.

2 SCREW THE LID ON TIGHTLY and shake the bottle to mix the contents well. Leave to stand for a few days.

Fine grains come to the top

Medium-sized grains settle in the middle

Coarse grains sink to the bottom

Graded bedding
Heavier grains sink more quickly, so the big grains tend to end up at the bottom. As this settling process can happen again and again, greywackes (turbidites) contain many bands of grains graded in this way (below). Graded beds like this are often deposited by turbidity currents (p.86).

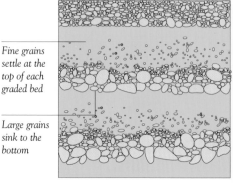

Fine grains settle at the top of each graded bed

Large grains sink to the bottom

Making sedimentary rocks

Over millions of years, loose sediment turns into solid rock, a process called "lithification". But you can make layers of sedimentary rock in just a few days with sand, food colouring, and wall filler.

The wall filler cements the grains of sand together, just as minerals like calcite do in real rocks. You can even put a "fossil" shell in between the layers.

YOU WILL NEED
- sand ● spoon
- food colouring
- wall filler ● plastic bottle ● shells
- scissors ● bowl
- petroleum jelly

1 MIX FOOD COLOURS with damp sand and wall filler. Build layers in the bottle and put in greased shells.

Your own layered "sedimentary rock"

2 LEAVE YOUR "ROCK" to harden for a few days. Then carefully cut away the bottle with scissors.

3 IF YOU WISH, you can break apart the layers to reveal the shell "fossil" and its imprint in solid rock.

▪ Layer cake

As the nature of sediments changes over a period of time, sedimentary rocks are always clearly "stratified" into layers ("strata") of different rocks. You can often see this stratification in cliff faces.

▪ Sedimentary rocks

The most common clastic rocks are conglomerate, sandstone, siltstone, and shale. Conglomerate is a solid mass of rounded pebbles, probably formed from beaches. Sandstone is made from grains of quartz sand held together by silica or calcite. Siltstone is made of even finer grains, while shale is a smooth rock made from brittle flakes of compacted clay.

The most common organic and chemical sedimentary rocks are limestones, so called because they are rich in calcium compounds. These include shelly limestones, made from fragments of sea shells, and chalk, made from the skeletons of microscopic sea creatures called coccoliths. Coal is made from the squashed remains of the swampy forests that covered much of North America, Asia, and Europe 300 million years ago.

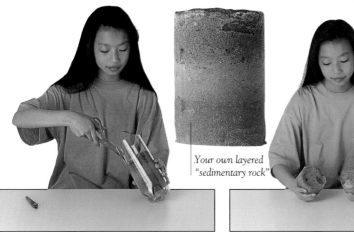

Conglomerate

Gypsum sand rose

Breccia

Sandstone

Coal

Clay

Shelly limestone

Chalk

Beds and joints

HAVE YOU EVER NOTICED how the rocks in many cliff faces have long horizontal cracks that make it look as if the rock was piled up like sheets of cardboard? These cracks are called "bedding planes" and, if you see them, you can be fairly sure the rock is sedimentary. Sedimentary rocks formed when layer after layer of sediments dropped on sea beds long ago; bedding planes simply show where the bed was when conditions changed a little. If the surface inside the crack is exposed, you may even see ripple marks and fossil shells, just as they were on the sea bed.

Bedding planes are usually flat, or tilted at an angle – depending on how much the rock has been crumpled up (pp.66–67). But there are often other cracks running at right angles to the bedding planes, especially in limestones. These are called "joints", and they were created when the rock slowly shrank as it dried out after being lifted up from the sea bed.

■ Turbidity currents

Graded beds (p.84) are created when a mix of sediments is dropped on the sea bed – often by "turbidity currents". These are undersea avalanches that cascade debris down the continental slopes (pp.46–47) and delta fronts.

Graded bedding will be seen as the current slows down

Turbidity current

Underwater avalanche
Make a turbidity current by pouring coloured water, sand, and scouring powder together down a funnel on to an underwater slope.

EXPERIMENT
Ripple marks

Sedimentary rocks provide a record of the motion of the sea millions of years ago. Tiny "laminations" or bedding planes in rocks like shale are traces of ancient tides, while small ripples are the imprint of waves washing through shallows long ago. Here, you can see how waves create such ripples.

YOU WILL NEED
● *tank, freezer tray, or large rectangular bowl*
● *clean sand* ● *water*

1 FILL THE TANK with water to a depth of about 10 cm (4 in). Spread about 1 cm (½ in) of clean sand evenly over the base of the tank. Gently raise and lower one end to make a wave.

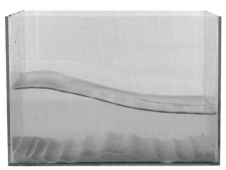

2 LET THE WAVE WASH SMOOTHLY to and fro. You will gradually see ripples developing in the sand. Once the water has settled down, the ripple pattern should be very clear.

■ Dip and strike

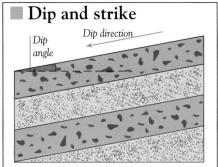

Dip angle

Dip direction

In folded rocks, bedding planes tilt at an angle called the "dip", at 90° to the fold (the "strike", p.95).

Bumpy bed
Parallel ripples like these form wherever waves flow in shallow water, such as on a beach or in a river. Water in waves moves in circles (p.142), and the ripples form where the circular motion of the wave touches the bed and moves the sand forwards a little way.

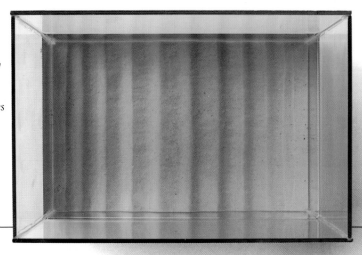

EXPERIMENT
Cross-bedding

Not all sediments are laid flat on the sea bed, so not all bedding structures are flat. Where a strong flow of water (or wind) keeps sediments moving in one direction, they are laid down in sloping beds, because the current is forever pushing new material forwards over the top of the slope. Often, a whole series of ripples or sand dunes may move forwards like this, creating a zig-zagging pattern of curved, sloping marks called "current-bedding" or "cross-bedding" (because they tend to cut across the main beds). This experiment shows one way of creating small-scale sloping beds.

YOU WILL NEED
- *guttering* • *jug*
- *sand* • *soil*

Pour water in the guttering to wash the sand down the slope

Slowly wash each handful of soil and sand down the guttering

Rest the guttering in a tray if indoors, but the experiment will work better outdoors, where the water can run away

Soil and sand beds begin to form

1 HOLD UP ONE END of the guttering to create a slope. Keep the other end just off the ground if outside (or resting in a tray if inside). Drop in a little sand, then wash it down the slope with water.

2 ONCE ALL THE SAND has washed away, sprinkle a handful of soil in the guttering. Slowly pour on water to wash this down the slope. Repeat, using handfuls of sand and soil in turn.

Sloping beds
From above, the alternate beds created by the soil and sand are very clear. If you could cut vertically through these sediments and scrape the material away, you would see the beds slope.

Sand layers

Soil layers

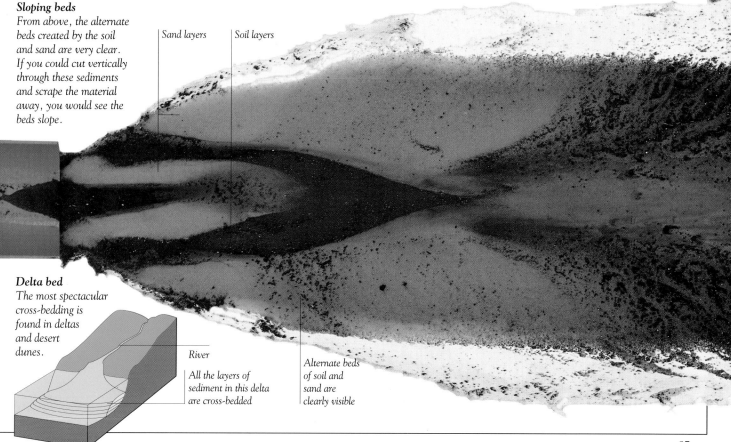

Delta bed
The most spectacular cross-bedding is found in deltas and desert dunes.

River

All the layers of sediment in this delta are cross-bedded

Alternate beds of soil and sand are clearly visible

Fossils

THERE WAS LIFE ON EARTH over 3.5 billion years ago. We know this because bacteria preserved in stone have been found inside rocks that formed that long ago. Stone remains like these are called "fossils" and can be found in many kinds of sedimentary rock. Any creature can be fossilized – providing its body is buried quickly by mud or sand before it rots away or breaks up. Because quick burial is most likely to occur in the sea, fossils of shells and sea creatures are much more common than those of land animals. However, lake and swamp sediments often hide the fossilized remains of plants and even dinosaurs.

■ DISCOVERY ■
Georges Cuvier

It was known what fossils were as long ago as the days of Leonardo da Vinci (1452–1519). But it was not until the French anatomist Georges Cuvier (1769–1832) began to study fossils that the science of "palaeontology" was born. Cuvier was an expert in animal anatomy and taught at the Museum of Natural History in Paris, then the largest scientific institution in the world. When he studied fossils, he used his skill as an anatomist to work out exactly what an animal had looked like from the remains of just a few bones. In this way, he was able to classify and study fossil "vertebrates" (reptiles and mammals) – even if they belonged to species that had been extinct for millions of years.

EXPERIMENT
Fossil cast

Many fossils preserve just the imprint of the creature, like a mould. To see what the actual creature was like, you can make a model in plaster of Paris or dental plaster, using the fossil as a mould.

YOU WILL NEED
● *fossil* ● *plaster of Paris* ● *spoon*
● *mixing bowl*
● *petroleum jelly*
● *brush*

2 MIX A SMALL QUANTITY of plaster and spoon it on to the fossil, making sure you fill all the cracks completely.

4 VARNISH OR PAINT your cast for display. If you have both halves of the fossil, why not make a cast of both?

Imprint of fossil   *Fossil body*

Cast of the fossil imprint recreates the original body   *Cast of the body makes a new imprint*

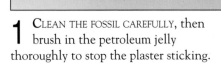

1 CLEAN THE FOSSIL CAREFULLY, then brush in the petroleum jelly thoroughly to stop the plaster sticking.

3 LEAVE THE PLASTER to harden for a few hours, then carefully prise the plaster away to reveal the cast.

Ammonite shell
Ammonites are now extinct, but they were common in the warm seas of Jurassic and Cretaceous times (p.92). Like squids and octopuses, they had tentacles and belonged to a group of creatures called "cephalopods".

■ Identifying fossils

Fossils give us a wonderful picture of the history of life on Earth. But it is a very blurred picture. Only a tiny proportion of the "species" (kinds of creature) that have ever lived are preserved in fossils. And the species preserved tend to be mostly small, shelled "invertebrates" (creatures without backbones like prawns) that live on the bed of shallow seas. Fossils of soft-bodied creatures (like insects and worms) and land-living animals (like mammals) are very rare.

What is worse, usually all that remains to tell us what the creature was like are the hard parts – shell and bone. So we have no idea what colour the creature was, whether or not it had fur, or even the size of its nose.

Fossils are not just plant and animal remains; traces of footprints and well-used trails are also preserved in stone. These can be just as misleading to study. Palaeontologists studying dinosaur footprints were baffled to discover that dinosaurs seemed far more numerous than their prey – until they realized that hunting dinosaurs moved around more, and so left more footprints. However, fossils do tell us a great deal about the history of the Earth, for they are the best way of dating rocks.

Nearly all the fossils you are likely to find are from small, shelled sea creatures from sea-floor sediments, especially limestones and shales. This page shows you some of the main groups.

Sea urchin
With their round knobbly shells, sea urchins make very distinctive fossils. Their skeletons are made of interlocking plates, some with spines on them. Geologists use fossilized sea urchins to date chalk deposits.

Graptolite
Known only from the saw-like marks they left on ancient shales and slates, these creatures died out 300 million years ago. They lived in little cups and probably dangled by threads from drifting seaweed.

Tabulate coral
Tabulate coral has skeletal plates that cross from side to side. It is one of the oldest forms of coral, dating back to Ordovician times (p.92), but it became extinct over 200 million years ago.

Snails
Like most snails or "gastropods", this Buccinum has a shell coiled in a spiral. Snails have existed for 500 million years, but only became common enough to help geologists date rocks from their fossils 65 million years ago.

Turitella
There are many different kinds of gastropod, including garden snails and slugs, and their shells are often preserved completely. This shell is a species called Turitella.

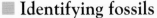

Bivalve
Bivalves such as cockles and mussels usually have a pair of identical shells, but Gryphea (above) has one shell very large and the other very small.

Precious rocks

WITHOUT THE ROCKS of the Earth's crust to supply us with minerals, life would be very different. Bricks for building, metals for machines, oil to burn, gems for jewellery, and many other materials come from rocks. Each mineral is formed by a special set of circumstances. Some metal "ores" (combinations of minerals) crystallize in magma. Gems often grow in gas pockets in igneous rock. Coal is found in sediments from the Carboniferous period. Because of this, we now know where to start looking for deposits.

EXPERIMENT
Growing crystals

Gems are crystals grown from minerals in solution. You can grow your own crystal from alum (available from chemists) or sugar. Start by dissolving the alum in warm water until it will not dissolve any more. Pour some of the solution into a saucer and allow it to evaporate. Soon small crystals appear.

1 SUSPEND ONE of the previously grown crystals in a jar of alum solution.

YOU WILL NEED
● *alum powder*
● *water* ● *cotton*
● *pencil* ● *jam jar*
● *saucer* ● *tweezers to pick up crystal*

2 LEAVE FOR A WEEK, by which time the crystal will have grown larger.

■ Precious minerals

While many gemstones are found in "geodes" (gas pockets in cooling igneous rock), many metals, especially lead, zinc, copper, and iron, may be concentrated in "veins". Veins are cracks in the rock where hot, watery fluids once ran. As the water cooled, the minerals crystallized outwards, creating solid veins. Metals are usually found as "ores" (that is, mixed with other elements) and must be processed before they can be used.

Emerald
Found in veins with calcite and pyrite.

Haematite
This kidney-shaped ore is a major source of iron.

Diamond
This is the hardest of all minerals.

Gold
Pure gold is often found on quartz.

Chalcopyrite
This copper ore occurs in veins.

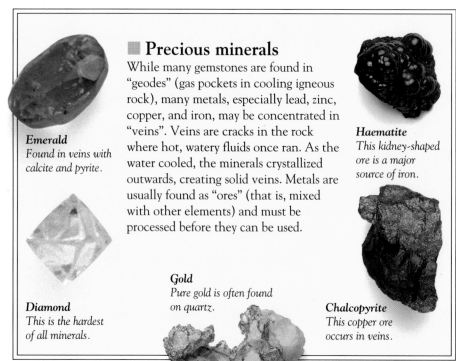

EXPERIMENT
Pebble polisher

Adult help is advised for this experiment

Gemstones are rare and precious, but ordinary pebbles from the beach can be very attractive if polished. The best pebbles to polish are the different kinds of quartz – agate, amethyst, and rose quartz – because they are very hard, but many others are also suitable. Pebbles can be polished in a rotating drum, along with a paste of coarse grit and water that wears off the rough edges. If you are a keen modelmaker, why not make your own polisher, as shown here.

YOU WILL NEED
● *tools as shown* ● *masking tape* ● *glue* ● *balsa wood cut as shown in red* ● *6 rechargeable batteries (1.5 volt)* ● *electric motor* ● *switch* ● *electric lead & tape* ● *metal strips* ● *coffee jar* ● *elastic band* ● *4 toy wheels with thin rods, or knitting needles, for axles* ● *2 grooved wheels to fit motor shaft & driving axle* ● *3 collars for rods* ● *screws* ● *paint & brush* ● *grinding paste*

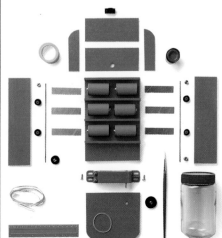

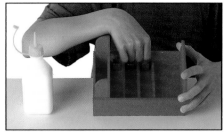

1 GLUE THE PIECES OF BALSA WOOD together to make the box as shown in the diagram below. Slot in the divisions for the batteries. Bend the metal strips to make U-shaped contacts for each battery as shown in the diagram.

2 STICK ONE CONTACT in each end of each battery compartment. Fit a switch in the end of the box. Drill a hole for the motor in the end panel. Slot the motor into the end compartment and secure with screws.

3 TAPE LEADS TO the contacts to connect them with each terminal of the switch, as shown in black in the diagram below. Connect the motor and place the batteries in compartments, as shown in the diagram.

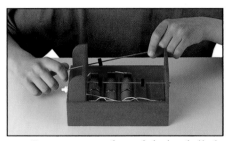

4 SLOT THE RODS through holes drilled in each end panel, with two wheels on each rod. Glue the wheels to the rod connected to the motor (the driving axle). Slot a wheel on to the end of the driving axle and secure with a collar.

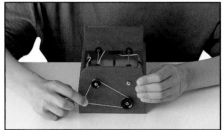

5 SLOT ANOTHER WHEEL on to the shaft of the motor. Remove the tyres from this and the other wheel to reveal the grooves. Stretch an elastic band around the grooves of both wheels. It should not be so tight that it pulls hard on the axle.

6 WRAP TAPE AROUND THE JAR and lower it on to the axles. Put grit, pebbles, and water inside. Switch on.

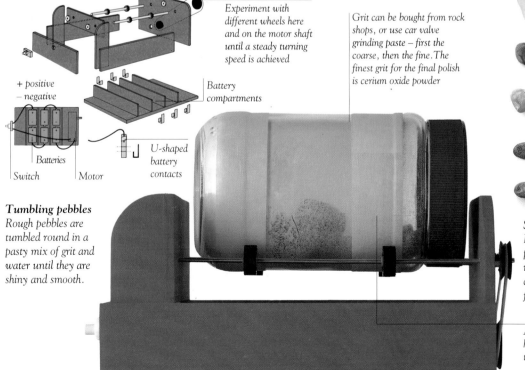

Experiment with different wheels here and on the motor shaft until a steady turning speed is achieved

Grit can be bought from rock shops, or use car valve grinding paste – first the coarse, then the fine. The finest grit for the final polish is cerium oxide powder

+ positive
– negative

Battery compartments

Batteries

Switch   Motor

U-shaped battery contacts

Tumbling pebbles
Rough pebbles are tumbled round in a pasty mix of grit and water until they are shiny and smooth.

Slow grind
It takes several days of grinding to polish pebbles to this extent. You need to change the grit from coarse, through medium, to very fine to achieve a good finish.

A circle of masking tape helps the driving wheels to grip and turn the jar

The geological clock

THE ROCKS OF THE EARTH'S CRUST could tell us the history of the world – if only we could understand them. We know so little about rocks from more than 590 million years ago that geologists call anything before this date Precambrian, even though the world is 4,600 million years old. Yet layers of more recent sedimentary rocks can often be read like the pages of a book. Since they were laid down one on top of another, the rocks at the bottom must be older – although the sequence may be tilted, twisted, turned upside down, or broken. Fossils in the rock, the position of igneous intrusions and ripple marks, and other signs all help give a clearer picture.

■ DISCOVERY ■
Charles Lyell

Until the early nineteenth century, most scientists believed that the Earth was relatively young, and that rocks and landscapes were shaped by a series of mighty catastrophes. It was the Scottish geologist James Hutton (p.78) who first suggested that the Earth might be very old, and had been shaped gradually by processes operating even today – a concept called "uniformitarianism". But it was the British geologist Charles Lyell (1797–1875) who made the idea widely accepted. Lyell was a lawyer by training, but his fascination with rocks took him on many geological expeditions. When his book *Principles of Geology* was published in 1830, it revolutionized people's way of thinking about the world and opened the way for Darwin's theory of evolution. It was also the first clear and accurate summary of basic geology, much of which is still accepted today.

■ The geological column

Geologists often refer to the "geological column" when talking about the history of rocks. The idea is that if sediments had remained totally undisturbed, you could cut a column right down through them to reveal the whole sequence, with the oldest rock at the bottom and the youngest at the top. Each bed of rock then becomes a division of geological time, with long eras (like the Mesozoic) split into short "periods" (like the Triassic). Of course, such a sequence exists nowhere on Earth, but it provides a useful guide.

Much of what we know about the relative ages of rocks comes from the study of fossils. Since certain fossils always appear before others in the sequence, whatever the rock type, we can say that one rock is older than another, or another younger, if it holds a certain set of fossils. But fossils cannot give the date in years. For this, geologists rely on radioactive elements in the rocks, such as uranium. By measuring how far these elements have broken down, they can work out the rock's age.

Early horse (Miocene)
Sabre-toothed tiger
Early primate
Flightless bird
Marsupial (Paleocene)

The Tertiary and Quaternary periods are divided into "epochs"

Holocene
Pleistocene
Pliocene
Miocene
Oligocene
Eocene
Paleocene

Quaternary
Tertiary

0.01 million years ago

Dinosaur Tyrannosaurus

Cretaceous
Jurassic
Triassic
Permian
Carboniferous

Early dinosaur

First bird

Early shark

Tree fern

Devonian

Lungfish

Silurian

Mollusc

Ordovician

Cambrian

Sea creature (trilobite)

Archaeocyathid sponge

Precambrian

590 million years ago

Quaternary Ice ages in the north; humans emerge
Tertiary Continents take present shape; birds and mammals replace dinosaurs
Cretaceous S. America and Africa split; dinosaurs die out
Jurassic Age of the dinosaurs
Triassic Pangaea splits up
Permian First reptiles
Carboniferous Swampy tropical forests in north
Devonian Desert sandstones form; early land plants
Silurian Most life still in sea
Ordovician Southern continents move to cold poles
Cambrian Life exists only in the sea

EXPERIMENT

Making a geological clock

Dating of radioactive elements of meteorites and rocks on the Moon (which is the same age as the Earth) suggests that the Earth is 4,600 million years old. Some evidence suggests that life began to emerge at least 3,800 million years ago, but it was not until just 200 million years ago that dinosaurs roamed the Earth. And it was less than 4 million years ago that our first primitive ancestors appeared. You can make your own simple geological clock to show how far apart these events are in the Earth's history. You will see that, if the Earth formed at noon, and we are now at midnight, the first human appeared less than half a second ago.

YOU WILL NEED

● coloured card ● ruler ● protractor ● pair of compasses ● scissors ● marker pen ● pencil ● paper fastener

2 STICK THE SEGMENTS carefully on a disc of card exactly as below, working round from 12 o'clock. Then mark in the details, as shown below.

3 DRAW THE ARROW POINTER on card and cut it out. Then attach it to the centre of the clock with a paper fastener to complete the clock.

The Phanerozoic eon began 590 million years ago. It is split into three eras: Palaeozoic, Mesozoic, and Cenozoic

In the last half a second, humans appear

Dinosaurs die out

Mammals evolve

Rise of the dinosaurs

Amphibians evolve from fish

First land plants

First shell fossils

4,600 million years ago – the Earth begins

The Archaean eon dates from the beginning of the world to around 2,500 million years ago. The oldest rocks were formed in these times

Solid crust forms

First living cells?

1,150 million years ago

3,450 million years ago

The Proterozoic eon is the age when the first real signs of life are seen on Earth – although life may have begun at an even earlier time

Green algae and bacteria evolve?

Earliest fossils

2,300 million years ago

Massive volcanic eruptions and earthquakes worldwide

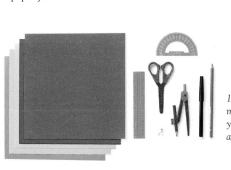

1 DRAW A LARGE CIRCLE on each coloured card. Measure the angle of each coloured sector on the clock (right) and then cut out each sector.

Geological time

Just as time on a clock is divided into hours, minutes, and seconds, so the Earth's history is divided into units of geological time: eons (longest), eras, periods, epochs, ages, and chrons (shortest). On our clock, each coloured wedge represents an eon. The Archaean eon (red), and the Proterozoic eon (yellow) are now known together as Precambrian time. The Phanerozoic eon (blue) covers the last 590 million years, and is divided into three eras (different shades of blue): Palaeozoic, Mesozoic, and Cenozoic. These in turn are divided into periods, beginning with the Cambrian, which are shown in the geological column on the left.

The geological map

IF YOU WANT TO KNOW WHAT KIND OF ROCK a range of hills is made of, look at a geological map. This will show you what kind of rocks appear where. Some of these maps just show loose surface material, such as peat and sediment carried by glaciers. These are called "drift maps". But most geological maps show the solid rock beneath. This is the rock you see exposed in cliffs, or the rock you would find beneath your feet if you dug far enough. These "solid maps" also show such things as faults, the dip and strike (p.86) of folds, and other structures in the rock.

Most geological maps are made from detailed surveys of the area. Surveyors study outcrops of bare rock, cliffs, quarries, and cuttings, and sometimes dig boreholes. But they also study the landscape. As some rocks are more resistant to erosion, geologists can work out where different rocks occur from the shape and position of hills.

EXPERIMENT
Make a clinometer

To measure the angle at which a rock bed slopes (the dip), geologists use a "clinometer". You can make your own from card, then use it to measure any slope, as well as the dip of rock beds.

YOU WILL NEED
- card ● fastener
- pair of compasses
- pen ● scissors
- protractor ● ruler

2 STICK THE RING ON CARD, then, using a protractor, mark off degrees, with 0° in the centre and 90° at each end. Pin a card arrow at the centre of the ring.

1 DRAW TWO HALF-CIRCLES on card, one just smaller than the card, the other even smaller. Cut along the circles with scissors to make a half-ring.

3 NOW TEST YOUR CLINOMETER on a slope, for which you already know the angle. The arrow should swing freely, pointing to the correct angle on the card.

EXPERIMENT
Rock structure

The main limitation with geological maps is that they show only the rocks as they appear at the surface. To get a full picture of an area's geology, you have to learn how to interpret the map and work out the structure of the rock beneath the surface. Geologists do this by looking for arrows showing the way the beds dip, lines showing faults, and contour lines showing the shape of the land. Then they draw cross-sections revealing the rocks you would see if you could take a slice down through the land. This experiment shows how you can build up your own "rock" beds, to get a better idea of how surface geology is related to the underlying structure.

YOU WILL NEED
- clear tank or dish ● sand ● food colouring
- card ● clinometer ● bowl ● spoon ● pencils

1 CUT A PIECE OF CARD to fit across the width of the tank. This will act as a fault plane (pp.70–71), on one side of which all the strata have slipped.

2 COLOUR THE SAND with food colouring. Pile it up neatly in the corner of the tank, making sure the slope remains straight and even as you go up.

3 NOW BUILD UP different coloured layers of sand. Continue each layer on the other side of the fault card, but at a slightly higher level, to show slippage.

4 CONTINUE ADDING LAYERS until you reach the top of the tank. Make sure the surfaces finish flat. Draw the coloured bands you see on top.

5 THE SLOPE OF THE SAND BEDS you see through the side may not be the dip (p.86), for the beds slope into the corner. Instead, measure the slope at the tank's end *and* side with the clinometer. The dip is halfway between the two.

Cross-section
The tilt of the beds and the way they are offset on either side of the fault is clearly visible in a cross-section.

Fault line | Tilted beds

End section
Even though this section is at right angles to the side view, the sequence of coloured layers of sand is exactly the same.

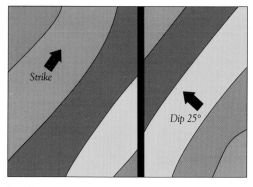

Plan view
The plan view shows how tilted layers appear on the surface as parallel bands of rock. See how the bands are offset on either side of the "fault" card.

Strike

Dip 25°

Simple map
With your sketch of the sand layers from the top, you can make a simple geological map of the structure you built up in your tank, as above. From this map, which shows the coloured beds and their strike (always at 90° to the dip direction), the fault line, and, most importantly, the angle and direction of dip, could you reconstruct the arrangement of sand layers beneath?

SOIL

SOIL IS THE FRAGILE LAYER OF LOOSE MATERIAL that covers most of the world's land, varying in depth from just a few centimetres to hundreds of metres. Without it, we would have no plants, no food, nor any of the vegetable products on which we rely. It is mostly weathered rock, with water, air, and rotting organic matter. But the rich plant and animal life of the soil and the complex physical, chemical, and biological processes going on all the time make it a dynamic, living system.

Cutting down forests can have a devastating effect on fragile tropical soils. It not only makes the soil highly vulnerable to soil erosion, but also accelerates the process of leaching, which washes valuable nutrients from the topsoil.

When rocks are exposed to the weather, they slowly crumble to form a thin veneer of loose material called the "regolith". Soils only begin to develop once the regolith is colonized by plants and animals. Gradually, organic remains accumulate and mix with the rotting rock to make a soil.

Just how the soil develops depends on five main factors: the underlying rock or sediment; organic activity; climate; time; and the lie of the land. In the 1940s an attempt was made to link these factors in a mathematical equation that would predict the nature of the soil. However, most pedologists (soil scientists) now think that the relationship between them is far too complicated to be simplified like this.

The extensive roots of grass indicate that the soils beneath the grasslands, such as the ancient plains of mid-North America, were at one time rich in organic matter.

Parent rock

The material on which a soil develops is known as "parent" material. Soil made mainly from the weathered fragments of the solid rock beneath is called a "residual soil". Soil made from fragments of rock carried by streams, waves, winds, or glaciers is called a "transported soil". Soils developed on glacial deposits (p.134), alluvium (p.124), and loess (p.136) are all transported.

Some parent materials have minerals that resist weathering,

such as the quartz in sandstone. This not only means that soils develop slowly and contain coarse grains; they also tend to be chemically similar to the parent material. In most soils, however, minerals from the parent material are broken down quickly. So in the long run organic activity and climate have far more influence on the nature of the soil than the parent material.

Soil life

Organic activity affects the soil in a number of ways. First of all, the leaves, bark, branches, roots, and so on, of dead plants rot to a jellylike mass called "humus", which is vital to soil fertility and structure (p.101). Plants also encourage infiltration of water and help retain mineral nutrients in the soil by drawing them up through their roots.

Meanwhile, micro-organisms such as bacteria and fungi feed on the organic matter and humus, helping to break it down and turn it into new organic compounds. Some pedologists estimate that there are a billion bacteria in a gram of soil. Then there are numerous larger creatures, such as earthworms, ants, termites, burrowing rodents, and so on, that stir up the soil, mixing organic material from the upper layers with the minerals from below. Earthworms are especially important, for they take soil in, pass it through their digestive tracts, and excrete it in

worm casts – not only mixing the soil but changing its texture and chemical nature. In the late nineteenth century Charles Darwin (1809–1882) worked out that English garden worms create 6.5 tonnes of soil casts per hectare (10–15 tons per acre). One study of a pasture in New Zealand suggested that the weight

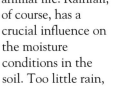

Hard salt crusts often form on the surface of soils in dry areas.

of worms in the soil was equal to the weight of the sheep grazing on the surface!

Climate and slopes

Of all the influences on soil formation, climate is perhaps the most important. It is no coincidence that many maps of world soil types match maps of world climate zones almost perfectly. High temperatures in the tropics, for instance, tend to restrict the accumulation of humus, yet speed up chemical reactions to such an extent that rock can rot hundreds of metres below the surface. Very low temperatures, on the other hand, inhibit plant and animal life. Rainfall, of course, has a crucial influence on the moisture conditions in the soil. Too little rain,

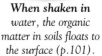

When shaken in water, the organic matter in soils floats to the surface (p.101).

and plants cannot grow; too much, and vital minerals are washed from the soil.

Yet the effects of climate are only fully realized if the soil has had time to "mature" – that is, fully develop. Volcanic landscapes and coastal sand dunes, for instance, may be so new that there has barely been time for soils to develop, let alone mature. Soils on many of the vast ancient plains of Africa, on the other hand, have often matured to such an extent that hard crusts of clay, lime, and silica form within the soil. Farmers have to break up these crusts by deep ploughing, or even by blasting them with dynamite, if they are going to be able to plant crops.

The lie of the land tends to influence soils mostly on a local scale. Soils are slow to develop on steep slopes, for instance, because water runs off so easily, and because any soil that does form is easily washed away. On level ground, however, run-off can be so limited that the soil gets waterlogged. Often, soils change downhill through exactly the same sequence, called a "catena", a phenomenon first observed in East Africa in the 1930s. On permeable rock, for instance, there might be a podzol (p.100) on the crest of a hill, brown earths on the slope, and peats in the valley.

■ Forming horizons

As any soil develops, differences gradually form down through the soil and often, especially in mid-latitudes, the differences develop into distinct layers. These are called "horizons" (p.98) and vary in thickness.

Horizons are created to a large extent by the way water trickles through the soil, washing down minerals and organic matter with it. In very wet regions, the slightly acid soils beneath heathlands are often subject to "lessivation". In this, water washes grains of clay down through root channels, worm tunnels, and gaps in the soil, and then deposits them in the subsoil. Here it tends to coat the soil grains with thin "cutans" (skins), making the soil sticky, damp, and hard to work.

A good soil must contain air as well as solid matter and water (pp.98–99).

Water can also dissolve minerals and wash them down through soil, a process called "leaching". In a similar way, organic material can be dissolved and washed down through the soil. This is the process known as "cheluviation". The effect of both leaching and cheluviation is to rob the topsoil of its food, sometimes leaving it both acidic and infertile. Often the dissolved minerals are "precipitated" (dropped) lower down in the soil. Precipitated iron can form a rock hard layer called an "ironpan".

Besides washing chemicals down into the soil, water can also carry dissolved salts upwards, especially in deserts where water evaporates faster than rain falls. The salts may then be left behind at the surface to form a hard crust when the water evaporates. In

Highly acid soils are often infertile, as soil nutrients tend to be very soluble and easily washed away. You can test soil acidity with red cabbage water (p.100); the pinker it goes, the more acid the soil is.

the dry season in many tropical areas of the world, a similar process takes place, sometimes creating solid layers of calcium ("calcretes"), iron ("ferricretes"), and silica ("silicretes").

Percolating water is not the only natural action that creates distinct horizons within the soil. Biological activities, such as those of plant roots and burrowing creatures, which were described earlier, also play their part. Other influences on the formation of horizons are the action of frost and human activities such as ploughing the land.

Soils on upland heaths and mountains tend to be highly acidic and infertile, and suitable only for grazing sheep and goats.

■ Soil erosion

Humans have had a marked effect on the Earth's soils, particularly through farming, since the beginning of history. Sometimes this has been for the better, sometimes for the worse. One of the most damaging impacts of human activity today is that of soil erosion. Soil has always been washed and blown off the land to some extent. But when forests are cleared away and replaced with farmland, it can have severe effects on the soil. Forests protect soil from splashing rain and from the wind, reduce the flow of water overland, and bind soil with their roots. If land is left bare, soil which has developed over thousands of years can disappear in months. Soil erosion that occurs after "deforestation" is especially serious in tropical and semi-arid areas. Even in the United States, the topsoil of agricultural land is being lost at a rate eight times faster than it is being formed.

Farming has substantially changed the nature of soils all over the world. Artificial fertilizers have altered the chemical balance of the soil, ploughing has changed the structure, and intensive production of crops has reduced the organic content.

What is soil?

THE WORLD'S CONTINENTS ARE COVERED in decay, for that is exactly what soil is – a mixture of rotting rock, plants, and animals. Soil is actually quite a complex substance, and there are many different kinds, but the basic ingredients are the rotting organic matter, which is anything derived from plants or animals, and fragments of rock from the bedrock below.

The tiny gaps between the decaying material are filled with air and water, along with vast numbers of bacteria, fungi, and tiny plants. Each of these subtly alters the chemistry of the soil, speeding up the process of decay, and making the soil a better home for larger plants and countless burrowing insects, worms, and larger creatures. In fact, more animals live in soil than in all the other environments of the Earth put together.

The basic texture of a soil depends on its bedrock, but the soil's character varies enormously with such factors as the shape of the landscape, the vegetation growing on it, and, above all, the climate.

EXPERIMENT
Measuring air space

Soil grains are covered in water, with air space in between. The amount of air depends on the soil's texture – where the grains are coarse, there is often more air. Fine silt and clay soils are easily waterlogged, and so are hard to cultivate. Coarse sands and gravels are easier to cultivate, but tend to dry out. The best soils are "loams", which contain both silt and sand. Why not test your own soil samples?

YOU WILL NEED
● beakers ● trowel
● measuring jugs
● soil samples
● water ● bucket

■ Soil profile

If you cut down through the soil to the bedrock below, you would see a "soil profile". In many profiles, you can identify about five layers, or "horizons". Each of these is given a letter, starting with O and running down through A, B, C, and D. The illustration below shows a fairly typical profile.

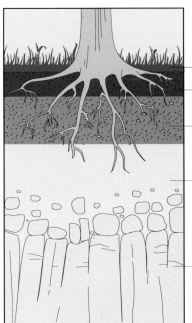

The O horizon is a thin layer of "humus" (dead leaves and other organic matter)

The A horizon is topsoil, dark and rich in humus

The B horizon is subsoil, poorer in humus, but rich in minerals from the topsoil

The C horizon is unfertile, weathered rock fragments

The D horizon is unfertile, solid bedrock

EXPERIMENT
What's in the soil?

Certain plants grow well only in certain kinds of soil, which is why it is important for gardeners and farmers to know about the make-up of their own soil. Expert gardeners can often tell a great deal about soil simply by picking up a handful. You can get an idea of the soil's texture, for instance, by rubbing the grains between your fingers. Gravelly soils are full of small stones. Coarse, sandy soil feels gritty; fine sand less so. Silty soils barely feel rough at all, while clay soil feels hard and smooth when dry; sticky when wet. But the best way to find out what soil is made of is to examine a sample in detail.

Pick out organic material with tweezers

Separate live animals from other organic material

1 WEIGH THE SOIL SAMPLE, then spread it on newspaper or a table. Examine it with a magnifying glass. Pick out live animals, corpses, and plants and put them in jars or bowls.

1 TROWEL THE SOIL from one sample into a measuring jug. Shake the jug gently until the soil surface is relatively level. Read off the quantity from the jug.

2 MEASURE OUT an identical quantity of water, then pour it all slowly into the jug containing the soil.

Calculating the air space
In our example, 200 ml of water was added to 200 ml of soil, which should have given a total of 400 ml. In fact, the combined total was 340 ml, so 60 ml (400 – 340 ml) was air.

The combined level of water and soil is less than you would expect, because some of the water fills the air spaces in the soil

The soil level rises slightly as air spaces fill with water

3 READ OFF the new water level and work out the air space as described above right. Now try again with a variety of soil samples, from very fine to coarse.

YOU WILL NEED
● *soil samples* ● *coarse-mesh sieve* ● *fine-mesh sieve* ● *storage jars* ● *magnifying glass* ● *scales* ● *trowel* ● *measuring jugs* ● *bowls* ● *tweezers* ● *paintbrush*

In each soil sample, there are different proportions of organic, coarse-grained, medium-grained, and fine-grained material, which you can discover by sieving and weighing

Coarse-grained material is left in the sieve

The fine-grained material passes through the sieve. Now you can weigh all three sieved materials to see what proportion of the sample they make up

Medium-grained material is left in the sieve

Sample from which coarse grains have been removed

2 TIP ALL THE SOIL on to a wide-meshed gardening sieve. Shake it through, then weigh the coarse material – stones and large particles – left in the sieve.

3 PUT ALL THE NON-COARSE SOIL into a fine-mesh sieve and shake it through. The soil trapped is the medium-grained; the soil that falls through is the fine. Now weigh the two.

Types of soil

IF YOU COULD DIG A HOLE in the soil beneath a tropical forest, and then dig another in arctic soil, you would see that the two are very different. For a start, tropical soil is much, much deeper than arctic soil, and the chemical make-up and structure of its horizons (p.98) is different, too. These two soils are extremes, but there is a wide range of soils in between.

Soil types depend largely on climate and vegetation. Where it rains heavily, minerals tend to move down through the soil, a process called "leaching". Fine grains are first "eluviated" (washed down), then "illuviated" (re-deposited lower down). But in deserts, water in the soil carries salts upwards, making upper horizons salty. Water may even evaporate to leave a white salt crust.

■ Different soils

There are so many different kinds of soil in the world that "pedologists" (soil scientists) cannot agree on a single way

Podzol
This is an ashy, acid soil which forms in cool, damp forests.

Desert soil
Desert soils have almost no humus. They are very dry and salty and may be topped by a white salt crust.

Gleysol
This is a dirty grey, or blue, wet soil that forms on loose sediments and is often waterlogged.

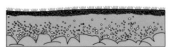

Chernozem
The light rain of the US prairies and the Russian steppes gives this soil a black, humus-rich upper layer.

Ferralsol
This deep soil is often found under tropical forests. Iron oxides turn it deep red or yellow.

of dividing them up. Some pedologists rely on soil profiles, like those shown here. The US Department of Agriculture groups soils according to certain key properties and the presence of a particular horizon. But the most popular way of grouping soils is by the "zonal" system, which relies mostly on the type of climate.

EXPERIMENT
Soil acidity

Some soils are more acid than others. This may be because they are rich in organic matter: both the decay and the breathing of animals create carbon dioxide gas, which makes an acid when dissolved in water. Or it may be because the rain is acid (p.106). Soil acidity is measured in pH numbers – the further the number is below 7 (which is neutral), the more acid the soil is. Here we show a simple way of testing soil acidity.

YOU WILL NEED
● *red cabbage* ● *purified water* ● *knife & chopping board* ● *saucepan* ● *jars* ● *sieve* ● *jug*

1 ASK AN ADULT TO HEAT 1 litre (2 pints) of purified water. Add half a chopped red cabbage and leave for 30 minutes. Sieve the liquid into a jug.

2 ADD A LITTLE RED CABBAGE water to different soil samples in each jar. The redder it gets, the more acid the soil is; the bluer it gets, the more alkaline.

Red cabbage water | *Very acidic soil* | *Slightly acidic soil* | *Slightly alkaline soil* | *Very alkaline soil*

EXPERIMENT
Organic content

The amount of humus (dead leaves and decaying animal matter) in the soil is crucial to its quality. Humus is not only food for the micro-organisms that make vital chemical changes to the soil; it also helps bind mineral grains into crumbs. Crumbs help soil to drain well without drying out, and keep minerals in the topsoil where they are available as food for plants. In the 1930s farmers in the American prairies learned a bitter lesson about the need for humus. For years, farmers planted wheat, cut the crop, and burned the straw. But no new organic matter was added, and the soil soon crumbled and turned to dust. During the years of drought that followed, winds carried off huge amounts of soil and the area became known as the Dust Bowl.

This experiment is a simple way of comparing the organic content of soil.

YOU WILL NEED
- *soil samples*
- *glass jars with lids*
- *trowel*
- *measuring jug*

1 PUT A DIFFERENT SOIL SAMPLE up to the same level in each jar. Then add the same amount of water to each jar.

2 SECURE THE LIDS on each jar, then shake each of them vigorously for about a minute.

3 LEAVE TO STAND FOR A DAY. Compare the amount of floating material in each jar. This is the organic content.

■ Minerals and plants

Early scientists thought that soil simply supported plants and provided a sponge for the water that plants needed to grow. Now we know that soil also provides tiny but vital quantities of a wide range of minerals. Experiments in the nineteenth century showed how important nitrogen, phosphorus, magnesium, potassium, sodium, and calcium were – which is why farmers often add these to the soil in the form of "inorganic" fertilizers. Plants also benefit from traces in the soil of sulphur, iron, manganese, zinc, boron, molybdenum, and selenium.

The CHANGING LANDSCAPE

Shaped by the elements

This hilltop tor (above) was once a single mass of granite. Over millions of years, weathering has broken up the granite, creating smooth, rounded boulders. In southwest China, rainwater has dissolved an immense block of limestone, leaving dramatic peaks and flat valley floors (left).

THE LANDSCAPE AROUND US seems to have a fixed shape, but if we could watch what was happening to any part of it, speeded up thousands or even millions of times, nothing would seem to stay the same. This is because all of the Earth's surface is constantly being reshaped, but most of these changes happen so slowly that we rarely notice them.

SHAPING THE LAND

MOUNTAINS, HILLS, AND VALLEYS may look tough and immoveable. But they are slowly being worn away by the weather, running water, waves, moving ice, wind, and various other "agents of erosion". The process is usually so gradual that you cannot see it happening, but over millions of years mountains have crumbled, hills have been flattened, and valleys have been broadened into huge plains as the landscape is steadily reshaped and "denuded" (worn away).

Crumbling and weathered rocks are a clear sign that the landscape is being slowly "denuded".

Four hundred years ago, most people in Europe believed the world was decaying – and had been ever since the biblical flood. For them, the world was like a decaying body, and mountains were just blemishes on the face of a once perfect world. The sixteenth-century geographer William Bourne was hardly surprised to observe that the "swiftness of the running of water dooth fret away the banks" of a river – it was all part of the general destruction.

Though geographers at this time could see that rivers had the power to erode, few realized that they carved their own valleys and played a major role in shaping the landscape. Most believed that mountains and valleys were the ruins left by huge catastrophes in the past, particularly the biblical flood, or Deluge. Only a few insisted on the role of "denudation" – the gradual erosion of the landscape by rivers, wind, waves, weather, and so on.

The long slope of crumbled rock below the cliff face indicates how this hill was being worn away. But scientists still disagree on whether slopes are mostly worn down, getting gradually gentler, or are mostly worn back, staying equally steep (p.113).

■ Early ideas

Among these few was the English scientist Robert Hooke (1635–1703). With remarkable insight, Hooke suggested that landscapes were shaped and reshaped by recurring "vicissitudes of change" (cycles of denudation). Each cycle begins with the landscape being worn down by rivers and waves. Eroded material is then washed into the sea and deposited as sediment on the sea bed. Sediments are cemented together or fused by heat to form new rock. Finally, the new rocks are lifted up to form a new landscape and the cycle begins again. Hooke thought it likely that each part of the Earth has been through several of these cycles.

At the time, no-one paid much attention to Hooke's theories, and it was 130 years before cycles of denudation were taken seriously again, this time in the theories of Scottish geologist James Hutton (1726–1797). By then the science of geology had advanced a long way (p.78).

In Hooke's time, most people had believed the world was barely 6,000 years old, as was implied in the Bible. This meant that there was not enough time for the gradual "fretting" of rivers and waves to have had much effect. Because of this, most geographers insisted that the land had been shaped by catastrophes. But by the time Hutton had published his *Theory of the Earth*, in 1795, these geographers had come to the conclusion that the world was much, much older. So there was time for denudation to have got to work after all.

Models of hillslopes give clues to how they are shaped (p.112).

■ Slow erosion

But geographers now faced a dilemma. If the world was God's creation, as many believed, why should God destroy his own perfect creation by denudation? Some suggested denudation might be improving the Earth, just as the sculptor's chisel shapes stone. Others argued that denuded material was continually recycled through the atmosphere, evaporating with water into the sky and falling again in the rain. Hutton solved the dilemma with his idea of denudation cycles. Though the landscape is always being denuded, he argued, all denuded material is deposited on the sea floor, changed into rocks, and then uplifted to form new landscapes. So the process was not destructive.

In Hutton's view, the Earth's surface had been shaped almost entirely by prolonged denudation,

Denudation can occur at different rates. Granite tors may result from faster denudation in the past (p.107).

especially by running water, and soon his supporters were finding more evidence to back his claim. They pointed, for instance, to granite intrusions, formed below ground, which had been exposed by denudation on a grand scale. You could see how much material had been worn away by working out the original rock structure.

In the early 1800s geologists began to venture out to see these processes at work. They learned to recognize the different ways rock is weathered, the ways that weathered material can move down slopes, how waves cut cliffs,

A simple experiment like this (p.106) demonstrates the immense power of water freezing – a power that can fracture solid rock.

and much more. Yet a bitter dispute over the role rivers played in landscape evolution remained.

■ River power

No-one denied that rivers were eroding their valleys now and would do so much more in the future. But many insisted that rivers had had little effect in the past – and the evidence seemed to be on their side. If rivers had really eroded their valleys, how was it that so many rivers were so much smaller than their valleys? Why did broad valleys often run into deep gorges? How did lakes form? And since rivers presumably erode most on their broad beds, why didn't they cut down vertically to give steep gorges, instead of broad valleys?

These were difficult questions for those who believed in the power of rivers (the "fluvialists").

Some argued that there were "pluvials" (wet periods) in the past when rivers were much bigger. A few thought that waters from the biblical flood might have been involved, and pointed to the vast sheets of sediments, which they called "diluvium", that seemed to cover much of northern Europe and North America. The problem with this was that there is no diluvium in the mid-latitudes or the tropics, and where it *is* found it seems too mixed up to have been dropped by floodwaters.

By the 1860s there were three different groups opposing the fluvialists: the "neo-diluvialists", who argued for the flood theory; the "marine erosionists", who believed only the sea had the power to affect the landscape significantly; and the "catastrophists", who thought the landscape had been formed by cataclysmic events – earthquakes, ice ages, and so on. Ironically, it was the success of one particular group of catastrophists that helped to tip the balance in the fluvialists' favour.

Few believed the geologist Louis Agassiz (1807–1873) when he first suggested that North America and northern Europe were once covered by vast ice sheets (p.135). But the evidence for Agassiz's glaciations mounted, and it soon became clear that

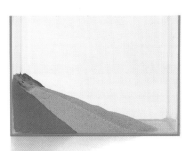

Rock crumbled by the weather slides downhill and is carried away by rivers and streams (p.111).

The shape of every hill and mountain depends on how it has been attacked by water and weather since it was first thrown up (p.113).

"diluvium" was dropped not by floodwaters but by ice. And if glaciers were extensive, as Agassiz suggested, then it was ice that had made so many valleys broad and had gouged out lake basins.

■ Further proof

The balance was tipped further in the fluvialists' favour by the detailed studies of pioneer "geomorphologists" (people who look at the way the landscape is shaped). Studies of the Colorado River in 1875 by John Wesley Powell (1834–1902), and of the Henry Mountains in Utah in 1877 by Grove Gilbert (1843–1918), showed how rivers could transform the landscape.

At much the same time, the geologist James Croll (1821–1890) compared the sea eroding the coast in the Gulf of Mexico with the amount of material swept down the Mississippi River – and showed that the sea changed the landscape at a tiny fraction of the rate of the river. And studies of southeast England showed no evidence of marine erosion, just hills and vales etched by rivers.

By 1900 few geomorphologists doubted that running water played a major role in shaping the land. The problem now was to work out just what that role was.

Places where igneous intrusions (p.60) have been uncovered provide strong evidence of just how much the landscape can be changed by gradual denudation.

Weathering

PEOPLE MAY SAY some things are "as solid as a rock". But even rocks do not stay solid forever. When rock is exposed to the air, and to sun and rain, it gradually starts to change, a process called weathering. Over thousands of years, weathering can change the hardest granite into soft, sticky clay.

Sometimes rocks are broken down by chemical reactions between the rock and the air, or by water trickling over it. Sometimes they are broken down physically by the effects of heat and cold and other changes in the environment. Water freezing in cracks, for instance, can expand so forcefully that it shatters even the toughest rock. Most rocks are weathered by both physical and chemical processes, though either may be more important in certain places. Weathering usually only affects rocks near the surface, but seeping water can carry its effects as far down as 185 m (600 ft).

EXPERIMENT
The power of ice

When water freezes and turns to ice, it expands with enormous force, as this experiment shows. Here we use the power of freezing to lift only a small weight, but scientists estimate that it can occasionally exert a pressure of up to 2,100 kg/cm^2 – equivalent to an elephant standing on a postage stamp. This is why water pipes burst in cold winters if they are not properly insulated. If water freezes in cracks in rock, it can prise the rock apart. In high mountain areas, vast slopes of broken rock called "screes" show the destructive effect of frost on bare rock. Frost action is most common on high mountains and in other cold parts of the world, but can happen in any place where the temperature dips below freezing point.

YOU WILL NEED
● *1–4 kg weight*
● *strong glass beaker*
● *saucer* ● *water*

1 FILL A STRONG BEAKER with water, then cover it with a saucer. Place a heavy weight (up to 4 kg/9 lb) on top.

2 PLACE IN THE FREEZER and leave for 24 hours. As the water turns to ice it expands, forcing up the weight.

EXPERIMENT
Chemical weathering

When a raindrop forms, it consists only of pure water. But as the drop falls through the atmosphere, it dissolves substances from the air around and becomes slightly acid.

If the rainwater then flows over a rock such as limestone, its acidity slowly dissolves the rock away. This is how caves form (p.120). The acidity of rain also helps erode the old stone on buildings and monuments, particularly where the air is polluted by acidic, man-made gases.

In this experiment, you can test the acidity of your own rainwater by pouring a little into a jar containing red cabbage indicator (see pp.100–101 for how to prepare the indicator).

The acid test
Acid will turn the cabbage indicator red. Rain is naturally slightly acid, but man-made pollution can increase acidity dramatically.

■ Scree slopes

Frozen out
Rock shattered by freezing may tumble down to form a "scree slope" of angular rock fragments.

■ How tors are formed

Tors are clumps of bare rock blocks. Most people think they were formed by weathering deep underground in an age when the climate was different. The weathered rock was then washed away, leaving just a few exposed blocks.

Underground
Water seeps down through joints, weathering the rock either chemically or by ice action, or by the two combined.

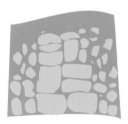

Weak points
Areas where joints are closely spaced erode faster, leaving the large "corestones" unaffected.

Rock sculpture
Weathered material is washed away, until only the relatively unaffected corestones are left standing.

EXPERIMENT
Cracking up

High up on mountains, the temperature often falls below freezing point at night, and then rises above it during the day. Using a freezer and some modelling clay, you can see what effect this cycle of freezing and thawing can have. With the modelling clay, you should be able to see some changes after just one or two cycles of freezing and thawing. From this, you can imagine what happens when rock is frozen and thawed out, not once or twice, but thousands or even millions of times.

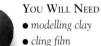

YOU WILL NEED
● *modelling clay*
● *cling film*
● *water*

1 MOISTEN SOME MODELLING CLAY and mould into two balls. Wrap both in cling film and put one in the freezer.

2 AFTER 24 HOURS, UNWRAP the cling film and compare the samples. Wet and re-freeze if the cracking is not clear.

The ball that has been in the freezer is broken up

The unfrozen ball remains intact

■ Weathering and surface area

A piece of rock that is full of cracks and joints weathers much faster than one that is smooth and solid, not only because its joints are weak points but also because it has a larger surface area.

You can see how important differences in surface area are by trying a simple experiment with sugar. Take a sugar cube and weigh it. Now measure out the same weight of granulated sugar. Pour some lukewarm water into two glasses, making sure that they are filled to the same level, and then add the sugar to each one. Then give them both a good stir and watch what happens. You will find that the granulated sugar dissolves almost immediately, because all the surfaces of each sugar crystal are surrounded by water. The cube, on the other hand, takes much longer to dissolve, because its total surface area is smaller. It slowly disintegrates, but may take another stir to dissolve completely.

The same thing is true of rocks. The more broken up a rock is, the faster it will weather. And once a rock starts to weather, the process will accelerate as the rock becomes more broken up.

Shifting slopes

AFTER ROCKS ARE BROKEN down into fragments by weathering, gravity starts to pull all the pieces downhill. But the journey is often slow, because friction between the weathered fragments works against the pull of gravity. Without friction, scree slopes would tumble downhill, sand dunes would collapse, and soil would slide away. The way friction holds slopes together, and makes some steep and others gentle, depends in part on the material from which the slopes are made.

EXPERIMENT
Angle of rest

Loose material, from large boulders to sand grains, always tends to form slopes at a particular angle, called the "angle of rest". Here you can see how different materials give different angles of rest.

YOU WILL NEED
● *various materials – lentils, gravel, earth, etc.* ● *thick card*
● *protractor* ● *jug*
● *pen* ● *notebook*

1 HALF-FILL A JUG with one of a range of materials, such as lentils, gravel, sand, and earth. Pour against a piece of card fixed or held perfectly upright.

2 AS YOU POUR, A SMALL MOUND will form at the bottom of the card. Mark the angle of the slope on either side, then clear away the loose material.

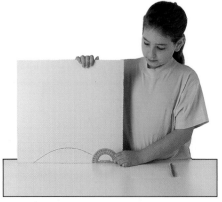

3 MEASURE THE ANGLE OF THE SLOPE with a protractor and make a note of it. Now try again, first with different materials, then from different heights.

EXPERIMENT
Sliding slopes

Friction holds weathered material together until it builds up beyond a certain angle. After this point, gravity overcomes the force of friction, and the material begins to tumble and slide. You can measure this "angle of failure" with loose material in a beaker. Like the "angle of rest" (left) it varies according to the material.

YOU WILL NEED
● *loose material*
● *beaker & cling film* ● *pen*
● *protractor*

1 HALF-FILL A CLEAR BEAKER (or a jar with a lid) with a test material. Seal the end and lay the beaker down.

2 LEVEL THE MATERIAL, then roll the beaker until the material starts to slip. Mark and measure the angle.

Gravel – irregular but steep

Peppercorns – low and scattered

Sand – smooth and steep

Earth – the steepest slope

EXPERIMENT
Shifting sand

Sand is actually rock that has been weathered into very small grains. Between the grains are small holes, called pores. In dry sand, these pores are filled with air. In wet sand, the pores are filled with water. The water, or lack of it, affects the way that the sand grains behave. Dry sand forms slopes, and in many ways acts like a solid surface. Very wet sand behaves more like a liquid. The "pore pressure" of the water pushes the grains apart, so that they can flow around each other with much less friction. In this experiment, you can see what happens to a weight sitting on sand as the pore pressure of the sand increases. You may need to ask a friend to help you set up and carry out the experiment.

YOU WILL NEED
● *thick card* ● *plastic tubing* ● *2 rubber seals or corks* ● *2 cut-off plastic bottles* ● *tape* ● *clip* ● *500 g (1lb) weight* ● *sand* ● *water*

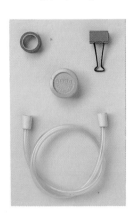

Working on a slope
On the gentle hillsides in this fertile landscape, nearly all the land is being farmed. Farmers have to be careful when cultivating sloping ground, in order to prevent soil from slipping away downhill. Plant and tree roots often hold the soil together on steep hillsides. If the plants are ploughed up or the trees cleared, the soil is all too easily washed away by rainstorms. Where the only available ground is on steep hillsides, the land is sometimes "terraced" into wide steps with retaining banks or walls, in order to keep the soil in position.

1 TAPE BOTTLES to the card, and attach the tube and clip. Fill a third of one bottle with sand, and pour water up to the same level in the other bottle.

2 PLACE THE WEIGHT in the sand container. Then fill the other bottle to the brim with water.

3 WHEN YOU REMOVE THE CLIP, the water will flow up through the sand. The pressure of water makes the sand "bell" up, and the weight sinks a little.

The weight sinks when water pressure pushes the grains of sand apart

With three times the depth of water in this side, water pressure is much greater

Mass movement

ALL OVER THE SURFACE OF THE **E**ARTH, weathered rock and soil is on the move, rolling, sliding, tumbling, and flowing downhill. Much of this "mass movement", as it is called, is far too slow to see – like the imperceptible downhill "creep" of soil on every slope. Sometimes, however, it can be sudden and catastrophic. An earthquake, or the undercutting of a cliff by the sea, can trigger a landslide that carries millions of tonnes of soil or rock away in a few seconds.

Mass movement is most rapid on steep slopes, or where the material has a low angle of failure (p.108). But saturation by water can dramatically reduce a slope's stability and increase the rate of mass movement.

EXPERIMENT
Holding together

Many materials gain their strength from cements that bind the grains together. How well slopes hold up depends on how easily the cements are dissolved. Calcium carbonate cements in limestones dissolve easily in acid rain, while silica cements in sandstones do not – which is why sandstones can support steep rock faces. You can see how important cements are in this simple experiment.

YOU WILL NEED
● *2 beach buckets*
● *large bowl* ● *sand*
● *distilled water*
● *salt* ● *tap water*
● *jug* ● *stirrer*

The salt from the saltwater acts like a cement, binding the castle together

The distilled-water castle has no "cement" and easily crumbles away

1 ADD SALT TO WATER and use this to make one sand castle. Make another castle using distilled water.

2 TURN OUT and leave to dry. Which is the strongest?

■ Slow and fast movement

Gravity pulls weathered material downhill in a number of different ways. You can see the steady downhill "creep" of soil only by signs such as tilting poles, or falling walls. "Landslips" can carry solid rock and entire sections of hillside away, leaving massive scars. "Slumps" occur when a mass of soil slips down, like jelly out of a bowl. "Mudflows" happen when soil becomes sodden with rain and flows downhill like treacle.

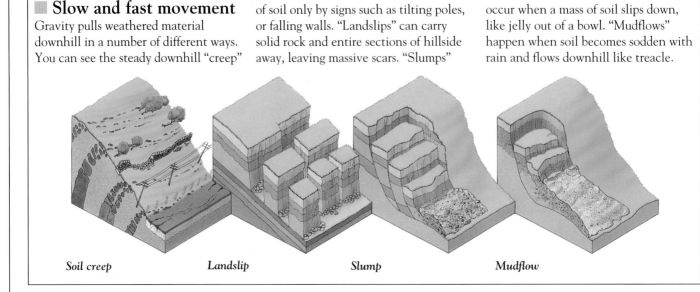

Soil creep   *Landslip*   *Slump*   *Mudflow*

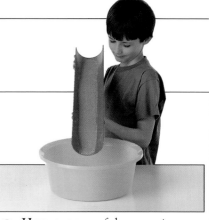

EXPERIMENT
Solid flow

A little water can help bind together fine material, such as sand and soil, but a lot of water can make the soil so runny that it flows away almost like a liquid. Some flows, called earthflows, are relatively slow, moving just a few metres a day or even a month. Others, called mudflows, are much more rapid, and are common in very dry areas after sudden storms. Here you can see how saturating sand can make it flow.

YOU WILL NEED
● *length of guttering* ● *washing-up bowl (if experimenting indoors)* ● *jug* ● *water* ● *sand*

1 FILL A SECTION OF GUTTERING – about 1 m (3 ft) long – with a deep, even layer of dry sand.

2 HOLD ONE END of the guttering over a bowl, then raise the other end until the sand starts to flow.

3 RE-FIILL THE GUTTER WITH SAND, then sprinkle the sand with water. This will help bind the sand together.

4 TEST THE FLOW of the sand again. Then repeat step 3, but this time really "drown" the sand with water.

EXPERIMENT
What's underneath

This experiment is in many ways similar to the one above, but it shows that it is not just the weathered material on top that affects how likely a slope is to slip, but also the material underneath. When a porous material like sand, which allows water through, lies over a material like clay, through which water cannot soak away, the sand may become sodden during rainstorms. The extra water it has retained makes it much more liable to slip – an effect often seen on road embankments after heavy rainstorms.

1 BUILD A CLAY slope against the tank's side.

2 POUR FINE, DRY SAND down on to the clay slope.

YOU WILL NEED
● *clear tank or deep dish* ● *modelling clay* ● *sand* ● *spoon* ● *jug* ● *protractor* ● *water spray*

3 MEASURE THE ANGLE of the dry sand slope. Spray with water until the sand slips and measure the new angle.

Because clay is impermeable (p.120), water cannot soak away

Wetting will make the slope much more unstable and shallow

Changing slopes

HILLS MAY LOOK PERMANENT, but over a long time they are slowly worn away by the weather, mass movement, and running water. Hillslopes in damp areas are often made "convex" (rounded out) near the crest by the effect of soil creep (p.110) and by rain splashing on weathered rock. Lower down, they are made "concave" (rounded in) by water washing over the surface. But exactly how these shapes evolve over millions of years – whether they wear down or wear back – is still not fully understood.

EXPERIMENT
The shape of slopes

How do slopes vary? Are slopes that face north different from slopes that face south? One way to find out is to make a model hillside that shows how gradients change. There are two ways of doing this: one is shown below, the other is shown on the right.

On maps, the height of the ground is often shown by contour lines, which link places of the same "altitude" (height). Contour lines are separated from each other by a set difference in height (10 m for example), so that the closer together they are in any one place, the steeper the slope is. You can use the information shown by contour lines to make an accurate scale model of a hill.

YOU WILL NEED
● *detailed local map showing contour lines*
● *pencil* ● *paper* ● *graph paper* ● *tracing paper*
● *ruler* ● *scissors* ● *thick card* ● *glue* ● *paint*

1 FIND A HILL ON YOUR MAP, lay a sheet of paper on a line from the summit to the base, and then mark off contours.

4 PLOT THE POINTS of the slope and connect them up. Transfer to card with tracing paper. Cut out the shape.

EXPERIMENT
Comparing slopes

In this project, you can make a model hill or landscape by building it up in layers of card or cardboard. Each layer follows a single contour line. Together, they stack up to show the different slope angles all around the hill. Try modelling a number of hills from the same map and comparing them. Do their steepest slopes always face in the same direction?

YOU WILL NEED
● *detailed local map showing contours* ● *tracing paper* ● *thick card* ● *pencil* ● *scissors* ● *paint*

2 PUT THE PAPER beside a horizontal "axis" drawn on the graph paper and transfer the contour marks.

3 SET A SCALE on the vertical axis that relates to the contours on the map, e.g. 1 cm for every 10 m interval.

5 REPEAT STEPS 1 TO 4 to make different profiles from around the hill. Colour, then glue together.

EXPERIMENT
Slippery slopes

A slope's shape or "profile" often depends on how fast rock is weathered and how fast it is carried away by mass movement. By using clay, sand, and "rain" from a water spray, you can see how water may help material slip downhill faster, flattening the lower slope. To begin with, the slope is straight, with an even sand layer. But as the sand gets wet, it begins to slip.

YOU WILL NEED
● *clear tank or deep dish* ● *sand*
● *modelling clay* ● *water spray* ● *jug*

1 BUILD A CLAY SLOPE at the end of the tank, with a sand layer on top. Spray water on the sand until it slips.

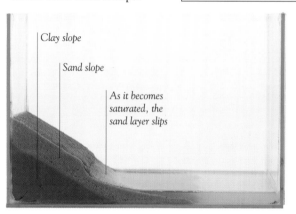

Clay slope

Sand slope

As it becomes saturated, the sand layer slips

■ Slow change

Slopes change so slowly it is difficult to know how they evolve. There are three main theories: "decline", in which slope shapes get gentler as crests are worn down; "parallel retreat", in which slopes are worn back, but stay equally steep; and "replacement", in which steep sections get shorter and shallow sections longer, until all the slope is shallow.

Decline
Summits are worn flatter.

Retreat
Slope wears back, not down.

Slope elements
In damp regions there are three elements in most slopes: a convex crest where rainsplash (p.119) and soil creep dominate; a straight mid-section shaped mainly by mass movement; and a concave lower slope shaped mainly by surface wash.

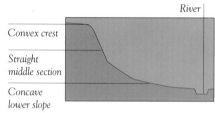

River

Convex crest

Straight middle section

Concave lower slope

1 TRACE THE CONTOURS of a hill from the map (select every second or third line only if the hill is very steep).

2 TRACE THE LINE of each contour on to thick card (or cardboard) and cut out the individual shapes.

3 PAINT EACH LAYER a different colour, then pile one on top of the other to build a model of the hill.

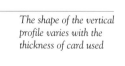

The shape of the vertical profile varies with the thickness of card used

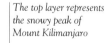

The top layer represents the snowy peak of Mount Kilimanjaro

The gently sloping approach to the mountain is seen in the more widely spaced lower contours

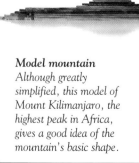

Model mountain
Although greatly simplified, this model of Mount Kilimanjaro, the highest peak in Africa, gives a good idea of the mountain's basic shape.

The evolving landscape

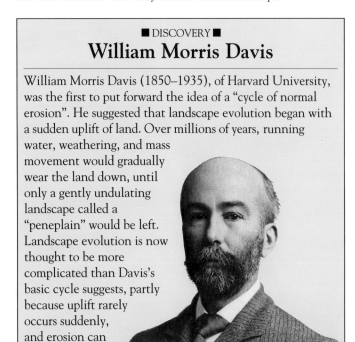

THE LANDSCAPE AROUND US is always changing. Instead of it having a fixed shape, it is constantly being built up and worn down. In the late nineteenth century, attempts were made to explain how these changes work together in a certain pattern, known as the "cycle of erosion". This cycle begins with a great mass of land rising high above sea level. Then streams form on the slopes and cut deeply into the land, producing steep valleys and sharp ridges. Over millions of years the land is worn down by erosion, until only gently sloping hills and rounded valleys remain. But geologists now know that this cycle can be disrupted at any time by further uplift (pp.66–67).

A "mature" landscape
Low hills and a wide river valley indicate a mature landscape.

From youth to maturity
The "cycle of erosion" theory suggests that a landscape develops through three main stages: from youth, through maturity, to old age – from massive uplift to bumpy plain. But as this model shows, different parts of the landscape can be at different stages in the cycle.

River valleys broaden as the land around them is eroded

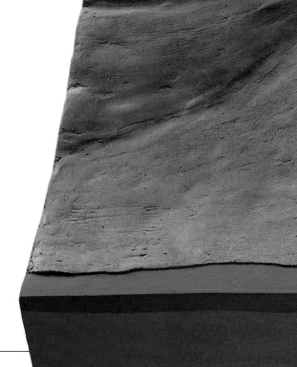

■ DISCOVERY ■
William Morris Davis

William Morris Davis (1850–1935), of Harvard University, was the first to put forward the idea of a "cycle of normal erosion". He suggested that landscape evolution began with a sudden uplift of land. Over millions of years, running water, weathering, and mass movement would gradually wear the land down, until only a gently undulating landscape called a "peneplain" would be left. Landscape evolution is now thought to be more complicated than Davis's basic cycle suggests, partly because uplift rarely occurs suddenly, and erosion can begin even while the land is rising.

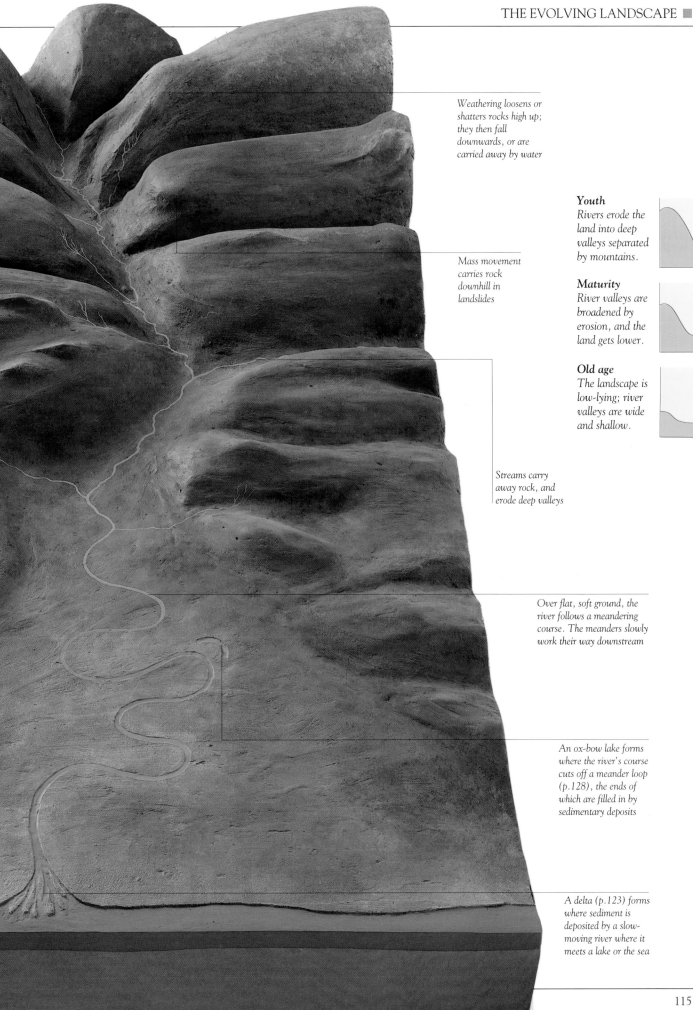

Weathering loosens or
shatters rocks high up;
they then fall
downwards, or are
carried away by water

Mass movement
carries rock
downhill in
landslides

Streams carry
away rock, and
erode deep valleys

Youth
Rivers erode the
land into deep
valleys separated
by mountains.

Maturity
River valleys are
broadened by
erosion, and the
land gets lower.

Old age
The landscape is
low-lying; river
valleys are wide
and shallow.

Over flat, soft ground, the
river follows a meandering
course. The meanders slowly
work their way downstream

An ox-bow lake forms
where the river's course
cuts off a meander loop
(p.128), the ends of
which are filled in by
sedimentary deposits

A delta (p.123) forms
where sediment is
deposited by a slow-
moving river where it
meets a lake or the sea

RIVERS AND STREAMS

Wɪᴛʜᴏᴜᴛ ʀᴜɴɴɪɴɢ ᴡᴀᴛᴇʀ ᴛᴏ sʜᴀᴘᴇ ᴛʜᴇᴍ, landscapes would be as jagged as the surface of the Moon. Indeed, in deserts, where rivers are few and far between, landscapes can look almost lunar. Rivers and streams gradually mould and soften contours, wearing away material here and depositing it there. Over millions of years, a river can carve a canyon thousands of metres deep through solid rock, or deposit a vast plain of fine silt hundreds of metres deep and dozens of kilometres wide.

Every stream tends to wind to and fro, and where rivers flow across broad plains, elaborate horseshoe-shaped meanders may develop.

For the Ancient Greeks, rivers were something of a mystery. Lives and crops depended on river waters, and rivers were the main transport routes. Yet the Greeks did not really know how rivers kept on flowing. Greek scholars, such as Thales (c.625–550 BC), had a good grasp of the water cycle (p.160) – how water evaporates from the sea, condenses into clouds, and falls back to Earth as rain. But as far as they could see, the water that falls as rain is not nearly enough to keep a mighty river running. To them, only oceans could supply this much water, so they guessed that rivers were fed from the sea by underground springs.

This kind of idea persisted for thousands of years. Even in the 1600s people imagined that beneath our feet flowed a vast network of underground waters, filled from undersea caverns.

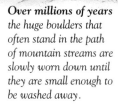

Over millions of years the huge boulders that often stand in the path of mountain streams are slowly worn down until they are small enough to be washed away.

Then in 1674 French scientist Claude Perrault (1613–1688) decided to find out if rainfall really could supply enough water to keep a river running. He measured the rain falling over the area in France drained by the River Seine and its tributaries – and found there was enough rain to fill the Seine six times over.

But if Perrault was right, and rivers were fed by rain, how do rivers flow when it isn't raining?

Six years later, another French scientist, Edmé Mariotte (1620–1684), learned that springs gush more water when it rains. Mariotte realized that, during intense downpours, rainwater not only runs directly *over* the ground ("overland flow"), but also seeps *into* the ground before emerging

Moving water moulds sand into ripples, even on a small scale, as in this experiment (p.124).

back on to the surface from springs ("groundwater").

Because it takes some time for water to trickle down through the ground, it starts to emerge from springs long after a rainstorm begins – and springs may go on flowing long after the rain stops. This "lag" is why groundwater often gives rivers a steady "base flow" all year, while overland flow provides "peak flows" when it rains. Rivers in humid regions often get over a third of their water from underground; the Mississippi River in America gets over half its water from this source.

But why, it was asked, does some water seep into the ground

and some flow away overland? In the 1930s an American engineer, Robert E. Horton (1875–1945), found that water flows overland only when a storm is so intense that the ground cannot soak up the water fast enough. This is known as "Hortonian overland flow". However, other "hydrologists" (people who study water resources) argue that overland flow occurs only after the ground gets so full of water that it overflows ("saturated overland flow"). In most places there is a mixture of both types.

■ River channels

Horton also studied the tendency of overland water to form into "dendritic" (branching) networks of streams, with tiny "rills" joining together to form bigger streams. He called a stream without tributaries a "first-order" stream; one formed by two first-order streams joining he called a second-order stream; one formed by two second-order streams, a third-order stream – and so on. When he analyzed rivers in this way, Horton found they had a very regular pattern. In every river basin, streams get

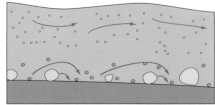

Rivers can carry small grains floating "in suspension"; larger grains are rolled and bounced along the bed.

fewer, longer, and less steep with each successive order – so the river goes from the many short, steep, first-order streams to a single, long, gently sloping, highest-order stream.

■ Speed of flow

In fact, if you trace a river along its course, you usually find it starts off steeply and slopes ever more gently towards the sea. Scientists were puzzled by this for some time. To look at a tumbling mountain stream and a winding lowland river, you might guess

Models of streams have taught hydrologists a lot about how rivers wear away material in some places and deposit it in others (p.122).

that streams run swiftly over high ground, where the slope is steep, and then dawdle lower down where the slope is gentler. This is what many scientists assumed 50 years ago. So the steep upper reaches, they argued, are a sign of "youthful" vigour – where the stream is wearing away its bed energetically, keeping the slope steep. The lower reaches, by contrast, are a sign of sluggish "old age", where the tired old stream drops its sediment. But appearances can be deceptive.

In the 1960s flow-meter measurements showed that rivers often run *faster* further downstream, not slower. This is because they are slowed down less by friction with the bed and banks. In the steep upper reaches of a stream, friction is high because the stream is shallow and tumbles over a rough bed of boulders and gravel. There may

be threads of rapid current, but water can slow almost to a standstill in places. In the lower reaches, friction is low and the flow is more even because the channel is deep and smoothly lined with fine silt. The discovery that rivers flow fast downstream demolished the idea of young and old streams. It also destroyed the explanation that sediments get steadily finer downstream because coarse particles are dropped first as streams get slower. If rivers run as fast downstream, this idea is wrong. The answer is that coarse particles are left behind, as fine ones are moved faster and more often.

Further research has shown that a stream channel is modified constantly by the way water and sediment interact with the material of bed and banks. Where a river flows through loose gravels, the channel tends to be wide and shallow. Where the banks are made of sticky silt, rivers are deeper and narrower.

■ Meandering

This constant interaction also seems to play a crucial role in a river's tendency to "meander" (wind to and fro) in certain places, especially as it nears the sea. The reason why meanders

Many rivers, like China's Yellow River, carry huge loads. This is a way of measuring the load (p.125).

develop is a mystery, though various theories have been suggested, including the idea that they are started by deflection from boulders, or by the effect of the Earth's rotation.

Yet far from being helped by lumps in coarse river material, meandering is hindered by them. It appears to develop best in smooth, fine silt. Actually, meanders are remarkably consistent and predictable in form. They are nearly always seven to ten times as long as the river is wide, bend every five to seven channel widths, and tend to develop towards the same horseshoe shape. This is the reason why most scientists believe that meandering is an inborn property of every stream channel. Since meandering is encouraged by a shallow slope and a large flow, scientists are sure it has something to do with the way energy is used in a stream.

Just how this works seems to depend on the interaction between water and sediments in the stream bed. Significantly, the alternate pools and riffles (deeps and shallows) that develop along the beds of even straight streams are nearly always five to seven channel widths apart – just the same as meander bends. In the 1950s comparisons of model streams and real streams by hydrologists showed that the "thalweg", the line of deepest water, tends to wind to and fro across channels – even straight channels – every five to seven channel widths. It seems a natural progression from the winding thalweg to the meandering stream (pp.128–129).

When rivers flood *after prolonged heavy rain, or when snow melts in spring, huge trees and even boulders may be swept along in the torrents of water.*

Mountain streams *may appear very fast-flowing as they rush over rocks – but even below waterfalls there are places where the water barely moves.*

Water on the land

EVERY YEAR, MILLIONS OF TONNES OF WATER fall on the land as rain. Untold billions of raindrops hammer against the ground's surface, slowly shifting it and shaping it. Gravity drags the water over the ground into streams, then into rivers, and finally once more into the sea.

When water reaches the ground, some of it sinks below the surface, forming "groundwater" (p.120). Some evaporates straight away into the air, or is taken up by plants and then evaporated through their leaves. The remainder runs away over the surface. This starts off as "overland flow" – that is, water that moves over the ground without following any particular path. But overland flow does not usually travel far. Within a short distance, the water finds its way into tiny gullies. From then on it becomes "stream flow" – water that follows well-defined channels downhill.

■ Drainage patterns

The patterns made by streams reveal a lot about the land over which they flow. Here are three common patterns: as an exercise, why not try finding them on a map of your area?

Dendritic drainage
A tree-like pattern forms where rock is flat and regular; the "twigs" can grow in any direction.

Parallel drainage
Streams like this form mainly where rock strata are eroded in parallel bands.

Radial drainage
This occurs where streams flow outwards and downwards from a high point, such as a volcano cone.

Rainwater that lands on slopes begins to run downhill as overland flow

During storms, overland flow runs down hillsides as sheets of water

"Runoff" can be collected from a hillside with a length of gutter, and channelled into a container for measurement

Measuring overland flow
Overland flow can be collected and measured with a gutter, buried in a slope, that leads to a container. It varies according to rainfall and the type of ground, and man-made changes can have an important effect on it. If a hill is covered in vegetation the flow is usually small, because the vegetation holds much of the water until it evaporates, or infiltrates the ground. But if the vegetation is cut down, there is nothing to hold the water. The overland flow increases, and the soil may be washed away. The result is often severe erosion and barren hillsides.

EXPERIMENT
Erosion by rain

In short, violent storms, the impact of raindrops on soft ground with little or no vegetation is quite enough to dislodge grains of soil. This is called "rainsplash erosion". You can see the effects of this, and how a harder layer of rock can protect the material below, in the following experiment.

YOU WILL NEED
● *plastic dish* ● *sand*
● *coins*

1 MAKE A MOUND of sand in the tray. Put a few coins on the sand. Now put the tray outside in an open place, where it is not sheltered from the rain.

2 RAIN WILL GRADUALLY wear the sand down. But the sand under the coins will not erode so quickly, leaving pillars standing up in the tray.

Pillars form where layers of hard rock (the coins) protect the softer rock from rainsplash erosion

EXPERIMENT
Splashing down a slope

If you drop a ball on level ground, it will bounce back vertically. But if you bounce it on sloping ground, it will gradually work its way downhill. Something similar happens to soil and rock as rain hits a hillside. When a raindrop reaches the ground, its energy is often enough to dislodge soil or rock fragments. The soil or rock is thrown outwards and downwards, so it lands further down the slope. But it doesn't always go straight downhill. At times, the impact of raindrops shifts material at an angle. The experiment shows this happening on a miniature "hillside".

YOU WILL NEED
● *protractor* ● *ruler* ● *pen* ● *scissors*
● *pair of compasses* ● *glue* ● *blotting paper*
● *sand* ● *tray*

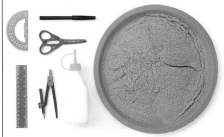

1 MARK OUT THE BLOTTING PAPER as shown, with lines crossing at the centre, surrounded by circles at equal intervals. Cut out the central circle.

2 PUT THE SAND IN THE TRAY, and level it off. Place the tray outside on a slope, cover with the paper, and glue or weight the sides down.

3 OVER THE NEXT FEW WEEKS, watch what happens to the sand. Can you see "rainsplash" forcing the sand out and down the slope?

Water underground

WHEN IT RAINS, THE WATER does not always flow away into streams and rivers. If it falls on rocks such as chalk or limestone, much of it disappears into the ground. It then becomes groundwater – water that very slowly passes through "pores" (air-spaces) or gaps in the rock, sometimes hundreds of metres below the surface. Groundwater saturates the bedrock (p.182), in some places forming huge natural reservoirs of pure water. The top of this saturated zone is called the "water table", which tends to follow the contours of the land. Groundwater often emerges lower down as springs, where the water table and surface meet again.

Groundwater can erode underground layers of rock, just as water does on the surface. Where the rock is limestone, the water, which contains carbon dioxide, gradually dissolves the rock. It seeps through cracks and widens them, eventually forming large caves.

Running beneath the surface
This underground cavern has been formed in limestone rock. Dripping water has created stalactites on the cavern's ceiling.

EXPERIMENT
Testing permeability

Rain falling on sandy ground quickly drains away. But rain falling on a tarmac road stays on the surface, so that slopes and drains have to be built to prevent flooding. Sand contains lots of spaces that water can drain through and is said to be very "permeable", while tarmac makes an almost waterproof barrier and is said to be "impermeable". You can test the permeability of different materials with this simple experiment. Are the coarser materials more permeable?

YOU WILL NEED
● *materials to test (sand, gravel, lentils, cleaning powder etc.)* ● *plastic bottle* ● *muslin* ● *pouring jug* ● *measuring jug* ● *elastic band* ● *scissors* ● *pen* ● *notebook* ● *watch*

1 CUT THE TOP OFF the plastic bottle to make a funnel. Using an elastic band, securely fasten a piece of muslin across the bottle's mouth.

2 PUT THE FUNNEL in the measuring jug. Fill the funnel with one of the test materials and mark the level it reaches on the side of the funnel.

3 FILL THE OTHER JUG with a measured amount of water. Make a note of the time before you start, then pour the water into the funnel.

4 MAKE A NOTE of how long it takes the water to flow through into the jug. Now try the other materials, filling the funnel up to the same mark as before.

EXPERIMENT
Seeping through

Even in places where the ground is full of air-spaces, or "pores", puddles of rainwater can be left on the surface after a heavy storm. This is because it takes time for water to "infiltrate" into the ground, once it is saturated. Here you can see how long it takes water to drain away through different soils. Notice that, once the soil is saturated, water drains through at the same rate, however much you pour on.

YOU WILL NEED
● *pen* ● *notebook*
● *funnel (top of a*
plastic bottle) ● *jug*
● *clock or watch*

1 BURY THE FUNNEL in the ground so that the top is level with the surface. Make a note of the time, and then pour in a jugful of water.

2 NOTE HOW LONG it takes for the water in the funnel to drain away. Try again with more water, then test the infiltration rate of other soil areas.

EXPERIMENT
Making a stalactite

In limestone caves, the steady drip of mineral-bearing groundwater over hundreds and sometimes thousands of years can form huge stalactites and stalagmites. With a solution of washing soda, you can grow a small one in less than a week. As the solution drips into a dish, some of the soda is left behind to grow down into a stalactite, and up from the saucer into a stalagmite. Minerals build into cave features in the same way.

YOU WILL NEED
● *wool* ● *paperclips* ● *jug* ● *dish* ● *spoon* ● *2 jars*
● *washing soda*

1 FILL THE JARS with very warm water. Add some washing soda to each one, and stir the solution. Keep adding soda until it can no longer dissolve.

2 CUT A LENGTH of wool. Attach clips to the ends of the wool and lower each end into the jars. Put the saucer in the middle and leave for 2 to 3 days.

Washing soda solution

Short length of wool weighted with paperclips at both ends

Capillary action draws solution out of jar and along the wool

Washing soda solution

A stalactite grows downwards from above, as the dripping water evaporates

Solution drips into saucer

A stalagmite grows upwards from below, as the water in the solution evaporates

Running water

 WITHOUT MOVING WATER to mould the landscape, the surface of the Earth would look more like the Moon. Streams and rivers wear away material here, deposit it there – all the time reshaping and softening the landscape. The process might seem slow, but deep valleys are the result of rivers cutting through solid rock, while vast floodplains of silt show the power that rivers have to move weathered material. Just how rivers shape the land around them depends on many factors, including how fast the water flows and what kind of rock it flows over.

■ The rough and the smooth

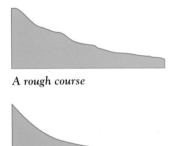

A rough course

A smooth course

Knickpoint

A new slope

At first, a young river's course from head to mouth is very uneven, with lots of waterfalls and rapids.

In time, the river erodes material here and deposits it there, to make the slope much smoother or "graded".

If the sea level drops, the river starts cutting back at "knickpoints" until the course is smooth again.

Rivers, like people, change as they get older. One way to see this is in the river's "long profile", which plots the height of its bed from head to mouth. When the river is young, its path is full of bumps and hollows. Through time, however, the river wears away the bumps and deposits material in the hollows, smoothing out the course. The profile becomes a shallow curve, sloping steeply at the top and gently at the bottom, as more and more water is picked up on the way.

Making a stream tray

Adult help is advised for this experiment

A stream tray is a river in miniature, and you can use it to see how rivers form and change over time. It is not the same as a full-size river, but you can adjust flow, gradient, and other factors to see how they affect the channel shape and the way material is eroded and deposited.

YOU WILL NEED
- *base 120 x 60 x 0.5 cm (48 x 24 x 1/4 in)*
- *2 ends 56 x 10 x 2 cm (22.5 x 4 x 3/4 in)*
- *2 sides 120 x 10 x 2 cm (48 x 4 x 3/4 in)*
- *smoothing strip 55 cm (22 in) wide* ● *props*
- *hose and connector* ● *adhesive tape* ● *sand*
- *bucket* ● *plastic sheet* ● *hammer* ● *saw* ● *drill*
- *panel pins* ● *ruler* ● *screws & screwdriver*

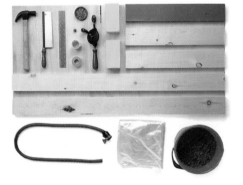

1 **F**IX THE SIDES AND ENDS to the baseboard by hammering panel pins through the board and into each piece. Make sure they line up at right angles.

2 **S**TRENGTHEN THE CORNERS by screwing the sides and ends together where they meet. Use a drill to make a pilot hole for each screw.

3 **S**AW A V-SHAPED NOTCH in the centre of one of the ends. This notch will allow water to drain away. Drill a hole directly beneath the notch.

4 LAY THE PLASTIC SHEET over the tray, spreading it out so that it follows the shape of the tray and tucking it into the corners. Tape down around the outside.

5 MAKE SURE THAT THE TRAY is securely supported. Next, line it with about 7 cm (3 in) depth of sand, taking care not to damage the plastic lining.

6 SET THE TRAY where the water can drain away. Tape the hose at the far end from the notch. Draw the wood across to completely flatten the sand.

■ Stream tray waterfall

Waterfalls are created where rivers flow over a band of hard rock on to soft rock. You can see how a waterfall develops in the stream tray by using a ruler to make a resistant ridge. Press the ruler across the stream's path until it is level with the bed. Now turn on the water, and watch what happens. The stream wears away the soft sand in front until a small waterfall forms.

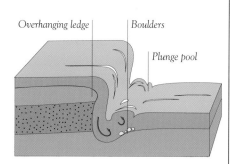

Overhanging ledge *Boulders* *Plunge pool*

Taking the plunge
In this waterfall, the river is flowing over two different types of rock. The central band of rock (purple) is soft, but the rock above and below (green) is more resistant. The stream cuts back quickly through the soft rock, and water pours over the ledge of hard rock into a "plunge pool" below.

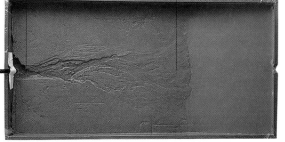

In the upper parts, the river picks up and carries sediment

Near the sea, the water slows and drops sediment

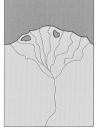 

7 PROP UP THE HOSE END of the tray with blocks of wood as shown in the top picture. Connect the hose to a tap and turn it on to give just a trickle. After an hour or so, the sand will become saturated and the stream will start to carve a channel. Look for changes every few hours, and notice how sand grains move through the channel.

Deltas
Deltas are fans of sediment left by rivers as they meet the sea. Some are arcuate (bow-shaped), like that of the Nile (above left). Others, like the Mississippi's, form like a bird's foot as sand between stream branches drops away (above right).

123

A river's burden

SOME RIVERS ARE SO CLEAR you can see almost every detail of the river bed. In others, the water is made so murky by the sand and mud being swept along that if you trailed your hand in the water it would disappear from sight. So thick is the broth of silt and water in China's Huang Ho that it is popularly known as the Yellow River.

The material carried along by a river or stream is known as its "load", and varies according to how fast the water moves and the kind of country through which the river flows. Most material is carried during short periods of flooding; when rivers like the Huang Ho flood, they move billions of tonnes of sediment downstream. Yet even the smallest, clearest stream carries a load.

■ Floodplain

If you could slice through a wide river valley, you would see that the floor is coated with layers of fine sand and mud called "alluvium" – deposited by the river as it floods after heavy rains. The river may flow inside raised mud banks called "levées", built up every time the river bursts its banks.

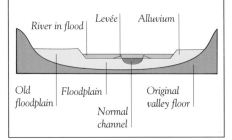

River in flood | Levée | Alluvium
Old floodplain | Floodplain | Original valley floor
Normal channel

EXPERIMENT
Making ripples

A stream cannot pick up material from its bed unless it is flowing quite fast. Once it is flowing fast enough, it starts to mould the bed, creating regular ripples called "dunes" that slope gently on the upstream side and steeply on the downstream. You can make these dunes yourself in a circular "flume" or channel, in which water is stirred around inside a bowl – a very simple way of creating a continuous stream. If you stir slowly, the water picks up no sand and the bed stays smooth. But as you stir faster, dunes begin to develop. They are most marked towards the outside of the bowl, where the flow is fastest.

1 HALF-FILL THE BOWL WITH WATER. Fill the plastic beaker with sand, and then put it into the centre of the bowl.

2 SPRINKLE A THIN, EVEN LAYER of sand into the bowl, then set up a circular motion in the water by stirring gently.

YOU WILL NEED
● round bowl ● sand-filled beaker or similar round, heavy object ● sand ● spoon ● water

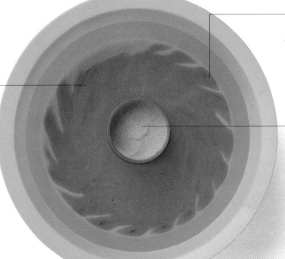

Thin, even layer of sand

Up to a point, the faster the water is stirred, the more the sand is picked up – and the more pronounced the ripples become

A sand-filled beaker makes a static central point, around which the water can run

■ Moving the load

A river's load moves in three different ways. Some substances are dissolved in the water ("solute load"). Small particles hang in the water ("suspended load"). Larger objects move along the bed ("bed load"), either by rolling and tumbling or by making small hops ("saltation").

Heavy stones and boulders hop and tumble along the river bed

Small particles stay suspended as long as the water moves fast enough

---

EXPERIMENT
Suspended load

Suspended load is harder to measure than bed load. Pushing a piece of white card below the surface gives a rough guide – the quicker it becomes invisible, the heavier the load. But you *can* measure the load with this simple device. It consists of two jars, each with an inflow pipe and an upward-pointing outflow pipe fixed through plasticine seals on the jars' mouths. Tape the jars to a stick at different heights and stand them in a stream, the straws facing upstream. Water flows into the jars and slows down, dropping most of its load. It then flows out again. After six hours, weigh the contents with a fine balance.

EXPERIMENT
Sampling the bottom of a stream

 Adult help is advised for this experiment

If you want to know how the load of a real stream varies according to the flow, why not take your own measurements? Pick a small stream you or an adult can safely wade in, and take samples at different times of year. Shown here is the technique for measuring bed load; the experiment below left shows the technique for measuring suspended load.

To measure bed load, make a square of muslin stretched over a wire frame as shown. Weigh the frame, then lower it carefully into the stream and lay it flat on the bed. After six hours, carefully lift the frame out of the water, keeping it level all the time. Leave it to dry, and weigh again. The difference between first and second weights is the bed load.

YOU WILL NEED
- *muslin material, about 25 x 25 cm (10 x 10 in)* ● *wire*
- *scissors* ● *stapler*

Testing the beds

A muslin load sampler lying on a stream bed will catch heavier debris travelling along the bottom or being dropped from faster currents above.

Collect your load sample from a shallow stream

Muslin fitted loosely around a wire frame will hold in the collected debris when lifted from the bed

1 BEND THE WIRE into a square and twist the ends into a handle. Put the wire on to the muslin, then fold in the sides and staple them together.

2 CHECK THAT THERE IS PLENTY of slack in the muslin "net", then place the sampler flat on the bed of a stream and leave for six hours.

Flowing streams

LOOK CLOSELY AT THE SURFACE of a river
and you can see it doesn't all flow at the
same speed. In the middle of the main
channel the water shoots along. But in the
shallows near the edges, flow may almost come to
a standstill – because it is slowed by friction with
the banks and bed. You may find it hard to
believe that water is affected by friction, but it is
true. In fact, a stream uses 95 per cent of its
energy overcoming friction. Indeed, this is why
rivers don't flow faster high in the mountains,
where they use energy tumbling over rocks and
boulders, but speed up lower down, where they
flow between smooth banks of silt and mud.

Water on the move
*As this stream flows over its rocky bed, different parts move at
different speeds. In the middle the water rushes by, but at the
edges it may hardly move at all.*

EXPERIMENT
Rough and smooth

If water is run slowly over glass, it flows
in perfectly smooth, even layers – a kind
of movement called "laminar" flow. But
this kind of flow is rare in real streams
and occurs only where flow is very slow,
near beds and banks. In most streams,
flow is "turbulent". Instead of flowing in
one direction, the water moves
chaotically, eddying around in all
directions. This is significant because it
is these eddies that help streams to lift
particles up or drill them on to the bed.
You can see for yourself how laminar
flow changes to turbulent flow simply by
pouring water on a tray. The change,
called "hydraulic jump", is actually quite
sudden, and can be seen very clearly.

Jumping water
*When the water hits the tray, the flow is at first
smooth and laminar. But within a very short
distance it leaps up to become turbulent flow.*

YOU WILL NEED
● *large tray (or use the bath or sink)*
● *jug* ● *water*

*Hold the jug about
20 cm (8 in)
above the tray and
pour steadily*

*The jump from
laminar to
turbulent flow
occurs in a ring
around the
spreading water*

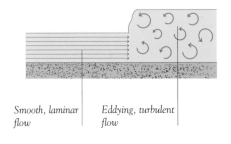

*Smooth, laminar
flow*　*Eddying, turbulent
flow*

EXPERIMENT
Speed of flow

The easiest way to see how fast a stream flows is to time a floating object over a measured distance. An orange makes a good marker because it floats just below the surface, picking up the flow more accurately than a stick on the surface. Drop the orange upstream, then time it over a measured length of bank.

YOU WILL NEED
● *watch* ● *tape measure*
● *orange or similar fruit*

Getting the average
Because water flows fastest near the surface, you need to multiply your answer by 0.8 to get a good average for the whole stream. For example, 100 m in 20 seconds would give a flow speed of 5 m per second. But multiplying by 0.8 gives an average of 4 m per second.

■ Flow profile
This flow profile shows how a river's speed varies with its depth. The faster the water flows, the further to the right the flow line extends. The flow is fastest just below the water surface, and slowest near the bed, where friction acts as a brake.

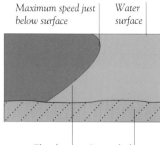

Maximum speed just below surface | *Water surface*

Flow line | *Stream bed*

■ Storm in a stream tray
When a storm suddenly pours water into a river's catchment area, the results can be dramatic. The water's energy is concentrated into a narrow region, and the river's ability to carry large objects (its "competence") increases sharply along with its "capacity", the total load it can carry. Not only vast quantities of sand and silt, but even giant boulders and trees can be swept away in the torrent. In real life, sudden floods like this can bring devastation. In August 1952, there was a dramatic flood in the tiny River Lyn in Devon, England, which dumped 100,000 tonnes of boulders on the small village of Lynmouth, sweeping away houses, bridges and cars. You can see the effect of this kind of sudden flow by using the stream tray (p.122).

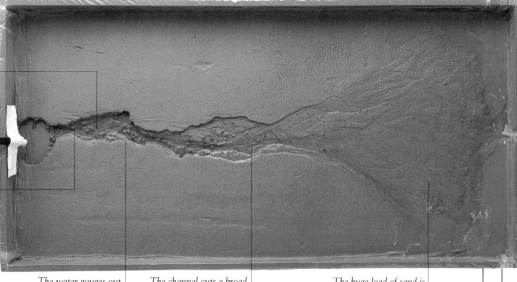

Even the largest grains of sand are swept away by the torrent

Increase the water flow to create a "storm" in the tray

The torrent carries huge quantities of sand, both fine and coarse, from one end of the tray to the other

The water gouges out a deep channel

The channel cuts a broad swathe through old meanders and bars

The huge load of sand is deposited in a giant alluvial fan, or delta (p.123), at the downstream end

Meandering

IF YOU DROP A HEAVY BALL on a slope it rolls straight down to the bottom. But running water winds backwards and forwards like a snake. This natural "sinuousity" plays an important part in shaping rivers. In fact, the bigger the river and the shallower its slope, the more likely it is to bend this way and that. As a river nears the sea, it tends to wind more and more, until it forms a series of regular, horseshoe-shaped bends called meanders. The bigger and wider the river, and the finer the material in its bed and banks, the bigger the meander will be.

Scientists have various theories to explain why meanders develop. But they know that both the way water spirals and eddies between the banks, and the way the river sweeps up sediment in some places and drops it in others, are important.

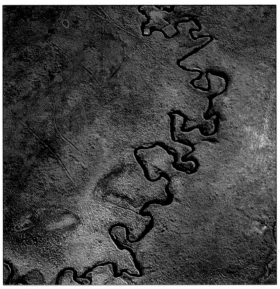

Ever-changing curves
This river shows extreme meandering. Some curves are so tight they may eventually touch. When this happens, water breaks through the curves. A loop of river bed is then completely cut off, forming an "ox-bow" lake.

■ Making meanders

By using the stream tray (pp.122–123), you can see for yourself how a shallower slope and a larger flow encourage meanders to form. Level out the sand and increase the flow of water a little above a trickle. Leave it for six hours. Now put the tray on smaller blocks to lower the slope significantly, and increase the flow even more. You will probably see distinct bends beginning to develop quite quickly.

After the stream has been left to run for a while, its course begins to shift more and more across the sand. Notice

Sand is carried away from the "upstream" end of the tray, creating a channel

To begin with, the stream follows an almost straight course

Further downstream, the water begins to curve across the sand

Sand carried downstream is deposited wherever the water flows slowly

■ How meanders form

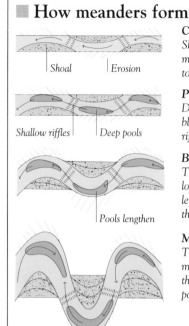

Shoal | Erosion

Shallow riffles | Deep pools

Pools lengthen

Curving begins
Shoals of deposited material divert water to create bends.

Pools and riffles
Deep pools (dark blue) and shallow riffles (lines) form.

Bends build up
The channel becomes lopsided as pools lengthen and move to the outside of bends.

Meandering
The size of the meander depends on the spacing of the pools and riffles.

■ Spiral flow

The flow is fastest on the outside of each bend, where the water is deepest

The flow is slowest on the inside of bends, where the water is shallow

Material is deposited on the inside of bends to form shoals and sandbars

Material is cut away from the outside of each bend to form cliffs

Line of fastest flow

Undercurrent from the outside to the inside of bends

In most rivers, water not only flows downstream, but across river too. Because it flows fastest on the outside of bends, water piles up here, and is then drawn across to the shallows on the inside, where the flow is slowed by sandbars. This "corkscrewing" of water through the meander is significant, but it does not, as once thought, scour material from the outside and dump it on the inside of bends.

how branches in the main flow develop into bends. As water strikes the outside of each bend, it cuts away the sand to form miniature cliffs, and on the inside, sand is piled up into sandbars. As long as the water flows, the pattern of meanders keeps changing. In reality, meanders tend to wander across the valley floor. This, along with occasional floods that spill across the whole valley, helps to create a flat plain of deposited material called a floodplain. Meanders also tend to move downstream, because erosion is concentrated on the downstream side of bends in the river.

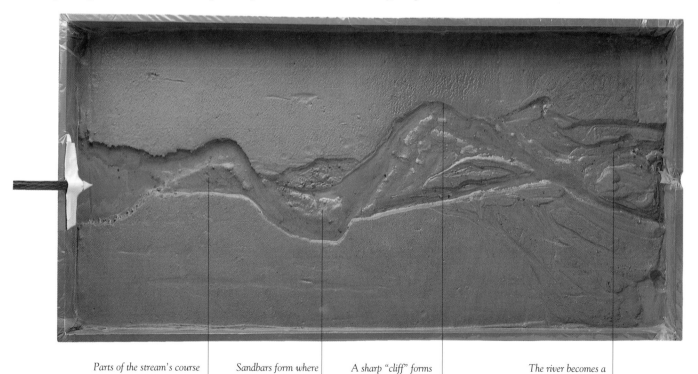

Parts of the stream's course are cut off as the water flows through new meanders

Sandbars form where sand piles up on the inside of each bend

A sharp "cliff" forms where the water strikes the concave bank

The river becomes a mass of intertwining channels, or "braids"

ICE AND WIND

Moving ice and air – just like moving water – can greatly change the landscape. Moving ice occurs in the world's glaciers and ice caps, which creep slowly downwards or outwards under their own weight. Today, only a tenth of land is covered by ice, and throughout the world many glaciers are slowly shrinking. But glaciers have not always been in retreat. Over the last 150 years, scientists have shown that these great masses of ice once covered much of the northern hemisphere.

The Mittens, in Utah's Monument Valley, are the remnants of a plateau that has been eroded by water and the wind.

In the summer of 1836 two men went on an expedition high into the valleys on the western edge of the Alps. One of them was Johann von Charpentier (1786–1855), a man who had a particular interest in glaciers, and the other was the Swiss naturalist Louis Agassiz (1807–1873).

The expedition had been arranged to resolve a friendly dispute. Some geologists had noted how high-mountain glaciers gouge their way through valleys, and carry rock from one place to another. Armed with this knowledge, they had then looked at the landscape much lower down, where no glaciers existed. To their surprise, they found exactly the same kinds of gouged valleys, and the same characteristic piles of rock. For Charpentier, the conclusion was clear: at one time, much of northern Europe had once been covered by an ice sheet.

Agassiz was sceptical. Although several scientific papers had been published about an earlier age of ice, he thought it unlikely that such an event had taken place. But the trip proved to be a turning point in his thinking. Instead of arguing against it, Agassiz decided that the evidence was overwhelming. From then on he became a leading supporter of the "Glacial Theory".

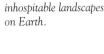

Windswept desert mountains make up some of the most inhospitable landscapes on Earth.

■ Evidence from ice

Since the 1830s geologists have found a great deal of evidence supporting the Glacial Theory. There is now little doubt that 18,000 years ago much of the northern hemisphere – including the land where New York and parts of London now stand – was covered by a thick sheet of ice. Ice also covered the Alps, and the tip of South America. Even in Australia and Africa, the highest ground was enveloped in a massive cloak of ice.

From observations of glaciers, we know that this ice would have been on the move, flowing very slowly but with tremendous power. And wherever the ice once flowed, it has left its imprint. Moving ice does this in two ways – by eroding the rock beneath it, and by carrying away stones and boulders, which are then deposited as mounds of debris, called "moraines", where the glacier ends and then retreats.

You can get some idea of the size of these ancient rivers of ice by the size of the rocks they carried, and the distances that they moved them. Some ice-borne boulders, known as "erratics", weigh hundreds of thousands of tonnes, and are over a kilometre long. On the east coast of Britain, there are boulders that come not from the underlying rock, but from near

Pressure melts ice into a layer of water along which a glacier can slide (p.133).

Oslo in Norway. So ice must have carried them a distance of more than 800 km (500 miles).

■ Changing climate

When geologists began to amass evidence to support the Glacial Theory, one of the first things they tried to establish was how far the ice had once spread. At this point, some strange discoveries were made. Parts of North America and northern Europe were covered with moraines, and these often overlapped. Moreover, in the 1870s, the remains of a forest were found sandwiched between two sheets of glacial deposits or "till".

It was clear from this that the glaciers had not simply come and gone. Instead, they had advanced and receded in at least four separate "ice ages". During each ice age, the ice left a different set

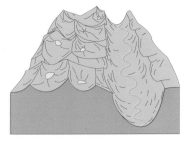

After glaciers have retreated, they leave behind a landscape marked by U-shaped valleys and bowl-shaped cirques.

of moraines, much as an ebbing tide leaves behind lines of seaweed on a beach.

These findings could only mean that the Earth's climate had alternately warmed up and cooled down. It was an important discovery, because it challenged the idea held by many geologists that the Earth always changed in a "directional" way, meaning that geological changes always followed the same path, and

"Plastic deformation" explains *how ice under extreme pressure flows like a liquid (p.132).*

never went back on themselves. The idea of warming and cooling, however, did not fit into this directional pattern of change.

Today it is accepted that the Earth's climate does go through periodic changes. The ice advances during "glaciations", when the average surface temperature falls, and retreats during "interglacials", when the temperature rises. At its maximum extent, ice may have covered nearly a third of the world's land surfaces. The land can sink under the huge weight of ice, but because so much water is locked up as ice, the sea level falls by up to 150 m (500 ft). In an interglacial – such as the one we live in now – the ice retreats so much that it may cover as little as 10 per cent of the land. This leaves much of the Earth's surface ice-free and habitable.

■ Sun and ice

Once the existence of separate ice ages had been established, the hunt began for their cause. Over

the last hundred years or so, many explanations have been put forward, yet the question still remains unanswered.

One of the most popular explanations was put forward by the Yugoslav physicist Milutin Milankovitch (1879–1958). He calculated that the Earth's distance from the Sun, and the angle of its tilt, both go through cycles. The first cycle lasts for 20,000 years, and the second for about twice that time. In 1938 Milankovitch worked out a graph showing the way these cycles would influence the amount of energy that the Earth receives from the Sun.

The "Milankovitch curve", as it is known, does seem to rise and fall roughly in step with the ice ages. However, when it was first published, few believed that it had a connection with the world's climate. Even today, many scientists do not think that it plays a part in ice ages. Some think that ice ages may be caused by volcanic activity, or even by inbuilt oscillations, with ice advancing and retreating like waves in a bath, without needing a "push" from outside.

■ Erosion by the wind

Compared with moving ice, moving air is weak. It can pick up only small objects, such as sand and dust grains. Even so, in some parts of the world wind erosion

The wind sorts sand particles *according to their size – the larger ones are dropped first, the smaller ones are carried much further (p.137).*

has done much to change the landscape. Like ice, wind works in two ways – by scraping things together, and by carrying things from one place to another – forming sand dunes and depositing fine layers of soil.

Icebergs are created *by glaciers shedding ice into the sea. As the icebergs melt, their shape becomes jagged.*

One of the most spectacular examples of wind erosion happened quite recently – in geological terms. On 20 March 1935 a giant dust storm swept through the American states of Colorado, Kansas, Oklahoma, and Texas. The dust formed a huge cloud nearly 4 km (2 miles) high, and it was so thick that day became almost as dark as night. It piled up around cars and tractors like a snowdrift, and people had to wear breathing masks outdoors.

When the wind eventually died down, farmers found that much of the precious topsoil on their fields had simply blown away. This great storm was just one of many that occurred during the 1930s – a time that came to be known as the decade of the "Dustbowl". During the Dustbowl years, some areas lost up to 1m (3 ft) of soil. It disappeared because farmers had removed the land's natural covering of plants through ploughing and overgrazing and because of years of drought. Once the soil was exposed, strong winds could then carry it off.

Ironically, many of the world's best croplands were created by wind erosion. In the American Great Plains, in the USSR, and in China, the most fertile soil is formed on a deep layer of "loess" – a silt blown by the wind from a distant place, and often thousands or millions of years old.

Sea ice forms when *the surface temperature falls below −2°C (28.5°F). It is never more than about 5 m (16 ft) thick.*

Erosion by ice

GLACIERS ARE GREAT STREAMS of ice that flow through mountain valleys, creeping lower and lower until they finally melt. The ice in them is not clear like ice cubes are, but opaque, because they are made from compacted snow, like snowballs. Glaciers rarely move more than 2 m (6 ft) a day, yet they are so large they can carve vast bowls in the rock, gouge valleys into enormous troughs, and truncate (cut off) entire hillsides.

Nowadays, glaciers are confined to mountain areas and polar regions. But in the ice ages (p.135), much of North America, Europe, Asia, and South Africa were covered by glaciers and vast ice sheets up to 3,000 m (10,000 ft) thick, and landscapes there are largely glacial.

■ Features of a glacier

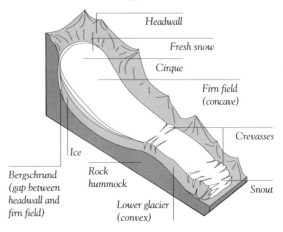

At the glacier's head, snow collects and turns into crystal grains called "firn". The firn is squashed into solid ice. The ice moves slowly downhill, forming crevasses as it passes over rock hummocks and as it spreads out at the glacier's "snout".

EXPERIMENT

Creeping ice

Glaciers move in two main ways – by "plastic deformation" and by "basal slip" (opposite). Plastic deformation happens in ice that is at least 30 m (100 ft) below the surface. The intense pressure from the ice above rearranges the ice crystals, so that they can slide over each other. Instead of behaving like a solid, the ice now behaves like a very thick liquid, and it slowly creeps downhill. You can see for yourself how plastic deformation works with a weight and a stack of cards. As you tip the stack upwards, the "ice" begins to flow.

YOU WILL NEED
● weight ● card or playing cards ● tray

1 STACK THE CARDS IN A PILE on the tray. Put the weight on top. The weight represents a thick layer of ice, the cards the flattened ice crystals beneath.

2 SLOWLY TIP ONE END of the tray upwards. The weight will gradually start to slip downhill as the cards slide over each other.

3 EVENTUALLY THE WEIGHT slides off the tray. Notice that the cards nearest the tray have moved least – just like the deepest ice in a glacier.

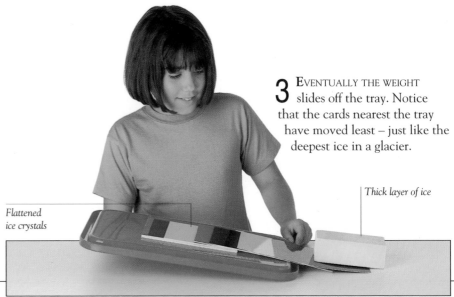

Flattened ice crystals

Thick layer of ice

EXPERIMENT
Scoured by ice

By itself, ice is too soft to carve rock. But as you can see in this experiment, ice containing rock is as harsh as sandpaper. Glacier ice collects rock by picking up – or "entraining" – rock fragments loosened by weathering. These pieces range from large boulders weighing thousands of tonnes, to "rock flour" – tiny fragments of sand with jagged edges. The glacier then scrapes these across the bedrock, wearing it away, and often leaving gouges or "striations" on the surface.

Armed in this way, glaciers can cause an immense amount of erosion. In just a few thousand years, they can change the shape of entire valleys, altering their cross-section from a V-shape to a U-shape. After a glacier melts, smooth, polished surfaces and rocks which have been carried from one region to another (pp.134–135) are revealed.

YOU WILL NEED
- ice cube ● sand
- softwood board

1 TAKE AN ICE CUBE out of the freezer. Wait until it is just starting to melt, and then dip it in the sand.

2 MOVING YOUR HAND in a circle, rub the sandy side of the ice cube on the wooden board. Keep dipping the cube in sand so that it stays sandy as you rub.

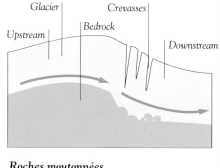

Glacier   Crevasses
Upstream   Bedrock   Downstream

Roches moutonnées
Moving downhill, glaciers may wear bedrock into hummocks, called roches moutonnées (French for "sheep-shaped rocks"). These are rounded on their "upstream" side and broken up by entrainment on the "downstream" side.

3 AFTER A FEW MINUTES, look at the board surface. The ice will have scraped the sand against the wood – just as a glacier scrapes against bedrock.

■ Sliding away
An ice cube melts quickly under a heavy weight, just as the deepest glacier ice can melt under the weight of the glacier, which then slides over the water. This is called "basal slip".

■ Glaciated landscapes

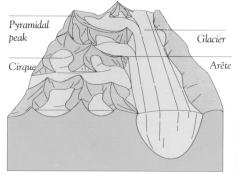

Pyramidal peak   Glacier
Cirque   Arête

During glaciation
Erosion at a glacier's head creates bowl-shaped "cirques". As they wear back, the ridges between are reduced to knife-edges or "arêtes", and the peak to a sharp "pyramid". Frost-shattering (pp.106–107) makes them even more jagged.

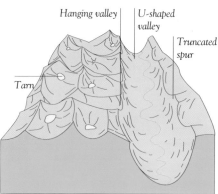

Hanging valley   U-shaped valley
                                  Truncated spur
Tarn

After glaciation
The melting ice leaves behind craggy mountains and deep, U-shaped valleys, with side-valleys that "hang" above the main valley floor. Small lakes, called tarns, often form in the bottom of the cirques after the ice has melted.

Dropped by ice

IT IS EASY TO IMAGINE GLACIERS as mighty rivers of sparkling ice. But if you get a chance to look at a glacier close up, you may be in for a surprise. Instead of being clean, the ice at the foot of a glacier often looks dirty. This is because the ice picks up a massive amount of debris – mainly rock fragments – as it flows. Some of the debris falls on to the ice from above, while the glacier itself scrapes out pieces of rock from below. When ice advances and retreats, all this debris, or " moraine", is left behind. These dumped fragments of rock, arranged in hummocks and twisting banks, are one of the hallmarks of a "glaciated" landscape.

■ DISCOVERY ■
Louis Agassiz

By comparing a glacier today with the same glacier in an old photograph, it's not too difficult to see if its shape has changed. But 150 years ago, the very idea that ice could advance or recede was not widely accepted. It was then that the Swiss-American naturalist Louis Agassiz (1807–1873) began to look closely at how glaciers worked, and what they could do to the landscape. Agassiz identified the effects of ice erosion in places where glaciers no longer existed, and suggested that at times in the past much of North America and Europe were covered in vast sheets of ice. It was through his work that the idea of "ice ages" (see right) became part of scientific knowledge.

EXPERIMENT
Making a moraine

With the help of a water-filled bag and some sand, you can demonstrate how a glacier can push rock fragments along, forming a "push moraine", a band of debris that forms a shallow embankment when a glacier retreats. In nature, moraines are formed by rock fragments of all sizes. Some fragments are as small as sand grains, while others can be as big as a car. Although you won't be able to see it in this experiment, the jumbled nature of these pieces of rock is a key feature of moraines. Unlike rivers, glaciers don't sort rocks as they carry them. Everything, no matter how big or how small, gets dropped together in the same place, whenever the ice stops.

YOU WILL NEED
● *plastic bag* ● *fork* ● *water* ● *sand* ● *tray*

1 PUT THE SAND IN THE TRAY and level it out. Fill the bag with water, and then tie it tight. Now put the bag on the sand and push it along sideways.

2 NOW TAKE AWAY the bag and you will see a "moraine" at the end and along the sides where your "glacier" was. Like a real moraine, it will be curved.

3 NOW PUT THE BAG BACK, give it a sharp prod with the fork, and pull it back. Water will flow out of the bag, just like a glacier melting as it retreats.

4 AS THE WATER FLOWS OUT, some of the moraine will be washed away, leaving a channel. The same thing happens when a real glacier melts.

■ Ice sheets

The largest expanses of ice in the world are the ice sheets of Antarctica and Greenland. In parts of Antarctica, the ice is over 4,000 m (13,000 ft) deep, and is so heavy that the rock beneath it has sunk far below sea level.

An ice sheet forms only over land, and is like a single giant glacier. Snow builds up in the centre, turning into ice that slowly moves outwards. Where the ice meets the sea, it breaks off and floats away, as shown in the picture on the left. In Greenland, this creates jagged icebergs, which are a hazard to shipping. In Antarctica, the ice forms huge floating shelves attached to the ice sheet. Parts of the shelves can break off to form flat "ice islands".

■ After the ice

The most obvious "leftovers" of a retreating ice sheet are moraines – low piles of rock debris, often heaped up along the margins of a glacier. Narrow banks of gravel, called "eskers", snake their way across the ground, having been created by streams of meltwater flowing underneath the ice. Retreating ice also reveals "drumlins", streamlined hillocks that point in the direction in which the ice once flowed; " kettle holes", depressions formed by lumps of melting ice; and "kames", either steep-sided terraced mounds formed by glaciers or undulating deltas formed by ice sheets.

During glaciation

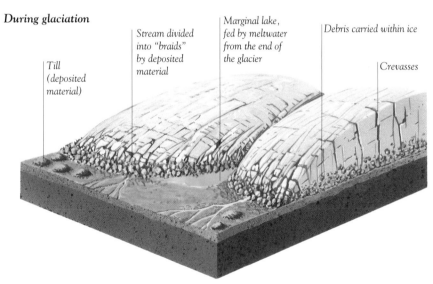

Till (deposited material)

Stream divided into "braids" by deposited material

Marginal lake, fed by meltwater from the end of the glacier

Debris carried within ice

Crevasses

After glaciation

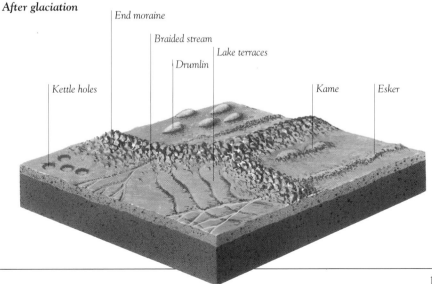

End moraine

Braided stream

Lake terraces

Drumlin

Kettle holes

Kame

Esker

Ice ages

Although people often talk about The Ice Age, the Earth has cooled and warmed many times, creating ice ages and "interglacial periods" of ice retreat. Average temperatures over the last 600,000 years are shown below.

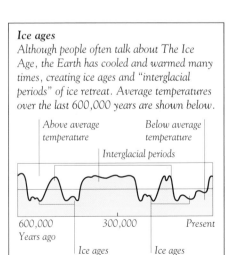

Above average temperature

Below average temperature

Interglacial periods

600,000 Years ago

300,000

Present

Ice ages

Ice ages

Wind in the desert

NOT ALL DESERTS are vast seas of sand. Some are rock-strewn plains; some are bare mountains; and some are made up of huge mountain blocks standing alone in wide basins. But they have one thing in common – they are all dry. This dry climate makes desert landscapes very different from all others, with the wind playing a major part in their formation. The wind "abrades", or erodes, the land by hurling sand and dust at the surface of rocks, creating many strange landforms. It rolls loose rocks along the desert floor, and lifts the lighter ones into the air, scooping out shallow depressions, called "blowouts". Powerful desert winds also pick up sand and dust and pile it into dunes, and carry silt to far places to lay it down as "loess", in thicknesses as great as 300 m (1,000 ft). Rain, when it comes, falls in sudden storms, creating an angular landscape of cliffs, deep gullies, and vast slopes called "bajadas".

Leftover landscape
This flat-topped hill, in the Monument Valley in Utah, is called a "mesa", and shows what water erosion can do in a desert region. Over millions of years, water has worn away the rock, leaving just a few isolated blocks – the mesas. The slopes gradually retreat inwards, until eventually the mesa shrinks to a pointed "butte".

■ Four different dunes

"Parabolic" dunes form more on coasts than in deserts, where there is lots of sand and where the wind is strong. Their long "horns" point into the wind, and are held in place by plants. Between the horns is the "blowout" area, where the wind has scooped out sand and blown it inland. Sometimes the blowout is blown out altogether to create two linear dunes.

"Transverse" dunes form at right angles to the wind. They form huge systems in deserts, and often build up behind beaches where there is a steady wind and abundant sand. A deep trough separates each ridge, with the steepest side facing away from the wind. On coasts, dunes furthest inland are often covered with marram (beach) grass, which anchors them in place.

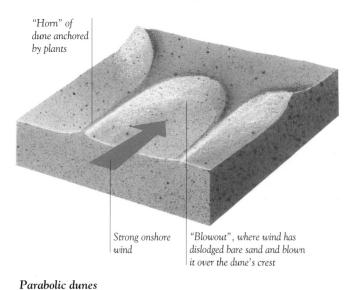

"Horn" of dune anchored by plants

Strong onshore wind

"Blowout", where wind has dislodged bare sand and blown it over the dune's crest

Parabolic dunes

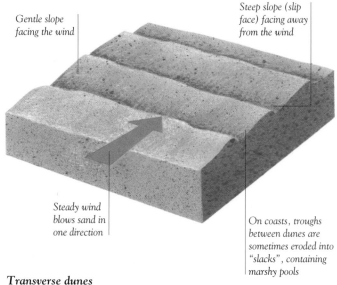

Gentle slope facing the wind

Steep slope (slip face) facing away from the wind

Steady wind blows sand in one direction

On coasts, troughs between dunes are sometimes eroded into "slacks", containing marshy pools

Transverse dunes

EXPERIMENT
Seeing sand jump

In a dust storm, clouds of dust are swept up high into the air. But sand grains are heavier than dust, and in a storm the sand rarely rises more than 1m (3 ft) above the surface – so your body could be engulfed in swirling sand, while your head and shoulders remained above it. As you can see in this experiment, a particle's size and weight determine how far the wind will carry it.

YOU WILL NEED
● *spoon* ● *hairdryer* ● *mix of coarse and fine sand*
● *wooden block* ● *ice-cube tray*

1 PUT THE WOODEN BLOCK at the end of the ice-cube tray. Spoon sand on to the top of the block to form a "dune".

2 HOLD THE HAIRDRYER close to the dune and turn it on so that it blows the sand into the tray. The finer sand should travel the furthest.

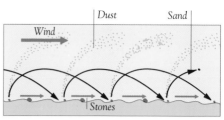

Sand on the move
In strong winds, sand grains hop through the air, a movement called "saltation". When they land, they collide with other sand grains and stones, pushing them forward in "surface creep". Dust is also blown upwards. Being lighter, the dust becomes "suspended" in the air, and travels much further than the sand.

Heavy grains travel the least distance

Light grains are blown furthest

Remains of "dune"

The smaller the further
The distance each grain travels depends on its weight. Heavy grains fall into the near end of the ice-cube tray; light grains reach the far end.

Crescent-shaped "barchans" form in "swarms", or sand seas, on hard, flat plains with very little sand, where a wind blows in one direction. The "horns" point in the wind's direction. Sand blows up the gentle slope facing the wind, then slides down the steep slope facing away from the wind (the "slip face"). In this way the dunes advance several metres a year.

In the great deserts, "linear" dunes can form a sea of giant ripples. One dune can be hundreds of kilometres long, and up to 180 m (600 ft) high. They form where sand is scarce, and where the wind is variable, but mainly from one direction. Linear dunes are called "seifs" in the Arab peninsula, and "sand ridges" in Australia.

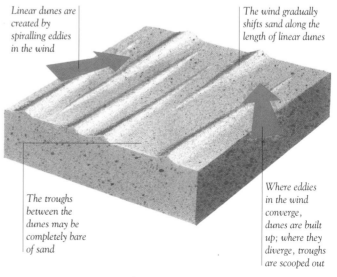

Steep slip face with a gradient of 30–33°

Linear dunes are created by spiralling eddies in the wind

The wind gradually shifts sand along the length of linear dunes

Steady wind blows sand in one direction

Gentle slope facing the wind

"Horns" move faster than the rest of the dune, and so point downwind

The troughs between the dunes may be completely bare of sand

Where eddies in the wind converge, dunes are built up; where they diverge, troughs are scooped out

Barchans

Linear dunes

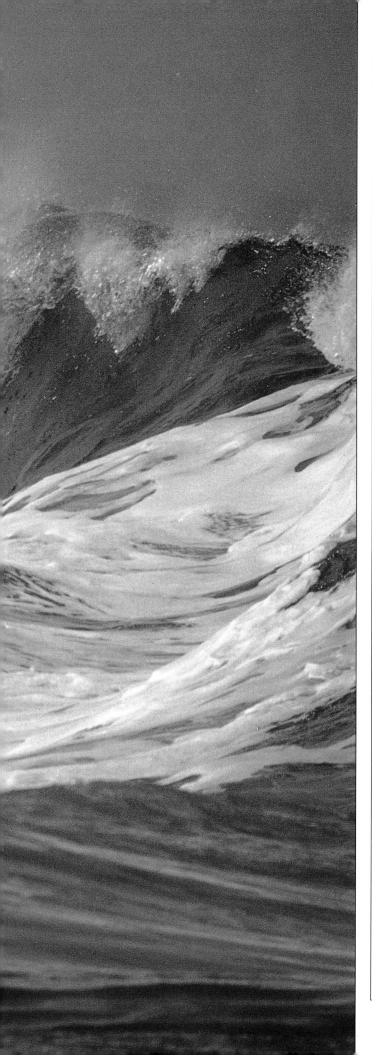

The OCEANS

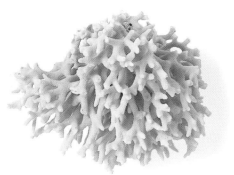

Little and large
*Coral skeletons like this one (above) build up
from tiny polyps to form gigantic reefs, which
often protect the land from the power of the sea.
In wide stretches of open ocean, huge waves
develop unhampered. When they finally crash to
the shore in places like Hawaii (left), they carry
an immense amount of energy, which can batter
and shape the coastline.*

NEARLY THREE-QUARTERS OF
our planet is covered by
seas and oceans. Sea water
is nearly always on the
move. Its currents transfer
the Sun's heat and help to
create the world's climates,
while its waves pound
against the shore, breaking
it down or building it up.

THE OPEN SEA

OVER TWO-THIRDS OF THE EARTH'S SURFACE IS UNDER WATER, submerged beneath seas and oceans to an average depth of 3.5 km (2 miles). The oceans are never still, but are kept in constant motion by the wind and the Sun. Winds whip the surface into waves and drive currents for thousands of kilometres across the oceans, while the heat of the Sun stirs the ocean deeps. This endless circulation of ocean currents also has a profound effect on the world's climate.

Where cold currents rise up from the sea floor, they carry minerals to the surface. These minerals act like a rich fertilizer, enabling tiny "planktonic" plants to thrive in the sunlit water. In this satellite image, cold plankton-rich seas are yellow; warm seas containing little plankton are pink.

The sea undermines cliffs and cuts into the coast, creating bays and headlands as the land is worn back.

On 26 May 1876, HMS *Challenger*, a British research ship, returned to port after an epic voyage. It had travelled over 125,000 km (77,000 miles), charting the deepest parts of the world's oceans and collecting animals that lived far beneath the surface. Its scientific staff had measured temperatures, analysed sea water, and timed currents in all the world's great oceans. It took 20 years for the expedition's findings to be fully documented, and when published they made up a series of reports that stretched to 50 volumes.

With the *Challenger* expedition the science of oceanography had finally come of age. A century before, very little was known about the world's oceans and how they worked. Sailors knew that sea water drifted in currents, and Isaac Newton (1642–1727) had explained how the Moon's gravity helped to produce tides (p.20). But what happened beneath the ocean surface, and indeed why the oceans existed at all, was a complete mystery.

■ Underwater Earth

One of the key figures in the study of the oceans was Matthew Maury (1806–1873), a US naval lieutenant. In the middle of the nineteenth century he became involved in one of the most ambitious engineering projects the world had ever seen – the laying of the Transatlantic Cable. Before the days of radio, all electrical communication was by "telegraph" – pulses of electricity sent down a wire. Cables had been laid across short stretches of shallow sea, such as the English Channel, but laying a cable across the Atlantic was an enterprise on a much bigger scale.

Maury was asked to bring together all the measurements on record, and prepare a map of the sea bed of the North Atlantic. His results were surprising. Instead of becoming gradually deeper towards its middle, the Atlantic seemed to do the reverse. About a quarter of the way across, from either side, the sea floor plunged to a great depth. But towards the middle, it rose again. Maury called the shallow central section the "Telegraph Plateau".

In Maury's time, the only way to measure the ocean's depth was to let out a weighted line until it hit the bottom. This method was slow and often inaccurate. But in 1917 Paul Langevin (1872–1946), a French physicist, devised a system of measuring distances by timing

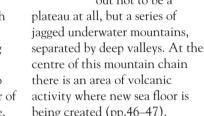

The slope of the shore decides whether the sea builds up the shore, or eats it away (p.144).

the echoes of high-frequency sound as it bounced off distant objects. Sound navigation and ranging (or "sonar", for short) works well even in very deep water, and it has enabled scientists to map the sea bed in much greater detail.

We now know that ocean floors are just as varied as the surface of dry land. In some places, huge seamounts rise from the depths, and in other places, trenches plummet 11 km (nearly 7 miles). Maury's Telegraph Plateau has turned out not to be a plateau at all, but a series of jagged underwater mountains, separated by deep valleys. At the centre of this mountain chain there is an area of volcanic activity where new sea floor is being created (pp.46–47).

But where did the *water* in the oceans come from? In many traditional accounts of the formation of the Earth, the oceans appeared first, and dry

A tsunami, a gigantic wave, is caused by an earthquake or volcanic eruption on the sea floor.

land second. But geologists think that events may have taken place the other way around. According to their theory, the oceans were formed as part of the same process that created the atmosphere (pp.150–151).

■ Origin of the oceans

To begin with, the Earth had neither oceans nor atmosphere. However, its heat was enough to evaporate some elements and compounds – such as nitrogen, carbon dioxide, and water vapour – and these formed a layer of gas, which was kept in place by gravity. Once the new atmosphere held as much water vapour as it could, water started to condense as a liquid, forming the oceans.

This process probably happened on other planets as well. But on the smaller planets between the Earth and the Sun, gravity was not strong enough to stop water vapour escaping into space. Temperatures were so low on the heavy, outer planets that any water formed ice. As far as we know, the Earth is the only planet in the solar system where water exists in three different states – solid, liquid, and gas.

■ Swirling waters

The water in the world's oceans does not stay still. Instead, it swirls about in a huge and complicated system of currents. The existence of some surface currents has been known for centuries, while the currents that flow over the ocean floor are a much more recent discovery.

In the second half of the eighteenth century Benjamin Franklin (1706–1790), the American politician and scientist, made some of the earliest studies of surface currents.

From first-hand experience he knew that ships crossing the North Atlantic were either helped or hindered by a current flowing in a northeasterly direction. He found that the current, which we know as the North Atlantic Drift, moves at about 6 km (4 miles) per hour.

Franklin also investigated the temperature of the current, and he found that it was warmer than the water around it. Instead of mixing with the surrounding water, the current kept together in one mass. The boundary between the warm and cold water was a sharp one, and Franklin showed how sailors could use thermometers to guide their ships into the current or out of it.

While winds drive currents at the surface, temperature difference is now known to be the driving force behind deepwater currents. Using temperature sensors and buoys that float at fixed depths, scientists found that the entire ocean is on the move, even in the deepest trenches. This gradual circulation, powered by the Sun, is essential to life in the sea. It dissolves oxygen from the atmosphere, and brings minerals up to the surface, where planktonic plants can use them.

A "diver" in a bottle shows how pressure, depth, and density are related (p.143).

■ In the dark

At depths greater than about 100 m (330 ft), the sea is completely dark, because the water filters out all the Sun's light. The water pressure is much greater than at the surface, and it goes on increasing

Waves curve around headlands as they slow down (p.145).

with depth. Where the sea is thousands of metres deep, the pressure is hundreds of times greater than the atmosphere.

Until this century, the only way to study this forbidding world was to dredge samples and bring them to the surface. In 1860 living starfish were hauled up from a depth of over 2.5 km (2 miles), proving that life existed even at this great depth. But it was only from 1948, with the invention of the bathyscaphe (a specially reinforced submarine), that humans could truly investigate the sea bed.

Exploration of the ocean floor has shown that some parts are cloaked in a deep ooze, while others are littered with nodules – lumps of minerals, rich in manganese, which have been built up by deposition from sea water. But perhaps the greatest surprise of the ocean floor has been its inhabitants. Even at great depths, spidery brittlestars glide over the ooze, while slug-like sea cucumbers burrow their way through it. These animals survive by feeding on the remains of surface-dwellers, which form a constant and nutritious "rain" from the sunlit world above the surface of the sea.

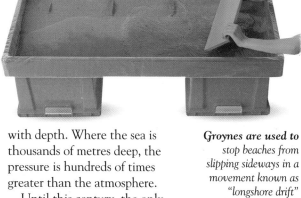

Groynes are used to stop beaches from slipping sideways in a movement known as "longshore drift" (p.147).

Waves are created by the wind's energy. The more water the wind passes over, the larger the waves can become.

Oceans on the move

SEA WATER IS ALWAYS ON THE MOVE – in waves (pp.144–145) and in currents. To see how it moves in currents, you need a full glass of water and some talcum powder. Scatter a small amount of the powder over the water, and then gently blow across the surface. The water will start to move, and the powder will swirl around in two circles – one turning clockwise, and the other anti-clockwise. This is what happens, but on a much bigger scale, in the world's oceans. As the wind blows across the water, it sets it in motion. Because the world is spinning, the water's path is altered by the Coriolis effect (p.158). Currents in the northern hemisphere rotate in a clockwise direction, while those in the southern hemisphere do the opposite.

But wind is not the only driving force behind currents; they are also caused by differences in water temperature and "salinity" (saltiness) and, once flowing, currents can be altered by coastlines. The result is a complicated mix of currents throughout the world.

■ Wave action

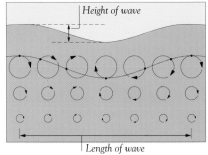

Height of wave

Length of wave

When you look at a wave, you might think that the water in it is rushing across the ocean. In fact, the water hardly moves at all. It simply goes round in circles, like the rollers beneath a conveyor belt. The wave's crest is the top of the circle; the trough is the bottom. Because the water does not move, an object floating on gentle waves just bobs up and down in one place – unless blown by the wind or carried by a current.

■ Coral reefs

Corals are small sea animals that live in warm, shallow water. Each coral "polyp" makes a hard outer skeleton, and, over thousands of years, vast numbers of these build up to form "reefs" (submerged barriers lying off coasts). Corals sometimes form ring-shaped islands called "atolls" (p.182).

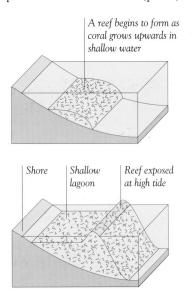

A reef begins to form as coral grows upwards in shallow water

Shore | Shallow lagoon | Reef exposed at high tide

EXPERIMENT
Making waves

When water is blown by the wind, waves always form. By blowing across a tank of water you can see that it takes only the lightest wind to set waves in motion. The larger your tank, the bigger the waves will be. This is because the size of the waves is determined, in part, by the "fetch" – the distance of open water over which wind blows. Coastlines like those of Hawaii, which face a huge fetch of open ocean, have very large waves.

Miniature waves
However gently you blow across the water, you will always make some waves.

EXPERIMENT
Making a diver

Air near the ground is much denser than air higher up, because it is compressed by the weight of the atmosphere above. But water cannot be "squeezed" like this – even in the deepest parts of the ocean its density stays roughly the same (though it can vary with salinity and heat). In this experiment, in which pressure is applied to air and water, the air in the pen-top becomes so dense that it is no longer buoyant enough to support the diver.

YOU WILL NEED
● *bottle* ● *water* ● *tightly fitting cork* ● *plastic putty* ● *lightweight pen-top*

1 FILL THE BOTTLE almost to the top with water. Fix plastic putty to the pen-top to make it float just below the surface, with air trapped inside.

2 PUT THE PEN-TOP "DIVER" in the bottle and insert the cork. When you press the cork down it will squash the air in the pen-top, but the water will remain uncompressed. The diver will now sink through the water. When you let go, the air will expand and the diver will rise – and sink if you press down again!

Under pressure
The "diver" sinks when the air trapped inside it is compressed, making it more dense than the water.

■ Ocean currents

Sea water has a high "heat capacity", which means that it takes a lot of energy to warm it up. But once it is warm, it takes a long time to cool down. This is why ocean currents have such an effect on the world's climate. Warm currents, such as the North Atlantic Drift, carry heat from the tropics and spread it to cooler areas. Without the North Atlantic Drift, the sea around Scandinavia and northern Britain would freeze in winter. Cold currents have the opposite effect.

The importance of currents can be seen when they change. On the west coast of South America, the Humboldt current normally brings cold water to the surface. With it come minerals and other nutrients that feed huge shoals of fish. But every three or four years, the current is blocked by a warm surface current, and the nutrients disappear.

Currents of the world
The map on the left shows warm ocean currents in red, cold currents in blue. The effect of these on life in the oceans can be seen in the satellite photograph below, which shows plankton density. This varies with the currents: red is most dense, then yellow, green, blue, and pink.

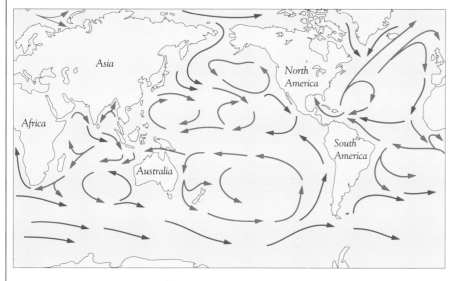

Wave power

NEXT TIME YOU ARE AT THE SEASIDE, watch what happens as a wave comes inshore. The wave starts out as a low, smooth front of water. But as it nears the shore, it slows down through friction with the sea bed, and becomes higher and narrower until it eventually topples over and "breaks", surging up the shore.

Waves – especially storm waves – can crash against a shore with enormous force. They wear rock away by pounding it to bits, hurling sand at it, and ramming air so hard into cracks that the rock bursts. In this way, waves undercut cliffs and carve broad platforms in solid rock – and reduce jagged boulders to smooth pebbles or sand.

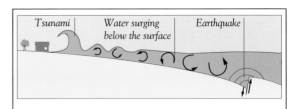

■ Tsunamis

A "tsunami" is a gigantic wave, usually triggered by an earthquake or volcanic eruption. The sudden movement sets up a powerful surge of water beneath the surface which travels outwards in all directions at about 1,000 kmh (600 mph). A tsunami is barely noticeable until it reaches shallow coastal waters, where it can suddenly roll up to a height of 40 m (130 ft), and cause havoc far inland. Most occur in the Pacific Ocean, and are set off by tremors in the "Ring of Fire" (p.62).

EXPERIMENT
Eroding shores

Where the sea meets the land, all the sea's energy is concentrated into the "shoreline", a line that varies with the tides (pp.146–147). Along the shoreline, waves constantly batter the land, and shift the material that makes it up. In some places the sea wears away the shore, but in others the waves build it up.

In this experiment, you can find out how the sea changes a sandy shore that has a steep slope. On a steep beach, the "backwash" (the wave's downward movement) is stronger than the "swash" (the wave's upward movement). In this way, material is pulled down the beach, so that the slope becomes gentler. The result is a gradually sloping beach, but with a much steeper slope beneath the low water mark. Beaches like this often have a strong current flowing down the underwater slope.

After you have tried this experiment, look at p.146 to find out how the sea affects shores with a shallow slope.

YOU WILL NEED
● *jug* ● *water* ● *tank or deep, clear dish*
● *sand* ● *spoon*

1 SPOON THE SAND into the tank so that it forms a steep slope against one of the narrow sides.

2 CAREFULLY POUR IN WATER without disturbing the sand. The water should reach about halfway up the slope.

3 GENTLY ROCK ONE END of the tank, so that waves form and run up the sloping "shore". The water will gradually erode the slope, shifting some sand downwards and under the water.

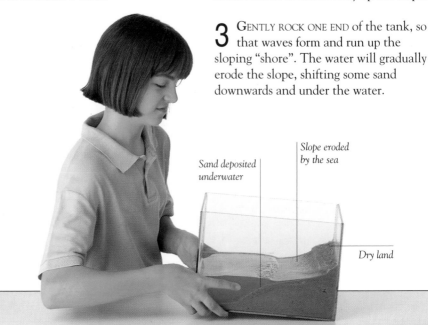

Sand deposited underwater

Slope eroded by the sea

Dry land

EXPERIMENT
Wave refraction

On the open sea, all the parts of a wave move at the same speed. But when a wave passes near land, things start to change. In shallow water, the wave drags against the sea bed, which slows it down. But the rest of the wave, still in deep water, moves on as before. Meeting an obstacle, like a headland, will also cause parts of a wave to move at different speeds. The difference in speed makes the wave take on a curved shape, with the slowed-down part lagging behind.

This effect is called "refraction", which means bending. You can make your own wave refraction with this simple experiment. Place a round object in a tank or bowl containing a shallow layer of water. Make a wave by pushing gently forward with a plastic lid. You should then see the wave change shape as it is refracted by the "headland".

Refraction is important in the way the sea moulds the shore, because the waves' energy is concentrated in particular places, such as rocky headlands.

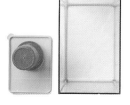

YOU WILL NEED
● tank or bowl
● water ● round, heavy object or filled beaker ● plastic lid

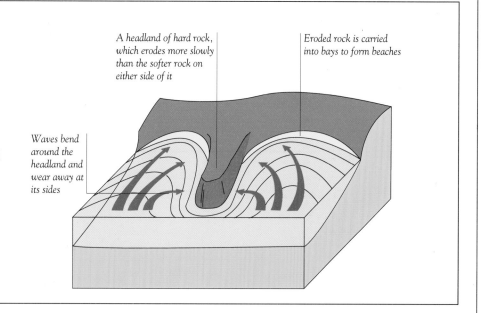

The outer part of the wave travels fastest, and so reaches the end of the tank first

The "inshore" part of the wave lags behind, giving the wave a definite curved front

"Headland" made out of a round object, such as a filled plastic beaker

The wave splits in two as it passes around the "headland"

Push the lid gently forwards to make waves

■ The changing coastline

The shore gets its shape from the different types of rock from which it is made. Part of the shore is often made of harder rock than the rest. The sea erodes this hard rock more slowly, leaving a headland that juts out to sea. The headland is then eroded into a rocky shape. As the waves bend around the headland, they erode its sides. Sometimes, the sea breaks through, leaving a natural arch that eventually collapses to form a rocky pillar called a "stack". The broken-up material of the headland is deposited in the bays, often forming beaches.

A headland of hard rock, which erodes more slowly than the softer rock on either side of it

Eroded rock is carried into bays to form beaches

Waves bend around the headland and wear away at its sides

Shifting shores

THE COASTLINE IS CONSTANTLY changing shape. It shifts backwards or forwards, and sideways as well. The movement is usually too slow to see, but you can often work out its direction from clues on the shore. On rocky coasts with high cliffs, dangling fences and landslips show that the sea is making headway into the land. On low coasts where the sea is shallow, banks of mud and sand, or bands of shingle, are signs that the coast is advancing. Here you can often see evidence of sideways coastal movement, such as "spits", which are strips of sand that stick out from the shore, or beaches where pebbles are larger at one end than the other.

Beach on the move
Low walls, or "groynes", are used to stop sand or shingle moving along the coast. Piled-up shingle shows that this beach drifts from left to right.

■ Building up the shore

On shores that have shallow slopes, the sea tends to erode material under the water and carry it up the beach – exactly the opposite of what happens where the slope is steeper (p.144). You can see this by using the stream tray (p.122). Make sure the tray is level, then add sand to make a very gently sloping beach. Pour in enough water to reach two-thirds of the way up the beach, then make gentle waves in the water with a wooden paddle.

Make gentle, regular waves with a wide paddle

Below the surface, the waves erode the sand and carry it up the beach

Sand is deposited on the beach, gradually making it steeper

Support the stream tray on strong boxes or chairs, making sure it is level

EXPERIMENT
Longshore drift

Waves often strike the shore diagonally. But as each wave falls back, gravity makes it flow away at right angles to the shoreline. Anything carried by the waves – sand or shingle, for example – moves along the coast in the same zigzag way.

This kind of movement is called "longshore drift". You can see how it happens with the help of the stream tray (p.122). Ideally, you should run water through the tray with a hose, but if you have nowhere to let the water drain out, you can mimic the action that causes longshore drift simply by making diagonal waves yourself, with a paddle.

Waves run straight back down the beach, taking sand with them

1 PILE UP SAND to form a sloping "beach" along one side of the tray. Then half-fill with water and make diagonal waves with a wide paddle, creating a "longshore drift" that runs from left to right.

Insert rulers at right angles to the shore to act as groynes

2 SMOOTH OUT the sand and try the experiment again. But this time put rulers into the sand, at right angles to the shore, to stop the drifting.

Sand is washed away from the side facing away from the waves *Sand builds up on the side facing the waves*

3 WITH THE GROYNES in place, diagonal waves no longer create longshore drift. Sand simply piles up on one side of each groyne.

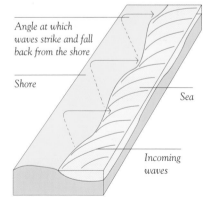

Direction of drift

River mouth

Spit

How a spit forms
Where there is a strong longshore drift, sand and shingle can build up on one side of a river mouth, forming a "spit" and diverting the river's flow. A spit always points in the direction of the drift. Some spits can be many kilometres long.

Angle at which waves strike and fall back from the shore

Shore

Sea

Incoming waves

Zigzag movement
Waves striking a shore diagonally fall back to the sea at right angles to the shore. Sand and shingle are carried by the waves and deposited in a zigzag pattern typical of longshore drift.

The ATMOSPHERE

Restless air
The weather has always been a source of wonder and mystery, and people have long valued devices like the barometer (above), which can help predict its effects. And yet weather is only the constant churning of the atmosphere (left).

OUR ENTIRE PLANET IS cocooned by a thin blanket of gases which we call the atmosphere. Without this thin layer, which is no thicker on the Earth than the skin is on an apple, our world would be as lifeless as the Moon. It gives us the air we need to breathe; it blesses us with a ready supply of clean water to drink; it keeps us warm; and, at the same time, it shields us from the harmful rays of the Sun.

LAYERS OF THE ATMOSPHERE

IT MAY SEEM AS IF OUR ATMOSPHERE IS NOTHING BUT THIN AIR. Yet scientists have only just begun to discover all its complexities. There are actually seven or more different layers in the atmosphere, each with its own characteristics – from the turbulent troposphere just above the ground, to the exosphere, which extends 1,500 km (930 miles) or more into the black nothingness of space. Without these layers to protect us, the Earth would be as inhospitable as the Moon.

High-speed winds *called jet streams blow at the top of the troposphere – the lowest layer of the atmosphere – and are revealed here in long, thin bands of cloud.*

The discovery, in the *seventeenth century, that a column of mercury could be supported by air pressure alone, showed that air had real substance.*

Our first ideas about the atmosphere probably came from people's desire to know what kind of weather was on the way. Some signs were obvious, like heavy clouds before rain. Others were worked out only after years of close observation. The Ancient Egyptians, for instance, knew from careful study of the stars that the dry season would end and the River Nile would flood when they saw Sirius, the Dog Star, in the sky before dawn.

Yet while many people learned to predict weather quite accurately, only in Ancient Greece was there any real effort to understand how the atmosphere worked. Thales of Miletus (c.625–c.550 BC) realized that water evaporated from the sea into the sky, turned into clouds higher up, and fell as rain. Then in the fourth century BC, Aristotle (384–322 BC) wrote his remarkable *Meteorologica* about the atmosphere. Although many of Aristotle's ideas were accurate, just as many were mistaken. But the power of Aristotle's name was such that for 2,000 years his book remained the unquestioned authority on meteorology.

In the Islamic world, scholars tried to find a link between the weather and the motions of the stars – a search that was taken up enthusiastically in Europe in the Middle Ages. By the end of the fifteenth century, astrological weather forecasts were so popular that dozens of weather "almanacs" began to appear every year, each of which contained a "prognosis" of the weather for the following 12 months. Indeed,

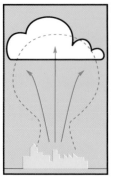

Weather houses like this one *(p.161) are simple hygrometers, indicating the weather by responding to changes in humidity.*

weather almanacs such as this were still popular in the late nineteenth century.

Only in the 1600s did scientific understanding of the atmosphere really advance further. A crucial factor was the development of instruments for measuring the air's temperature (thermometers), moisture content (hygrometers), and pressure (barometers). Many of these devices originated in Florence, where a group of gifted scientists and craftsmen gathered in the *Accademia del Cimento*

(Academy of Experiments) run by the Grand Duke Ferdinand II.

■ Measuring air

It was in Florence in 1593 that the brilliant Galileo Galilei (1564–1642) first made a crude thermometer. The Academy developed his idea further and made a mercury thermometer in 1657. It was in Florence, too, that Galileo's protegé, Evangelista Torricelli (1608–1647), discovered air pressure (p.157) and invented a method of measuring it – the barometer.

Within a few years, French mathematician Blaise Pascal (1623–1662) showed, simply by taking a barometer up a mountain, that air pressure decreases with height as the air gets thinner. If this is so, some scientists realized, the atmosphere must eventually fade to nothing.

Over the next 150 years, scientists used these instruments to observe the air in detail, and their understanding of the relationship between wind and pressure (pp.158–159), and between temperature and humidity (p.160), grew steadily. At the same time, laboratory experiments revealed that air is essentially a mixture of two gases, nitrogen and oxygen, plus invisible water vapour. Tiny traces of other gases were found later. But all their knowledge was

The Ancient Greeks *realized 2,500 years ago that rising warm air forms clouds.*

confined to the air just above the ground. Scientists began to wonder if all the atmosphere was the same.

In 1749 the Scottish astronomer Alexander Wilson (1766–1813) tried, without much success, to measure temperature in the upper air with a thermometer tied to a kite. Then, in 1783, the French Montgolfier brothers made the first balloon flight. Shortly after, an American called John Jeffries (1745–1819) made a balloon flight over London, armed with a barometer, and several other instruments and canisters with which to collect air at various heights. By 1804 the French scientist Joseph-Louis Gay-Lussac (1778–1850) had soared to 7 km

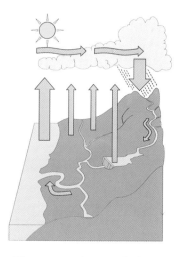

The water cycle – in which water evaporates from the sea, turns into clouds, and falls again as rain – was described by Thales 2,500 years ago.

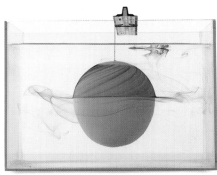

The spinning of the Earth affects the way the atmosphere moves, deflecting winds just as the dye on this spinning ball is deflected (p.158)

(23,000 ft) to see if air was chemically the same at this height. It was.

Over the next century scientists risked their lives in balloons to find out what the upper atmosphere was like. But no-one could go higher than 10 km (33,000 ft) or so, because the thin air made it impossible to breathe. Then French meteorologist Teisserenc de Bort used unmanned balloons carrying clockwork recording instruments. With these, he showed in 1902 that the air grew colder with

height, as expected; at 12 km (40,000 ft) or so, it was about –55°C (–67°F). But beyond this, temperatures seemed to stay steady. De Bort suggested that the atmosphere had two layers: a turbulent lower layer with winds and weather, which he called the "troposphere"; and a calm upper layer, the "stratosphere", above the level where warm air stops rising (the "tropopause").

◼ Higher spheres

With "radiosonde" balloons, which transmit measurements by radio, scientists could explore higher still. In the 1930s they found that temperatures in the stratosphere actually *increased* with height – an effect they later found was due to the concentration here of the gas ozone. The ozone is warmed up by absorbing ultraviolet rays from

Winds are air masses circulating between zones of different pressure, just as the hot and cold water circulates in this experiment (p.158).

the Sun – rays that would otherwise reach the ground.

At the same time, British physicist Edward Appleton (1892–1965) solved a mystery that had baffled scientists ever since Marconi first sent radio signals across the Atlantic in 1901. Since radio waves travel in straight lines, how did they get round the Earth's curved surface? Appleton showed that they bounced off a layer of charged particles ("ions") high in the atmosphere. In fact, there are five of these layers, and together they are known as the "ionosphere".

◼ Rocket high

Radiosonde balloons reach their limit 30 km (20 miles) up, and in the 1940s scientists began to use rockets to probe even higher, finding that above 50 km (30 miles), in a band called the "mesosphere", temperatures drop again, falling to –100°C (–148°F) at 80 km (50 miles). They also discovered that the mesosphere is colder in summer than in winter, though it is not clear why.

Knowledge of the "thermosphere" (the layer above 80 km/50 miles) progressed in the late 1950s, when scientists studied the way satellites were slowed by friction with the atmosphere. Temperatures vary wildly here, from 500°C (930°F) at night, to 2,000°C (3,630°F) at midday, but the air is so thin that it doesn't hold the heat.

Space flights have since extended our knowledge of the atmosphere, and more layers have been identified – the "heliosphere", a layer of helium, and the "protono-sphere", which extends over 60,000 km (37,200 miles) before fading to nothing.

Storms are created by swirling eddies in the troposphere. In contrast, the higher layers in the atmosphere are always completely calm.

Up in the air

LOOK UP AT THE SKY on a clear day and you can see the Earth's atmosphere stretching some 700 km (430 miles) above you. Without this blanket of gases to protect us, we could not live; we would be scorched by the Sun during the day and frozen solid at night. Most of the atmosphere is a thin mix of gases which are as calm and unchanging as space beyond. But the lowest 11 km (7 miles) – the layer in which we live and breathe – contains all the weather we experience, and is thick with gases, water, and dust. As the Sun warms the land and sea beneath it, the heat keeps this thick broth forever churning. It is the constant swirling of this lowest layer, called the "troposphere", that gives us everything we call weather, from the gentlest summer showers to raging hurricanes and tornadoes.

EXPERIMENT
Height and heat

The higher you go in the troposphere, the colder it becomes – as you can see from the snow that covers mountain peaks. Indeed, it gets colder at a steady rate, called the "lapse rate", which is about 6°C for every 1,000 m (3.5°F per 1000 ft). Only under special conditions, called "inversions", does it get warmer. When warm air rises up through the atmosphere it becomes cooler, because it moves into less and less dense air and its heat is spread more thinly, a process that is called "adiabatic cooling". You can see this when you try out these tests with a bicycle pump.

Pumping heat
When you pump air into a tyre, you squeeze it into a smaller and smaller space, which makes the air hot. You can see this by pumping hard and then feeling the connecting tube.

Cooling out
Now try feeling the cold draught as you press the valve to let air out of the tyre. It is cold because the air squeezed into the tyre is spreading out and cooling adiabatically.

EXPERIMENT
Rising air

Air becomes thinner the higher you go, and rising air spreads out more and more as it rises. You can see this if you blow a bubble up through oil. The bubble gets bigger as it rises, just as a bubble of air rising through the atmosphere would. This is why air cools "adiabatically" (see below left).

YOU WILL NEED
● *bottle of cooking oil*
● *plastic tube*

1 PUSH THE TUBE all the way down to the bottom of the bottle. Carefully blow one bubble from the tube. You may need a little practice.

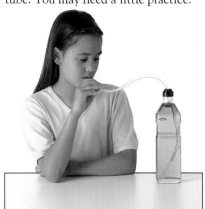

2 WATCH THE BUBBLE CLOSELY as it floats up through the oil. You will notice that it grows bigger and bigger the higher it rises.

EXPERIMENT
What's in the air?

More than 99 per cent of the atmosphere consists of just two gases: nitrogen and oxygen. Of these, nitrogen makes up 78 per cent of the atmosphere, but it is oxygen we need to breathe, and which is needed for burning. The remaining 1 per cent includes carbon dioxide, water vapour, and minute traces of gases such as helium, neon, and ozone.

The fact that air was basically nitrogen and oxygen was proved by Antoine Lavoisier in 1774. But a century earlier an English doctor named John Mayow (1641–1679) had shown that air contained oxygen with his famous experiment explained below – or, rather, he showed that air contained a substance needed for burning. Mayow called this substance "nitro-aerial spirit"; Lavoisier later showed this to be the gas oxygen. Mayow conducted a similar experiment with a mouse in the jar instead of the candle.

YOU WILL NEED
● candle ● candle holder ● bowl
● jam jar ● coloured water
● matches

1 SECURE THE CANDLE in the holder and place this in the bowl of coloured water. Now light the candle.

2 LOWER A JAM JAR carefully over the burning candle. Make a note of the level of water in the jar.

Burned out
Air bubbles out of the jar as it gets hot and expands. Soon all the oxygen is used up and the candle flame dies. As the air in the jar cools and contracts, water is drawn back up into the jar.

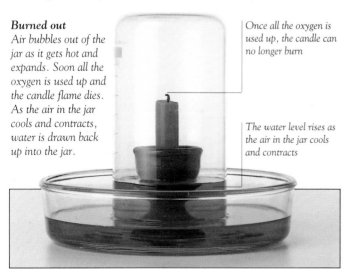

Once all the oxygen is used up, the candle can no longer burn

The water level rises as the air in the jar cools and contracts

■ DISCOVERY ■
Antoine Lavoisier

The French chemist Antoine Lavoisier (1743–1794) was one of the most brilliant scientists of all time. One of his most important discoveries was that air was composed mainly of nitrogen and oxygen. In 1774 the English churchman Joseph Priestley conducted a famous experiment – finding that when he heated mercuric oxide, it created a gas that made a candle burn brighter. He had discovered oxygen, although he did not realize how significant this was. A few months later, however, he told Lavoisier, who repeated the experiment and went on to show that air is a mixture of two gases. A fifth of this mixture was the gas Priestley had found, which was needed for breathing and burning. Lavoisier called this oxygen. The rest of the mixture was an inactive gas which Lavoisier called *azote* from the Greek for "no life" (this was later called nitrogen). Tiny traces of other gases in the air were found in the 1890s.

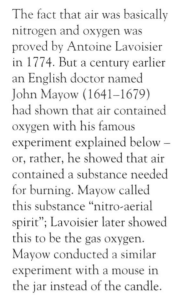

■ Layers of the atmosphere

Scientists divide the atmosphere into distinct layers, beginning with the troposphere at the bottom and stretching up 700 km (430 miles) to the very thin air of the exosphere, where satellites orbit the Earth (not shown here).

Thermosphere
Temperature in this layer increases with height.

Mesosphere
This layer gets colder with height, reaching –120°C.

Stratosphere
This extends from 11 to 50 km, holds 19% of the atmosphere's gas, and gets hotter towards the stratopause at 50 km.

Troposphere
80% of the atmosphere's gas and all weather is in this layer. Temperature decreases until the tropopause is reached at 11 km.

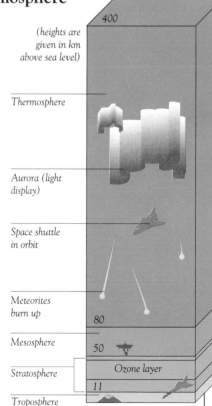

(heights are given in km above sea level)

400

Thermosphere

Aurora (light display)

Space shuttle in orbit

Meteorites burn up

80

Mesosphere 50

Stratosphere
Ozone layer
11

Troposphere

Heat from the Sun

WITHOUT THE SUN, we would not only be very cold – we would have no weather at all. It is heat from the Sun that stirs the atmosphere into motion, creating wind, clouds, rain, and snow. But the Sun's heat varies around the world, at different times of the day and the year (pp.18–19) – partly because of the angle of the Sun in the sky, and partly because clouds block off some of its rays. The Sun climbs so high in the tropics that they receive almost three times as much heat as the polar regions. Yet at the equator, the Sun's heat is cut in half by clouds before it reaches the ground.

Sun burn
The Sun's rays can burn a hole in paper if you focus them with a magnifying glass. Sunshine recorders work in the same way, using a glass ball to make the Sun burn its own record in paper.

EXPERIMENT
Solar power

The lower the Sun is in the sky, the less heat it provides. This is partly because its rays have to travel much further through the atmosphere, and partly because when the Sun strikes the ground at an angle, its heat is spread over a much wider area – as you can see from the long shadows at sunset. Why not try this experiment, which tests whether the angle of a surface affects the heat it receives from the Sun?

Shapes cut from 30-cm square (12-in square) polystyrene tiles

Lid hinged with tape

YOU WILL NEED
● *polystyrene tiles* ● *black card* ● *tape*
● *plastic tubes* ● *cups* ● *thermometer*
● *ruler* ● *knife* ● *glue* ● *scissors*

Plastic tubes taped to back of card and led into cups

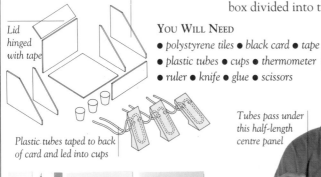

1 CUT OUT THE SHAPES (below left) and glue together to make a three-sided box divided into three compartments.

2 CUT OUT THE BLACK card shapes (below left) and tape a loop of tube to the back of each. Fold and glue flaps.

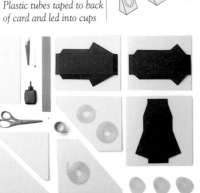

Tubes pass under this half-length centre panel

3 BRING THE CARD SLOPES to the half-length centre panel. Fill the cups with water and position in the rear compartment. Put one end of each loop in the water and fill the tubes by sucking. Now put the loose ends into the cups and fix the slopes in position. Stand the box out in the sun at noon, check the temperature of the water in the cups, and close the lid. Check again an hour later. Has the water heated up at different rates?

The angle of the slopes affects how much of the Sun's heat is absorbed

EXPERIMENT
Stevenson screen

If you step into the shadows on a warm spring day, you may suddenly feel cold, because the difference in temperature between direct sunlight and shade can be dramatic. So meteorologists always take temperature readings in the shade, to make sure they are consistent. In fact, weather stations keep thermometers in special boxes called Stevenson screens, which are painted white to reflect the Sun's rays, and have louvred sides to let a current of air pass through. You can make this simple version of the screen for your own shade temperature readings.

YOU WILL NEED
- balsa & plywood • knife & saw • set square
- plasticine • white paint • ruler & pencil
- thermometer • glue

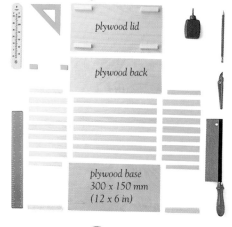

plywood lid

plywood back

plywood base
300 x 150 mm
(12 x 6 in)

1 MAKE 7 FRONT SLATS 280 x 20 mm (11 x ³/₄ in), and then 14 side slats 125 x 20 mm (5 x ³/₄ in). Use a set square to mark positions on uprights.

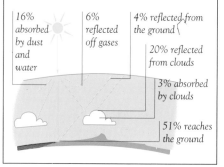

Where the Sun's heat goes
Half the Sun's heat is absorbed on its way through the atmosphere. But the Earth stays warm because some gases in the air trap heat like a greenhouse (p.184).

16% absorbed by dust and water

6% reflected off gases

4% reflected from the ground

20% reflected from clouds

3% absorbed by clouds

51% reaches the ground

2 GLUE THE ENDS of the slats and stick them in a slanting position between the two uprights, until you have built up the front and the two sides.

3 GLUE THE BACK BOARD at a right angle to the baseboard. Check with the set square. Stick the side pieces to the base and check the angle again.

4 GLUE THE FRONT SLATTED PANEL on to the baseboard and side panels. Cut four short blocks and glue them in the corners of the lid to keep it in place.

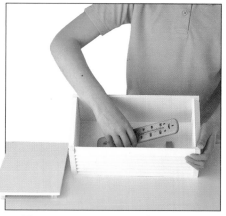

5 PAINT THE ENTIRE BOX white – it may need two coats. Finally, place the thermometer inside the box on two lumps of plasticine and put the lid on.

Sun trap
Place the "screen" outside, well away from any obstruction, and ideally 1.2 m (4 ft) above the ground. If you can, use a maximum and minimum thermometer in the screen. Otherwise, take readings at sunrise and midday.

Air pressure

WATCHING A SHEET OF PAPER FLUTTER to the ground, it is hard to believe that air can exert any force. Yet it does, all the time. The air around us is pushing constantly in every direction – up, down, and sideways – with a force equivalent to an elephant standing on a card table.

People used to think that this pushing force – known as "air pressure" or "atmospheric pressure" – was simply the weight of hundreds of kilometres of air pressing downwards. Now we know that it is the constant bombardment by billions of air molecules as they zoom this way and that.

Air pressure is greatest at sea level, because the air is densest there and contains the most molecules. When air pressure figures are given, they are usually for sea level. The pressure gets less the higher up you go, and so evenly that aircraft altimeters can work out how high a plane is simply by measuring pressure. Above 5,000 m (16,400 ft), the air pressure is so low that it becomes hard to breathe, so climbers have to wear oxygen masks, and airliners have to be pressurized to protect passengers.

■ Held up by air

A simple way to demonstrate the existence of air pressure is to fill a glass under water, then turn it upside down in the water and lift it up until the rim is just below the surface of water in the bowl. Air pressing down on the water in the bowl will stop the water in the glass running out.

High water
Air pressure on the water is enough to hold up not just a glass of water but a column 10 m (33 ft) high. It can even hold up 76 cm (30 in) of mercury (the heaviest liquid).

EXPERIMENT
Making a barometer

Air pressure is usually measured on a device called a "barometer". Barometers can be quite sophisticated and expensive, but you can get a rough idea of when pressure is changing from this very basic design. One of the important things to remember about air pressure is that it is closely related to weather, and changes in air pressure can give a useful indication of weather to come. A sharp drop in pressure, for instance, indicates the onset of a front or depression (pp.174–175) – and so the coming of rain and a storm. High pressure, on the other hand, is a sign of fine, dry weather.

YOU WILL NEED
● *long-necked bottle*
● *straight glass* ● *jug*
● *food colouring*
● *marker pen*

1 POUR COLOURED WATER into a glass. Invert a bottle in the glass so the mouth hangs just above the base.

2 MARK THE GLASS DAILY to show the changes in the level of water in the neck of the bottle.

When the water level in the bottle is high, it means the air is pressing down hard on the surface of the water in the glass, pushing the water up the bottle. This indicates high air pressure

When the water level is low, the air is only pressing down lightly on the water in the glass, indicating low air pressure

EXPERIMENT
Pressure power

In 1654 a German scientist named Otto von Guericke (1602–1686) demonstrated the power of air pressure by fitting the two halves of a brass ball together, then pumping all the air out. The air pressure outside the ball was so great that 16 horses could not pull the two halves apart. You can test the power of air pressure more simply by using a plastic bottle.

YOU WILL NEED
- *plastic soft drinks bottle* ● *funnel*
- *jug of hot water* ● *ice* ● *bowl*

1 STAND THE BOTTLE in a bowl. Pour a jugful of hot water in through a funnel.

2 SCREW THE TOP on the bottle, lay it down, and cover with ice and cold water.

3 STEAM FROM the hot water is now trapped inside the bottle. As this cools back into water, a part-vacuum forms. Greater pressure of air outside now crushes the bottle.

▪ Aneroid barometer

Changes in air pressure can be measured by the height of a column of mercury. But today most people use an "aneroid barometer", which has a metal box containing a part-vacuum. As the box gets bigger or smaller with changes in pressure, a needle moves a pointer along a dial marked in "millibars" (mb). At sea level, pressure is about 1,013 mb, but can vary between 800 and 1,050 mb. Some old barometers, like the one below, mark the changes in inches of mercury.

▪ DISCOVERY ▪
Evangelista Torricelli

The existence of air pressure was first discovered by Evangelista Torricelli (1608–1647), a pupil of the famous Italian scientist Galileo Galilei. In 1641 Galileo set him the task of finding out why water could never be pumped up more than 10 m (33 ft). To find out, Torricelli filled a 1-metre (3-foot) glass tube with mercury, the heaviest liquid. He then turned it upside down and held the open end under the surface of a bowl of mercury. The mercury in the tube dropped to about 76 cm (30 in), leaving what could only be a vacuum in the top of the tube. Torricelli concluded that it was the pressure of the atmosphere on the surface of the mercury in the bowl that prevented the mercury in the tube from falling any further. In fact, there could have been other explanations for this phenomenon, and for a while not every scientist agreed with Torricelli. But over the next 20 years, the evidence in favour of his theory mounted and, by the end of the seventeenth century, the concept of air pressure was widely accepted. Moreover, in 1647, the philosopher René Descartes added a scale to Torricelli's mercury tube so that it could be used as a barometer, relating changes in air pressure to changes in the weather.

Wind and pressure

WHEN AIR BEGINS TO MOVE, it becomes wind. A light breeze springs up when air moves slowly; gales and hurricanes tear through the skies when air moves very quickly. Slow or quick, wind always begins in the same way – with a difference in air pressure. Wherever air is warmer and lighter than the surrounding air, it tends to rise, reducing air pressure. Wherever the air is cold and heavier, it tends to sink, increasing the pressure. Winds blow from high pressure zones (called "anticyclones" or highs) to low pressure zones (called "cyclones", "depressions" or lows).

Pressure differences are shown on weather maps by lines called "isobars", which join places with the same pressure. Where the isobars are close together, there is a steep pressure gradient – that is, a sharp difference in pressure. Where they are far apart, there is a shallow pressure gradient – a gradual difference in pressure. The steeper the pressure gradient, the stronger the wind blows. When you see tightly packed isobars around a low pressure zone, you can be sure it will be very windy.

EXPERIMENT
Coriolis effect

Winds do not blow in a straight line from high to low pressure zones; they are deflected by the effect of the Earth's rotation – to the right in the northern hemisphere and the left in the southern hemisphere. This is called the "Coriolis effect" after the French physics professor Gustave-Gaspard Coriolis (1792–1843), who first realized how it worked in 1835. This experiment uses a ball to mimic the effect on the Earth of this important force, which also deflects ocean currents, controls the rotation of hurricanes and typhoons, and affects the flights of aircraft and space vehicles.

YOU WILL NEED
● *ball* ● *thread*
● *deep dish* ● *ruler*
● *matchstick* ● *food colouring* ● *dropper*

EXPERIMENT
Cold to warm

Put simply, winds blow because air is squeezed out by sinking cold air masses, and sucked in beneath rising warm air masses. So winds blow, at ground level, from cold places to warm places. Higher up, however, there is a current of air returning from warm to cold. This circulation is demonstrated here with warm and cold water.

YOU WILL NEED
● *2 plastic bottles* ● *tubing* ● *bowls*
● *plasticine* ● *clips* ● *food dye* ● *ice*
● *bradawl* ● *drill & block* ● *scissors*

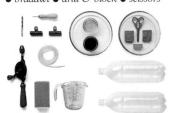

1 CUT THE TOPS off the bottles. Drill two holes top and bottom in the same places on each bottle.

2 CUT TWO EQUAL lengths of tube and insert the ends in the holes. Seal the joins with plasticine.

3 STAND ONE BOTTLE in hot water and one in ice, clip the tubes and pour different coloured water into each.

Circulation
Heat will create rising currents in the heated bottle and sinking currents in the iced bottle. When you unclip the tubes, water flows from the cold bottle through the lower tube and back through the upper tube.

Rising warmth creates a return circulation, with warm water passing to cold at high level

Winds act just like the water, flowing from cold to warm areas at low level

1 MAKE A SMALL HOLE in the ball and fill with water. Tie a matchstick to the thread and push through the hole.

2 SUSPEND THE BALL from the ruler and set it spinning smoothly. Then drop in a little food colouring at the "pole".

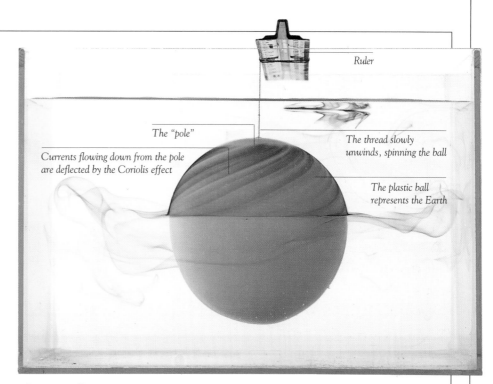

Ruler

The thread slowly unwinds, spinning the ball

The "pole"

Currents flowing down from the pole are deflected by the Coriolis effect

The plastic ball represents the Earth

Spinning off
The food colouring is deflected more and more to one side, just as winds blowing from the pole to the equator are. Winds blowing up from the equator are bent the other way.

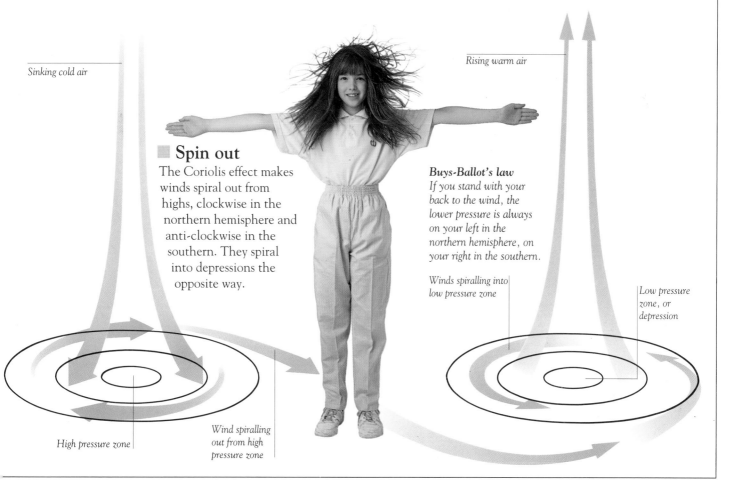

Sinking cold air

Rising warm air

▓ **Spin out**
The Coriolis effect makes winds spiral out from highs, clockwise in the northern hemisphere and anti-clockwise in the southern. They spiral into depressions the opposite way.

Buys-Ballot's law
If you stand with your back to the wind, the lower pressure is always on your left in the northern hemisphere, on your right in the southern.

Winds spiralling into low pressure zone

Low pressure zone, or depression

High pressure zone

Wind spiralling out from high pressure zone

Humidity

EVEN WHEN IT IS NOT RAINING the air is often very wet. This is because it contains invisible water vapour. When you dry wet clothes, the water does not simply vanish, it "evaporates" – that is, it turns into water vapour. It will "condense" – turn into water again – when the air becomes saturated. The amount of water vapour in the air at any one time is known as its "humidity". But the warmer the air is, the more moisture it can hold, so that meteorologists usually refer to "relative humidity" (r.h.), which is the amount of moisture in the air relative to the maximum it can hold at that temperature.

As air rises and cools, water vapour condenses to form clouds

Water droplets in clouds grow and fall to the ground as rain and snow

Water evaporates from the surface of seas and lakes

Water falling on the land runs back to the seas and lakes in rivers and under the ground

■ The water cycle

All the water on the Earth is constantly being recycled. Water is continually evaporating from the seas and lakes, which cover 70 per cent of the planet, to create water vapour in the air. As the air cools, the water vapour condenses into water droplets to form clouds. This water falls back to the Earth as rain and snow, where it runs underground and in rivers to the seas and lakes. At any one time, just 1 per cent of all the water is in the atmosphere; 97 per cent is in the oceans.

EXPERIMENT
Wet and dry bulb

Measure relative humidity with two thermometers, one kept dry, the other always wet. The smaller the difference in temperature between them, the closer is the air to its maximum moisture content.

YOU WILL NEED
- *pen & ruler*
- *two thermometers*
- *board* ● *balsa pieces* ● *muslin*
- *bottle top* ● *glue*

2 GLUE THE THERMOMETERS to balsa tabs on the board. Then glue the bottle top to the base and fill with water.

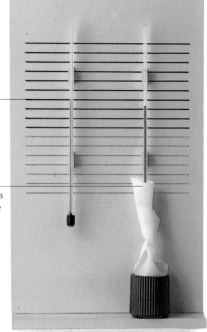

Lines drawn across the board make it easier to compare readings

Muslin absorbs water from the bottle top

1 DRAW LINES ACROSS THE BOARD, then glue it on to the base, using triangular balsa pieces to keep it upright.

3 WIND DAMP MUSLIN around the bulb of one thermometer, then down into the bottle top. Take readings once a day.

EXPERIMENT
Weather house

If the air is very humid, it is often a sign of wet weather to come; if it is dry, the weather will probably stay fine. This is why people have always used indicators of humidity to help predict the weather. Weather houses were once very popular as predictors. They work with a human hair, which stretches or shrinks as the humidity changes. When the air is moist, a hair in the house stretches and allows the wet-weather man to come out; when the air is dry, the hair shrinks, pulling the man in and letting the fair-weather woman come out. Provided you can find a long enough hair, you can make your own weather house very simply.

YOU WILL NEED
● *human hair*
● *card to make shapes below*
● *scissors* ● *screw-eye* ● *strips of balsa*
● *craft knife* ● *glue*
● *coloured pencils for cut-out figures*
● *tools for adult to cut baseboard*

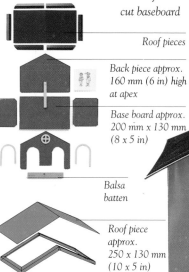

Roof pieces

Back piece approx. 160 mm (6 in) high at apex

Base board approx. 200 mm x 130 mm (8 x 5 in)

Balsa batten

Roof piece approx. 250 x 130 mm (10 x 5 in)

Balsa peg through hole to hold hair in place

Screw-eye

1 ASK AN ADULT TO CUT OUT the baseboard. Cut out the card walls, as shown below left, and glue them first to the baseboard, then to each other.

2 GLUE A STRIP OF BALSA between the front and back walls near the apex of the roof. Cut out and colour the card figures, then glue them to a balsa batten.

3 ATTACH THE SCREW-EYE to the balsa batten and tie on the hair. Thread the other end through a hole in the cross-bar above and fix with a balsa peg.

4 FOLD A RECTANGLE of card in the middle to make a sloping roof. Then make a frame from card strips (shown left) and fix the roof on the house.

Fair and foul
If you turn the screw-eye very slightly in or out of the batten, you can set your weather house so that the gloomy boy with the umbrella comes out in damp weather, and the smiling girl in beachwear comes out when it is dry.

Clouds

MANY CLOUDS HAVE SUCH DEFINITE SHAPES that they look almost solid. But they are nothing more than parcels of minute water droplets and ice crystals floating in the air. Clouds get their different shapes from the way they form, and from the balance of water droplets and ice crystals within them.

Clouds are formed by rising air. Because air gets cooler as it rises (p.158), it becomes less and less able to hold invisible water vapour. There comes a point – called the "dew point" – when the air becomes so cold that the water vapour "condenses" (pp.170–171) to form tiny, but visible, droplets of water, or even ice crystals.

Sometimes, air rises rapidly over just a small area to form puffy "cumulus" (heap) clouds, which rarely last for more than a few hours. At other times, air can rise slowly over a wide area to form vast, shapeless "stratus" (layered) clouds, which cover the entire sky and last for days. The darkest clouds contain the most water – either because they are very thick or very dense. The water simply blocks the Sun from view. That is why dark, grey clouds are most likely to bring rain.

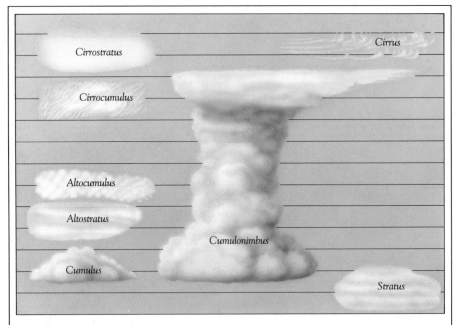

Cirrostratus

Cirrus

Cirrocumulus

Altocumulus

Altostratus

Cumulonimbus

Cumulus

Stratus

■ Types of cloud

Clouds are grouped according to their shape and the height at which they form. Clouds that form so high up that they are almost all ice are called "cirro-form" clouds, while those at medium height are called "alti-form". Clouds that form at all heights are either "strati-form" or "cumuli-form", according to their shape.

■ Condensation clouds

Take a very cold drinks can from the fridge into a warm room. It is soon covered in water drops, as water vapour from the air condenses on the cold can.

Hold a cold dish above a bowl of hot water; it is soon covered in water droplets. In the same way, rising warm air creates cloud droplets as it cools.

Breathe on a cold mirror and the invisible moisture in your breath will form a misty cloud of minute droplets.

EXPERIMENT
Cloud cover

The amount of sunshine reaching the ground depends on how much of the sky is covered by cloud. This is measured in "oktas", which is the number of eighths of the sky occupied by each type of cloud. So the sky may be three-eighths (3 oktas) covered by cirrus and two-eighths (2 oktas) by cumulus. You can estimate cloud cover by eye alone, but this grid makes it much easier, and helps make your estimates consistent.

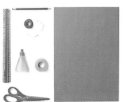

YOU WILL NEED
- card ● thread
- glue & tape ● ruler
& pencil ● scissors
- mirror

2 FOLD OVER ABOUT 1 CM (1/2 IN) of the diagonal edges of the side pieces to form flaps, and glue them to the edges of the frame as shown.

3 STRETCH THREADS OVER THE FRAME to form an even grid (the squares can be any size). Check that the threads are equally spaced, then secure with tape.

1 CUT OUT A RECTANGULAR FRAME from one sheet of A4 card, then cut diagonally across another two sheets to form two side pieces.

4 ESTIMATE THE CLOUD cover in each sector of the frame, either by holding it up to the sky or by laying it over a mirror set to reflect the sky clearly. Write down the cloud cover for each sector, add them all up, and divide by the number of sectors.

■ How a heap cloud forms

On warm days, the Sun heats up the ground in some places more than others. Bubbles of warm air form over these hot spots and rise through the cooler, denser air around them, rather like hot-air balloons. As each bubble rises into low pressure air, it expands and cools. A cloud forms when the air has risen and cooled so much that the water vapour it contains condenses into water droplets (p.171).

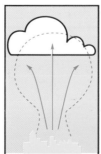

Cloud birth
These three diagrams show how a cumulus cloud forms when a bubble of warm air forms above a hot spot on the ground (far left), rises into the air and expands (middle left), and finally cools beyond its dew point (near left).

Frontal cloud
Clouds often form where warm, moist air slides up over a wedge of cold air along a front (pp.174–175). The base of this cloud shows the boundary between the warm air and the cold air.

Sky colours

HAVE YOU EVER WONDERED why clear skies are sometimes deep blue and at other times almost white? Or why some sunsets are fiery red and others watery yellow? The reason is that the mixture of particles in the atmosphere is constantly changing. Every colour in the sky comes from the Sun. Sunlight is white, which means it is a mix of every colour in the rainbow. But as it passes through the atmosphere, gases, dust, ice crystals, and water droplets split it into the various colours, bouncing some towards our eyes and absorbing others. The colours we see depend on which colours are reflected and which are absorbed. Clear skies are blue because gases in the air reflect mostly blue light from the Sun. The sky gets paler when extra dust or moisture reflects other colours, diluting the blue. Sunsets are yellow (or red, if the air is dusty) because the Sun's rays have to travel so far through the lower atmosphere that all but yellow light is absorbed.

Circular rainbows
From the ground, a rainbow forms only part of a circle. But from an aeroplane, you can sometimes see rainbows forming a complete circle on the tops of the clouds below you.

■ Rainbow colours

Rainbows are simply the reflection of the Sun in raindrops – which is why they appear after sudden showers, and why they are always seen opposite the Sun. The colours come from the way the raindrops split sunlight into a "spectrum" (a complete range) of colours, in the same way as a prism does. Since the sunlight catches each raindrop at a different angle, we see a different part of the spectrum reflected from each drop. The colours always appear in the same order: red, orange, yellow, green, blue, indigo, and violet.

Colour drops
When we see a rainbow, we see different parts of the spectrum reflected by each of the millions of raindrops in the sky.

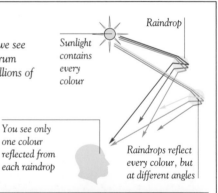

Raindrop

Sunlight contains every colour

You see only one colour reflected from each raindrop

Raindrops reflect every colour, but at different angles

EXPERIMENT
Red and blue skies

It is not always easy to believe that all the colours in the sky come from the different way particles in the atmosphere reflect and absorb sunlight. But you can demonstrate it for yourself with this very simple experiment. The effects are quite subtle, and not always easy to see, so you need to conduct the experiment in a very dark room. Fill a straight glass with cold water, then add half a teaspoonful of milk. Now try shining the torch at the glass from different angles and watch how the colour of the milky water changes very slightly. Hold the torch close to the glass for a better effect. Add another half-teaspoonful of milk and repeat. Finally, add a full teaspoonful of milk, and try shining the torch at the glass from a variety of different angles.

YOU WILL NEED
- *straight glass*
- *torch* ● *milk (or powdered chalk)*
- *teaspoon*

■ Red sunsets
Old weather lore says that red sunsets indicate good weather to come, and there is some truth in this. The reddest sunsets occur when the air is heavy with water drops or dust – which is often the case towards sunset in calm, high-pressure weather (p.156), before a misty night. High-pressure weather tends to be stable and fine.

Start with just half a teaspoonful of milk. Too much too soon will spoil the effect.

■ Bluest skies
Skies appear blue because of the way light from the Sun is reflected off the molecules of gas in the air. Dust, water droplets, and other particles dilute the intensity of the blue by reflecting other colours. So the bluest skies are seen when the air is at its purest. In Europe, for example, the bluest skies occur when bright sunshine is combined with a strong northerly wind, which sweeps the lower atmosphere clean and gets drier as it moves south into warmer air.

Blue sky
When you shine the torch at the side of the glass, you see only reflected light, giving a bluish tinge.

Yellow sun
If you look at the torch through the glass, it looks yellow, like the Sun during the day.

Pink sunset
When you add more milk, the glass becomes pinker, as other colours are absorbed.

WEATHER PATTERNS

Sᴛᴏʀᴍꜱ, ᴡɪɴᴅꜱ, ʀᴀɪɴ, ꜱɴᴏᴡ, ᴄᴀʟᴍ – all these are simply the air moving as it is stirred up by the heat of the Sun. You can see all the swirls and eddies clearly picked out by the clouds on a satellite picture (p.172). The swirling looks chaotic, but over the last 250 years meteorologists have gradually identified, within the chaos, distinct circulation patterns and weather systems, such as depressions and fronts (pp174–175), each bringing a particular kind of weather.

The angle of the Sun has a strong influence on the world's weather patterns. Winds tend to blow away from the cold polar regions, where the Sun is low in the sky, and towards the equator, where the Sun is always high in the sky.

Sailors knew a great deal about wind and weather patterns long before scientists began to understand what created them. They had to, because their lives depended on it. Sailors crossing the Atlantic, for example, soon discovered that to get to the Americas they had to sail south into the tropics to find the northeasterly winds that blew there. To find the westerly winds they needed to get home again, they would sail north, away from the tropics, before striking out across the ocean. We now know they were using two of the world's major systems: the trade winds that blow steadily in the tropics towards the equator from northeast and southeast, and the westerly winds that blow throughout the mid-latitudes.

■ Heat driven

Sailors exploited these winds for hundreds of years before scientists began to understand why they blew so regularly. The first hint of an explanation came from English astronomer Edmond Halley (1656–1742), who became fascinated by the trade winds while visiting the island of Saint Helena in the South

Benjamin Franklin proved lightning was electricity, and studied how storms move.

Atlantic. Halley suggested that the extra heat of the Sun at the equator made air rise, and that the trade winds were drawn in to replace it.

■ Why winds curve

This explained what drove the winds. But why did the winds blow at an angle to the equator – that is, northeast and southeast – and not straight towards it? Halley thought the rising air might be following the westerly movement of the Sun during the day. The true answer, as English meteorologist George Hadley (1685–1768) suggested in 1735, was that winds are affected by the spinning of the Earth. The Earth spins much faster at the equator than at the tropics, Hadley argued, so as air moves towards the equator it lags behind the Earth more and more. Since the Earth spins eastwards, winds blowing towards the equator swing off to the west.

In fact, as the French physicist Gaspard Coriolis (1792–1843) showed 100 years later, anything (wind or water) moving across a spinning surface follows a curved path – called the "Coriolis effect". This means that all winds (and ocean currents) in the northern hemisphere swing to the right, while those in the south swing to the left.

Hadley had another important idea. He

A tornado spirals like water down a plughole, but is not affected by the Earth's spinning (p.178)

suggested that the warm air rising over the equator moves towards the poles in the upper air, before cooling and sinking to the ground – then to be drawn back towards the equator. This circular movement of air was later called a "Hadley cell". We now know that Hadley cells do not extend as far as the poles, as Hadley had thought, but only just beyond the tropics (about 30° latitude). Here, upper air from the equator does sink to the Earth's surface and return to the equator – but not all of it. Some flows towards the poles and is swung to the east by the Coriolis effect, helping create the westerly winds of the mid-latitudes. A similar pattern occurs in the polar regions. Cold air sinks above the poles, pushing air outwards, and creating easterly winds as the air is swung round by the Coriolis effect.

■ Winds and storms

By 1850 most meteorologists knew of these three elements in the global wind circulation – the trade winds, the westerlies, and

In the 1920s it became theoretically possible to forecast weather by numbers (from numerous observations), but early devices like this took many hours to make the calculations.

In winter, frontal cyclones can bring blizzards, with winds howling at 110 kmh (70 mph) or more, and snowfalls over 60 cm (24 in).

the polar easterlies. But they still had only a vague idea about how the winds related to storms and changes in the weather.

People had known, almost since the invention of the barometer, that a drop in pressure indicated a coming storm. In the 1700s French physicist Jean de Borda (1733–1799) had noticed how changes in pressure were related to changes in wind speed and direction. In October 1743 American statesman and scientist Benjamin Franklin (1706–1790) was intrigued by a storm that seemed to move across Philadelphia from southwest to northeast – while at the same time the wind blew in the opposite direction.

■ Pressure zones

Slowly, meteorologists realized that storms are associated with moving zones of low pressure. In the 1830s American meteorologist William Redfield (1789–1857) suggested that in tropical storms winds circle around a calm centre of low pressure. Fellow American James Espy (1785–1860) argued that winds head straight for the eye of the storm, drawn by warm air rising like smoke up a chimney.

In fact, both men were partially right, because the winds spiral around the eye of the storm much as Redfield suggested, but they are drawn there by the rising warm air. Winds don't head

straight for the eye because they are deflected by the Coriolis effect – which is why winds blow around storms anticlockwise in the northern hemisphere and clockwise in the southern hemisphere.

Although they are different in size and intensity, storms or "cyclones" take this form in both the tropics and the mid-latitudes. But while tropical cyclones like hurricanes and typhoons all move westwards (like the trade winds), "extra-tropical" cyclones move northeast or southeast (like the westerlies). Only in recent years has the relationship between cyclones and the major wind patterns become clearer.

■ High-level winds

In fact, the westerlies are not part of global circulation in the way that trade winds are; they are

Experimenting with a saucepan, Carl-Gustaf Rossby showed how waves may be created by the spinning of the Earth affecting air moving from the poles to the equator (p.173).

simply the winds that blow around cyclones, and so are less reliable than trade winds. But there are strong, steady westerlies blowing at high altitude.

In the 1940s Swedish-American meteorologist Carl-Gustaf Rossby (1898–1957) found that huge meanders up to 2,000 km (1,243 miles) long, called "Rossby waves", often form in these high-level winds. Recent research suggests that as shorter Rossby waves migrate westwards, they draw cyclones with them,

steered by the longer waves. Rossby also found that in places within the waves there are narrow bands of specially strong wind called "jet streams", and that these may play a crucial role in generating storms.

None of this would have made sense, however, without the work of meteorologists in Bergen, Norway, after the First World War of 1914–1918, especially the work of Vilhelm Bjerknes (1862–1951). Scientists had assumed that the worst weather in a storm surrounded the low pressure centre. In fact, it follows two lines radiating in a V from the centre, bringing a very distinct sequence of weather (pp.174–175). As Bjerknes showed, these lines mark the boundary, or "front", between two masses of very different air – warm, moist air blown up from the tropics by the westerlies, and cold air blown in by the polar easterlies.

Indeed, the V of the fronts is simply a deep kink in the wavy boundary between warm tropical air and cold polar air that runs all the way around the globe, a boundary Bjerknes called the "polar front". The polar front is where, as Bjerknes put it, the tropical air and the polar air battle for supremacy – and this conflict is what generates storms.

Waves in the polar front correspond so closely with Rossby waves that meteorologists are convinced they are linked in some way. But the exact nature of the link is not yet fully understood.

In a tropical cyclone, such as a hurricane, winds spiral around the calm low pressure centre, or "eye", drawn in by the vigorously rising warm air.

Weather often changes with wind direction, as the influence of a particular air mass is blown in (p.168).

Wind

 THERE IS AN OLD SAYING that "every wind has its weather", and it is true. Some winds bring sunny weather. Others bring rain, snow, or mist. In the USA, for instance, winds from the north bring cold weather; winds from the west bring rain. In fact, wind direction tells you a great deal about what weather to expect, because different winds bring the influence of different air masses with them, each with its own characteristics. Air masses from above continents are dry; those above sea are moist. Tropical air masses are warm; polar air masses are cold.

■ DISCOVERY ■
Sir Francis Beaufort

The first system for comparing wind strength was the Beaufort Scale, devised by the English admiral Sir Francis Beaufort (1774–1857) in 1806, and still often used today. Beaufort realized that a simple way to judge wind strengths was to compare the way sailing ships must be rigged in different winds. His scale had thirteen wind strengths, with calm at Force 0 and hurricane at Force 12. The scale was later adapted for use on land, using indicators such as rising smoke, breaking trees, and falling chimneys.

EXPERIMENT
Wind station

Adult help is advised for this experiment

If you want to find out which winds bring different kinds of weather, why not make this wind station, and keep a record of the wind direction and the weather at a particular time every day? This design also includes a wind meter, or "anemometer", to tell you the wind's strength (speed in km or miles an hour).

YOU WILL NEED

● dowel ● 2 softwood strips 380 x 12 x 6 mm (15 x ¹/₂ x ¹/₄ in) ● plywood sheet 320 mm (13 in) square ● copper tube ● plastic bottle & top ● nuts, bolts & screws ● wire ● plastic card ● glue ● tools & instruments as shown ● paint

1 DRAW THE COCKEREL and the other shapes on a square of plywood, then clamp it firmly in a vice and get an adult to cut round the outlines with a fretsaw.

2 CUT SLOTS in the ends and middle of the two wood strips, join together, and glue in the arrow head, tail, and cockerel. Screw in the braces either side.

4 CLAMP THE COPPER TUBE in a vice and carefully drill a small hole through both sides. File the dowel ends to a point and fit in tube (see diagram opposite).

5 DRILL A HOLE in the bottle top, slot it over a length of dowel, and glue it half-way down. Screw the dowel into the braces and glue the wind meter in place.

■ Land and sea breezes

Land and sea breezes are the local winds that blow across tropical coasts every day. Sea breezes blow from sea to land during the day; land breezes blow from land to sea at night. Sea breezes blow because the Sun heats the land in the day, making air rise. This pushes air seawards higher up and draws cool air in from the sea lower down (the sea breeze). At night, the situation reverses: the sea stays warmer, creating land breezes.

Land breeze
By night, air circulates from sea to land high in the air, and from land to sea at ground level, creating a land breeze.

Sea breeze
By day, the circulation reverses and air blows from land to sea high in the air and back from sea to land at ground level, creating a sea breeze.

Jet stream
Straight bands of clouds in this satellite picture reveal the presence of a "jet stream", a narrow channel of very strong wind that blows high up in the atmosphere for thousands of kilometres.

Mounting the vane
Complete the assembly as below and set up in the open where there is no obstruction to the wind, about 1.3 m (4 ft) off the ground. A mark every 10° on the meter will show changes in wind speed in 30-kmh (19-mph) steps.

3 Cut slots in both ends of four short pieces of dowel, and glue the slots around the ring cut from plywood. Cut out the animal shapes and glue them in.

Animal winds
Why not use these animal shapes to indicate direction? Use a compass to find the points – polar bear for north, kangaroo for south, buffalo for west, and panda for east.

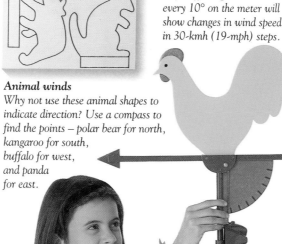

6 Make loops in either end of a piece of wire. Bend one loop 90° and bolt to the wind cup (base of plastic bottle). Bolt the other loop so it swings freely.

Rain

ASK ANYONE WHERE RAIN COMES FROM and they will say it comes from "clouds". Yet why do some clouds give rain and others not? Every cloud contains billions of water drops, ice particles, and crystals, which are so tiny they usually float on air. To fall as rain, they must grow at least a hundred times bigger, and this happens only when the air rises and cools so much that it releases more water by condensation (p.162). Air is forced to rise in three main ways: by convection (p.183) – that is, on warm updraughts of air; "cyclonically", as warm air is forced up by a wedge of cold air at a "front" (p.174); and "orographically", when air runs up against hills and mountains. The faster the air is forced to rise, the shorter and heavier the showers will be. The heaviest downpours come from cumulonimbus clouds; layered "stratus"-type clouds tend to give much longer, gentler showers.

Summer shower
In summertime, and in the tropics where it is sunny all year round, the hot morning sun often heats the surface of the ground, causing pockets of warm air to rise strongly. By mid-afternoon, the rising air can build up into large thunderclouds which may tower 10 km (6 miles) into the air. These then suddenly and dramatically unleash their store of water in a brief but intense downpour.

EXPERIMENT
Rain gauge

Weather stations have kept detailed rainfall records for centuries, but rainfall patterns can vary so much over even a small area that it is worth keeping your own records. You can make a rain gauge very simply with a plastic soft drinks bottle. To make sure that your records are in line with official measurements, mount your rain gauge so that the rim is 300 mm (12 in) above the ground. Every 500 cc of water you collect in the bottle is roughly equivalent to 1 cm ($^1/_2$ in) of rain. If you keep rainfall records over a long enough period, you may learn when to expect rainfall and when not to.

YOU WILL NEED
● *marker pen &*
ruler ● *scissors*
● *plastic shampoo*
bottle ● *plastic soft*
drinks bottle
● *measuring jug*

1 WITH A SHARP PAIR OF SCISSORS, cut the top off both the shampoo bottle and the plastic soft drinks bottle, taking care to get a straight edge.

2 FILL THE MEASURING JUG with exactly 100 cc of water, then pour this into the shampoo bottle. Mark the water level on the bottle with the marker pen.

3 NOW ADD ANOTHER 100 cc of water, and mark the level on the bottle. Repeat until you have a series of marks every 100 cc (2 mm/ $^1/_{10}$ in of rain).

4 EMPTY THE SHAMPOO BOTTLE and stand it inside the soft drinks bottle. Then invert the soft drinks bottle-top to funnel water into the shampoo bottle.

EXPERIMENT
Making raindrops

Cloud droplets only turn to raindrops when they are heavy enough to overcome air resistance. You can see how this happens on a much larger scale by spraying droplets of water on to a pane of glass or a mirror. The drops will not run down the glass until they have grown large enough to overcome surface tension.

YOU WILL NEED
● *water spray* ● *pane of glass or mirror*

Little drops
Spray a little water evenly over the entire surface of the glass. These first droplets are quite small and light, and surface tension – the attraction between the atoms of the glass and the atoms of water – is enough to stop them from running down the pane.

Running down
As you spray more and more water on to the pane, some drops will land close enough to others to join with them. Once enough drops have joined together, they will be heavy enough to overcome surface tension and run down the pane in rivulets.

▦ Annual rainfall

At the end of the year, you can plot monthly rainfall totals on a bar graph like this. Typically, the winter months are wettest and the summer months are driest. Can you spot any other patterns?

Rain forecasting
If you compare your rainfall records over a few years, you may be able to predict how much rain will fall in a particular month.

5 SET YOUR RAIN GAUGE outside, in a stable position 300 mm (12 in) above the ground surface. Check the level of water in the shampoo bottle each morning, and keep a record.

Collected rainwater

▦ Two types of rain

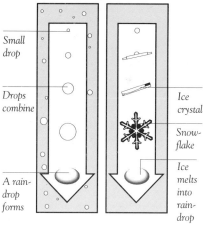

Small drop

Drops combine

A rain-drop forms

Ice crystal

Snow-flake

Ice melts into rain-drop

Raindrops grow in two main ways. In the tropics, most raindrops grow by "coalescence", which simply means that small drops bump into larger drops and join together (above left). Outside the tropics, raindrops usually grow by "aggregation" (above right), in which water vapour from the air condenses directly on ice crystals, so that they grow bigger and bigger. The crystals may then fall as snowflakes, or melt into rain as they fall.

Global weather

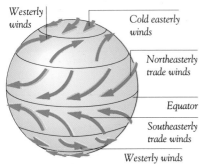

SOMETIMES IT IS HARD TO BELIEVE that there is is any order to the weather. Yet the world has a clear pattern of wind circulation, which sailors have known about for centuries. This pattern depends on the combined effect of the Earth's rotation and the way the Sun's heat is distributed. Because hot air rises at the equator (where the Sun is strongest) and sinks at the poles, there is a constant movement of ground-level air from the poles to the equator – from high to low pressure. This is balanced by a reverse movement high in the atmosphere. This general circulation is split into three zones, each with its own wind pattern: dry northeasterly and southeasterly trade winds (p.187) in the tropics; warm, moist westerlies in the mid-latitudes; and cold easterly winds in the polar regions.

Westerly winds
Cold easterly winds
Northeasterly trade winds
Equator
Southeasterly trade winds
Westerly winds

Twisted winds
Winds do not blow in a straight line between the poles and the equator, but are twisted at an angle (pp.158–159). So trade winds blow towards the equator from the northeast, not the north.

Circulating air masses
Polar cell
Polar front
Polar front, where warm air meets cold air
Pole
Mid-latitude cell
Tropics
Tropics
Hadley cell
Equator

Vertical pattern
The vertical circulation of air in each hemisphere is split into three "cells", mainly because the warm air blowing from above the equator cools and sinks to the ground near the tropics.

■ Swirling atmosphere

World circulation patterns are often clearly revealed in pictures of cloud patterns from space. Spiralling depressions of the westerly wind zone, in the mid-latitudes, are usually the most obvious. Often equally clear is a band of cloud above the equator, where hot air rises at the "Intertropical Convergence Zone", the meeting point of the trade winds blowing from the north and south.

Clear air over the tropics where the trade winds blow

South Atlantic

Spiralling depressions in the westerly wind zone

Equator

Thick cloud along the Intertropical Convergence Zone

Africa

Wind patterns

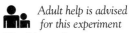
Adult help is advised for this experiment

World wind patterns are created by cold at the poles, heat at the equator, and the spinning of the Earth, as shown here.

YOU WILL NEED
● dish & beaker ● elastic ● wheels ● handle
● dowel ● wood blocks & base ● washers ● ice
● aluminium powder ● candles ● glue ● tools

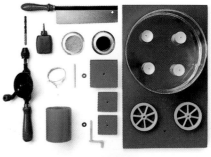

1 CUT TWO WOOD BLOCKS, drill a hole in the centre of each, and glue them to a baseboard in the positions shown.

2 MAKE A CRANKED HANDLE from dowel and balsa, glue it into the wheel, and fit to the block with a washer between.

3 GLUE A SIMILAR BLOCK to the centre of the underside of the dish and glue a wheel to the block.

5 LOOP THE ELASTIC around both wheels, stretch slightly taut, then carefully staple the ends together.

4 MAKE AN AXLE out of dowel for the dish-wheel, push into the base block, and slide the washer and wheel on to it.

6 SET A BEAKER OF ICE in the centre of the dish, light candles under the rim, and fill the dish with water and a spoonful of aluminium powder. Now wind the handle to get the dish turning smoothly.

The movement of the aluminium powder should mimic the patterns of the world's winds

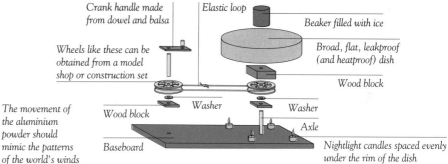

Crank handle made from dowel and balsa

Elastic loop

Beaker filled with ice

Wheels like these can be obtained from a model shop or construction set

Broad, flat, leakproof (and heatproof) dish

Wood block

Wood block

Washer

Washer

Axle

Baseboard

Nightlight candles spaced evenly under the rim of the dish

Winds and waves

In this experiment, the water is the world's atmosphere, the powder is the wind, the beaker of ice the pole, and the hot rim the equator. Turning the dish mimics the world's rotation. It is not a simple experiment to make work well – you may need to try it with more candles and more ice, or with a different material to show up the circulation patterns. Swedish scientist Carl-Gustaf Rossby used it to mimic both the wind circulation between the equator and the poles, and the appearance of a series of tongue-like "lobes" running around the pole, along the polar front (p.186). Called "Rossby" waves, they play a crucial role in the development of depressions.

Fronts and lows

WHEN IT RAINS FOR HOURS ON END, or your house is lashed by howling gales, you are probably beneath one of the vast spiralling weather systems called "depressions", which often appear in the mid-latitudes. These begin as tiny blips of low pressure along the polar front (p.186) and slowly grow as they sweep eastwards around the globe, bringing cool weather, cloudy skies, rain, and blustery winds. In every depression, a wedge of warm air extends right to the middle, like a slice of cake, and this is surrounded by a mass of cold air. The worst weather usually occurs along the "fronts", where warm air meets cold air. At the leading edge of the wedge of warm air is the "warm front", where warm air slides up over the cold air; at the trailing edge is the "cold front", where cold air pushes in underneath.

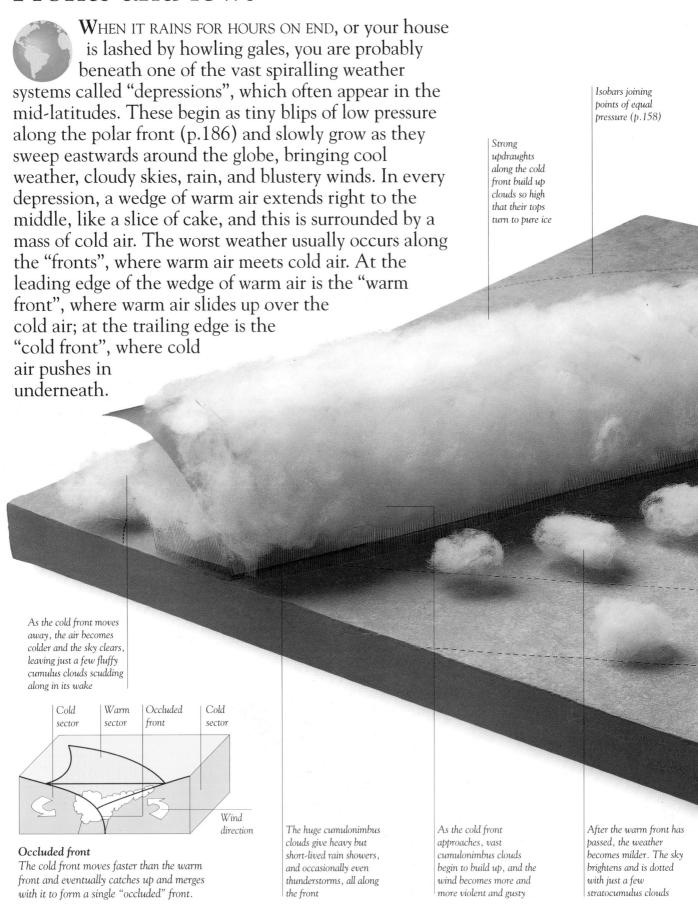

Isobars joining points of equal pressure (p.158)

Strong updraughts along the cold front build up clouds so high that their tops turn to pure ice

As the cold front moves away, the air becomes colder and the sky clears, leaving just a few fluffy cumulus clouds scudding along in its wake

Cold sector | Warm sector | Occluded front | Cold sector

Wind direction

Occluded front
The cold front moves faster than the warm front and eventually catches up and merges with it to form a single "occluded" front.

The huge cumulonimbus clouds give heavy but short-lived rain showers, and occasionally even thunderstorms, all along the front

As the cold front approaches, vast cumulonimbus clouds begin to build up, and the wind becomes more and more violent and gusty

After the warm front has passed, the weather becomes milder. The sky brightens and is dotted with just a few stratocumulus clouds

Model of a depression

This model shows the main features of a depression, including the warm front (pink) and the cold front (blue). The centre of the depression is where the two fronts meet – the warm sector lies in between. The whole system moves gradually from left to right, so if you were standing underneath it, the warm front would pass over you first, followed by the warm sector, then finally the cold front.

■ The life of a depression

Many depressions begin over the sea, where warm, moist tropical air collides with cold polar air along a line we call the polar front. The sequence begins when the tropical air bulges polewards over the polar air. The cold polar air slides in underneath the warm tropical air, and soon they begin to spiral around each other as cold chases warm and warm rides over cold.

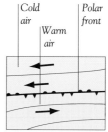

Polar front
A front forms as cold polar air meets tropical air from the south.

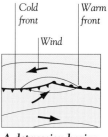

A depression begins
The depression starts with a bulge in the polar front.

Spiralling around
Warm and cold begin to spiral.

Occlusion
The cold front catches up with the warm and they merge.

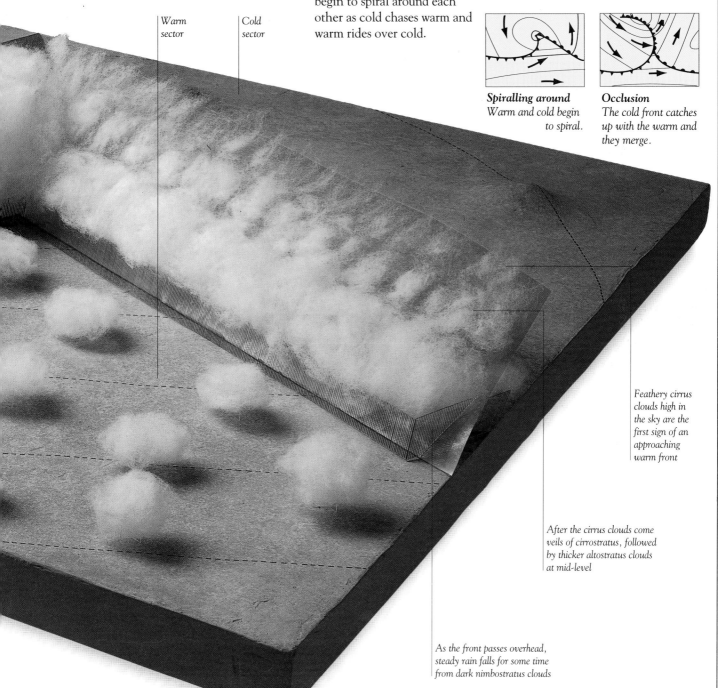

Warm sector

Cold sector

Feathery cirrus clouds high in the sky are the first sign of an approaching warm front

After the cirrus clouds come veils of cirrostratus, followed by thicker altostratus clouds at mid-level

As the front passes overhead, steady rain falls for some time from dark nimbostratus clouds

Thunder and lightning

THUNDERCLOUDS ARE HUGE and awesomely powerful. Very big thunderclouds tower 16 km (10 miles) or more into the air and contain enough energy to light a small town for a year. No wonder, then, that they can unleash such devastating storms.

It takes very strong updraughts of air to build such huge and powerful clouds, which is why they tend to form along "cold fronts" (p.174), or over ground heated by strong sunshine. Violent air currents sweep up and down inside the cloud, tearing the water droplets and ice crystals apart and then crashing them together again. These collisions load the cloud particles with a charge of static electricity – just as rubbing a balloon on a pullover does. Lightning is the sudden release of the charge built up on millions of particles within the thundercloud.

How lightning strikes
When cloud particles become electrically charged by bumping into each other, positively-charged particles collect at the top of the cloud, while negatively-charged particles stay at the bottom (upper right). Once a big difference in charge builds up, "sheet" lightning flashes between the two to cancel it out. Often, however, lightning discharges not within the cloud but towards the positively charged ground (lower right). This creates dramatic forks of lightning.

■ Storm sounds

Thunder is made by lightning as it scorches through the air. A flash of lightning heats the air along its path so dramatically that it expands at supersonic speed. This expansion causes a deafening crash of thunder.

You can create your own thunderstorm sounds very simply. To make thunder, try flapping a sheet of hardboard or thick card (right). The rapid movement of the sheet squeezes the air suddenly – just as the expanding air in the path of a lightning flash does – and the shock creates a crash of thunder.

You can create the sound of rain, too, by pouring dried peas on a metal tray (below left). This is a simple version of a method once used in theatres to make the sound of rain (below right), in which the peas are poured between zig-zagging metal plates inside a wooden tube.

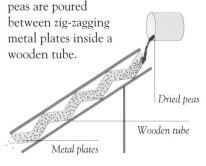

Dried peas

Wooden tube

Metal plates

EXPERIMENT
Making lightning

You can make a tiny and harmless lightning flash of your own with just a metal dish and a sheet of polythene. By rubbing the dish over the sheet, you create a static electrical charge – just like the particles that rub together inside a thundercloud. If you then hold a metal object close to the dish, the electrical charge you have built up will be released by a small spark, just like a miniature flash of lightning.

YOU WILL NEED
- metal dish ● plasticine ● metal tin lid
- polythene sheet ● scissors ● tape

1 TAPE THE SHEET OF POLYTHENE to a table or other flat surface with masking tape. Use fairly thick polythene if you have it, or fold it double.

2 STICK A LUMP OF PLASTICINE firmly in the middle of the dish as a handle. Then, touching only the plasticine, rub the dish round vigorously on the sheet.

3 AFTER A MINUTE'S RUBBING, the dish should have a strong charge. Create a spark by holding a metal object about 2–3 mm ($^1/_{10}$ in) from the dish.

Bright spark
The spark created as the static electricity discharges from the dish to the tin lid should be clearly visible in a darkened room.

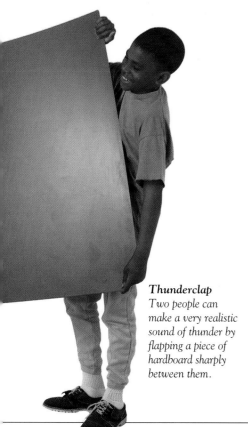

Thunderclap
Two people can make a very realistic sound of thunder by flapping a piece of hardboard sharply between them.

■ DISCOVERY ■
Benjamin Franklin

It was the brilliant American statesman and inventor Benjamin Franklin (1706–1790) who discovered the true nature of lightning. Franklin knew that scientists could create a spark of static electricity by rubbing glass and sulphur together. He wondered if lightning might be the same thing. To test his idea, he sent a kite up into the air during a thunderstorm, with a metal key attached to the kite string by a silk thread. Static electricity from the clouds flowed down the wet string through the silk to the key. When Franklin put his hand near the key, he felt a mild electric shock and saw small sparks – just like those created by static electricity generators. He had proved his point, but was lucky to be alive; many who tried to repeat the experiment afterwards were killed – and it is not an experiment you should ever try.

A few months later, in 1752, Franklin invented the lightning conductor, an iron rod mounted on the top of a building and wired to the ground. This protects buildings by discharging lightning harmlessly.

Hurricanes and whirlwinds

OVER WARM TROPICAL SEAS spiralling depressions (p.174) can turn into the most violent of all storms – the hurricane. Known as typhoons in the China Seas, and cyclones or "willy-willies" in Australia, they begin as small thunderstorms over sea. If the water is warm enough (over 24°C/ 75°F), several storms may then cluster together and whirl around as one. This new, larger storm spins over the ocean, drawing in warm, moist air and gaining energy as it goes. By the time it reaches the far side of the ocean, it is a massive spiral with huge clouds, driving rain, and devastating winds. At the centre is a tiny "eye" of calm, often 35 km (20 miles) wide.

■ Hurricane watch

The huge spiral of clouds that makes up a hurricane is very clear in this picture from an orbiting spacecraft – as is the tiny button-like eye in the centre. Pictures from space have made tracking hurricanes and predicting their paths much easier. Further vital information comes from special aircraft that fly through the storm again and again to take measurements from the eye.

EXPERIMENT
Making a vortex

 Adult help is advised for this experiment

The small-scale spinning of a whirlwind is what scientists call a vortex. Vortexes are not altogether understood, but you can see how they work quite clearly by watching the water running down the plughole of a bath, or by making your own vortex bottle as shown in this experiment. Contrary to popular belief, vortexes do not depend on the Coriolis force (p.158), so water does not run down the bath plughole in different directions in each of the world's hemispheres. Nor do whirlwinds spin in opposite directions in the two hemispheres (unlike hurricanes). As this experiment shows, the direction in which a vortex whirls depends on the direction of the initial movement.

YOU WILL NEED
● *2 soft drinks bottles*
● *saw* ● *car radiator hose* ● *potato* ● *food colouring* ● *knitting needle* ● *knife & cutting board*

1 CUT A SLICE FROM A POTATO, then use a bottle to cut out a disc of potato that will fit tightly into the bottle neck.

2 USING A NEEDLE OR A KNIFE, make a neat 7 mm (1/3 in) hole in the potato disc. Push the disc into the bottle neck.

3 SAW A LENGTH of radiator hose just over twice as long as the thread section of the soft drinks bottle.

4 PUSH THE HOSE over one bottle neck, half-fill the other with coloured water and push the hose on to the neck.

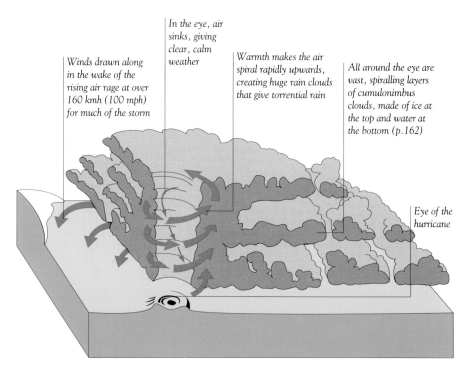

Winds drawn along in the wake of the rising air rage at over 160 kmh (100 mph) for much of the storm

In the eye, air sinks, giving clear, calm weather

Warmth makes the air spiral rapidly upwards, creating huge rain clouds that give torrential rain

All around the eye are vast, spiralling layers of cumulonimbus clouds, made of ice at the top and water at the bottom (p.162)

Eye of the hurricane

■ Anatomy of a hurricane

A typical hurricane is about 1,500 km (1,000 miles) across, and is built up of gigantic circular bands of cumulus and cumulonimbus clouds (pp.162–163) that spiral round the centre of the storm, known as the "eye". Within these bands of cloud, warmth makes the air rise very quickly. This rapid uplift of air builds up huge rainclouds that give torrential rain, and also draws in winds at hurricane speed, gusting up to 360 kmh (220 mph). Only in the tiny eye of the storm do the winds lose some of their force. Here the air is sinking and the sky may be clear. The lull in the storm while the eye passes over is short-lived, however, for the raging winds and pouring rain soon return and may continue for a further 18 hours or more before the hurricane has passed over completely.

5 INVERT THE BOTTLES. Hold the lower bottle in one hand, grip the necks in the other, and twist the bottles quickly. Try it a few times, then twist the other way.

Vortex

Coloured water

Rubber hose

■ Whirlwinds and tornadoes

Whirlwinds and tornadoes may be tiny compared with hurricanes, but they can wreak havoc. They are just 100 m (330 ft) or so across, and roar past in just a few minutes, but they can toss people, cars, and even buildings into the air. They seem to start deep within vast thunderclouds called supercells, where a column of rising warm air is set spinning by high winds roaring through the top of the cloud. As this spinning vortex becomes stronger, it projects down through the cloud base like an elephant's trunk, spinning violently and sucking up everything in its path.

Weather forecasting

To make an accurate weather forecast meteorologists need observations – millions of them from all around the world. Every minute of the day, weather stations, weather ships, satellites, balloons, and radar are making detailed recordings of temperature, pressure, wind direction, and so on, and feeding the data into the Global Telecommunications System (GTS). All this information is constantly fed into powerful supercomputers to build up a complete picture of atmospheric conditions. From this picture, the computers are able to generate forecasts for up to a week ahead.

Stormy weather
The cold front symbols on the weather map (blue lines with triangles) indicate stormy weather like this approaching.

■ Long-range forecasts

Modern forecasting techniques can predict the weather up to a week ahead with a fair degree of accuracy, but beyond that they are less reliable. What forecasters can do is predict the *type* of weather for the following week. They may know, for instance, that the wind always tends to bring in cold, dry continental air at that time of year, or that a "block" has developed, keeping out storm-bearing weather systems. For periods longer than a few weeks, forecasters can do little but search for weather patterns from the past.

■ Synoptic chart

Weather charts like these are usually drawn up by computer. They are called "synoptic", which means "seen together", because all the observations should be made at exactly the same time. In practice, some of the observations may be made at slightly different times.

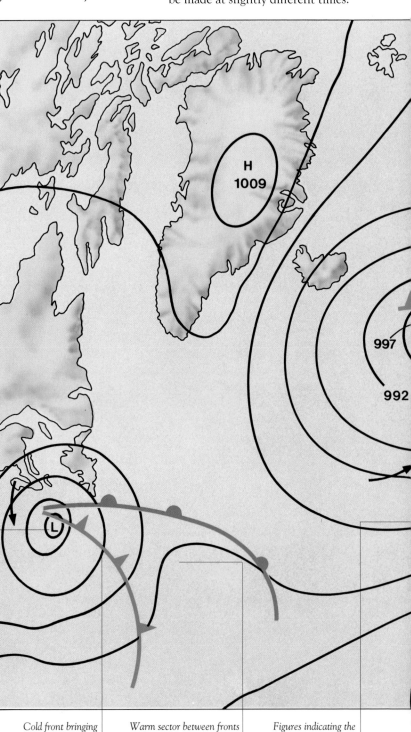

Depressions move steadily eastwards, from bottom left to top right

Cold front bringing stormy weather and heavy rain

Warm sector between fronts bringing milder weather and a break from the rain

Figures indicating the pressure in millibars for the isobar (p.157)

Strong winds spiral in towards the centre of the depression

In winter, highs often sit over large land masses, bringing cold, clear nights and heavy frosts

High pressure zone, or "anticyclone", giving fine weather with clear skies for days on end

Trough of low pressure

Ridge of high pressure

Isobars

Ridges and troughs
Pressure systems are what drive the world's weather machine, so the location of high and low pressure zones, ridges of high pressure, and troughs of low pressure is crucial.

H
1013

Isobars link points where the pressure is equal

These isobars will move steadily towards the top right corner, and pressure will drop, warning of stormy weather to come

Closer isobars bring stronger breezes. High cirrus clouds indicate a warm front is coming

Ridge of high pressure

Centre of depression or low, where pressure is at its lowest

Occluded front (p.174), where a cold front lifts a warm front off the ground

Warm front, bringing hours of steady rain

■ DISCOVERY ■
Lewis Richardson

Modern weather forecasting involves feeding numbers into computers and getting numbers out – which is why it is called "numerical" forecasting. The English meteorologist Lewis Richardson (1881–1953) first came up with the idea in 1922. He believed the best way to forecast weather was to take a wide range of observations simultaneously from evenly spaced points (grid points) throughout the world. From these, an accurate forecast could be made. Richardson tried to use this early calculator (right) to make the vast calculations involved, but it was really inadequate for that purpose. It is only the development of modern supercomputers that has made numerical forecasting a reality.

GLOSSARY

AA A Hawaiian word for type of runny basalt lava given a black, cindery look by gases bursting through cooling surface. *See also* Pahoehoe.

ABLATION The loss of glacial ice or snow cover by melting, evaporation, or the wind.

ABRASION The wearing away of the Earth's surface through the grinding action of sand and rock carried by streams, glaciers, wind, and waves.

ABYSSAL PLAIN A deep, flat ocean bed covered in ooze.

ACID RAIN Rain made acid enough to damage the environment by air pollution.

ADIABATIC Heating or cooling due entirely to expansion or contraction. The adiabatic lapse rate is the rate at which rising air expands and cools.

ADVECTION FOG A fog formed when warm, moist air flows over a cool surface.

AIR MASS A vast part of the atmosphere that is equally warm and dry, or cold and wet, throughout.

ALBEDO The proportion of the Sun's heat reflected by a surface. Fresh snow has an albedo of 85 per cent, meaning that it reflects 85 per cent of the Sun's heat.

ALLUVIAL FAN A fan of sand dropped by a river as it emerges from a mountain valley on to a flat plain.

ALLUVIUM Any material deposited by running water.

ALPINE GLACIER A moving stream of ice in a high mountain valley.

ALTO The prefix for medium-altitude clouds, such as altocumulus, altostratus.

ANABATIC WIND Warm air that blows up a valley as hill slopes are heated (*see p.184*).

ANEMOMETER A meter for measuring wind speed.

ANEROID BAROMETER A device showing air pressure on a dial.

ANGLE OF REST The greatest angle at which a slope of loose material is naturally stable and does not slide.

ANTICLINE An arched fold in layers of rock.

ANTICYCLONE Area of high atmospheric pressure, usually giving periods of fine weather.

AQUIFER Rock that absorbs water. It may be a source of water for wells or springs.

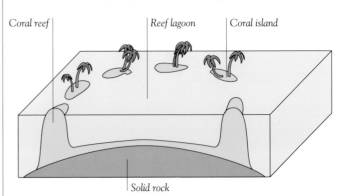

Coral reef   *Reef lagoon*   *Coral island*

Solid rock

ARÊTE A sharp ridge between two glaciers.

ARTESIAN WELL A well fed by groundwater that flows to the surface under its own pressure (*see below left*).

ASTHENOSPHERE The layer of the Earth's mantle directly under the lithosphere.

ATMOSPHERIC (AIR) PRESSURE The force with which the air presses on any surface. It is usually measured in millibars.

ATOLL A ring-shaped coral island surrounding a lagoon (*see above*).

AUREOLE A halo of metamorphic rock around an igneous intrusion.

AURORA Displays of coloured light above the Earth's poles.

BACK SLOPE The gentle slope on one side of a cuesta.

BAJADA A series of alluvial fans merging into a single slope in dry mountain areas.

BARCHAN A crescent-shaped sand dune that creeps along with the wind.

BAROMETER A device for measuring air pressure.

BASALT A fine-grained volcanic rock formed by the cooling of non-acidic lava that wells up through fissures in the Earth's crust wherever tectonic plates move apart.

BASE LEVEL The lowest level at which land can be eroded by running water.

Coral atoll
An atoll is a ring-shaped island made entirely of coral. They are thought to build up from rocky bases, in some cases volcanic islands that have slowly subsided.

BATHOLITH A huge domed igneous intrusion composed of granitic rock.

BEAUFORT SCALE The 13-point scale of wind strength devised by Admiral Beaufort in 1805.

BEDDING PLANE The flat boundary between two layers of sedimentary rocks, often marked by a crack.

BEDLOAD The heavier material that is rolled, dragged, or bounced along the bed of a stream.

BEDROCK Solid, unweathered rock beneath the soil.

BENIOFF ZONE Area where earthquakes are generated as one tectonic plate shudders down beneath another.

BERGSCHRUND A deep crack at the head of a glacier, created as the ice pulls away from the valley wall.

BLOCK MOUNTAIN An area of high land bounded by faults.

Artesian well
In an artesian well, water is pumped up from saturated underground strata under its own pressure. Pressure comes from the head of water – that is, water higher up in the same strata in nearby hills.

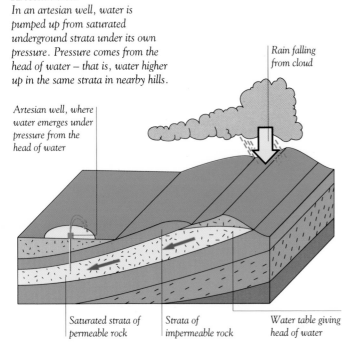

Artesian well, where water emerges under pressure from the head of water

Rain falling from cloud

Saturated strata of permeable rock   *Strata of impermeable rock*   *Water table giving head of water*

BOLSON An enclosed desert basin, often below sea level. Also called a playa.

BRAIDING The dividing of a stream into several branches.

BRECCIA Sedimentary rock containing a mixture of angular stones.

CALDERA A large circular basin created by a massive explosion destroying part of a volcanic cone or by the collapse of a volcano into its magma chamber.

CARBONIFEROUS A geological period that began 345 million years ago and lasted for 60 million years. Most coal deposits are the remnants of forests of this period.

CATASTROPHISM The theory that the world has been shaped by a series of major catastrophes rather than gradually by small-scale processes. *See also* Uniformitarianism.

CATCHMENT AREA The area from which a single river system receives its water.

CENOZOIC The most recent era in geological history, dating from 65 million years ago.

CINDER CONE A conical volcano made mostly of ash and other solid rock fragments rather than lava.

CIRQUE A deep bowl-shaped area gouged out by the head of an alpine glacier.

CIRRUS High, feathery clouds made entirely of ice crystals.

CLASTIC ROCK Sedimentary rock made from fragments of other rocks deposited in layers on the sea bed.

CLEAVAGE The tendency of rocks to break along a particular plane.

CLINOMETER A device to measure the angle at which a rock bed slopes.

CLINT Flat blocks of rock separated by grikes in limestone pavements.

CLOUD A mass of minute water droplets and ice crystals floating in the air.

COMPOSITE VOLCANO A type of volcano built up from alternating layers of ash and lava.

CONDENSATION The turning of invisible water vapour into water drops and ice.

CONGLOMERATE A type of sedimentary rock that contains rounded pebbles and boulders.

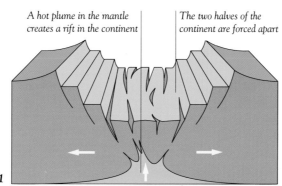

The rift widens and fills with water

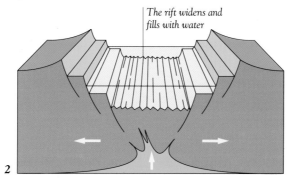

A hot plume in the mantle creates a rift in the continent

The two halves of the continent are forced apart

Continents splitting
Oceans can open up in the middle of a continent, when hot plumes in the Earth's mantle push up under the continental crust until it cracks (diagram 1 above). This crack grows into a wide "rift", which grows into an ever-widening ocean as hot currents in the mantle go on pushing up (diagram 2 above).

CONRAD DISCONTINUITY The boundary between an upper

granitic and a lower basaltic layer in the continental crust.

CONSTANT SLOPE The middle section of a hillslope, where mass movement is dominant.

CONTACT METAMORPHISM The process of rocks being remade through contact with the heat of an igneous intrusion.

CONTINENTAL CRUST That part of the Earth's crust beneath the continents and the continental shelf.

CONTINENTAL DRIFT The theory that the present continents came into being when a single massive continent broke into parts, which then drifted away.

CONTINENTAL SHELF The shallow underwater plain that borders continents.

CONTINENTAL SLOPE The steep undersea slope that extends from the continental shelf to the ocean floor.

CONTOUR A line on a map joining all points that are the same height above sea level.

CONVECTION The rising of hot air or a fluid because it is lighter than its cooler surroundings. In the atmosphere, convection is the driving force behind all winds, and creates clouds and rain. Convection in the Earth's mantle probably makes tectonic plates move and volcanoes erupt.

CORE The incredibly hot, metallic centre of the Earth, probably liquid on the outside and solid on the inside.

CORIOLIS EFFECT The deflection of winds and water by the spinning of the Earth, to the right in the northern hemisphere and to the left in the southern hemisphere.

CREEP The slow downward movement of soil on a slope.

CREVASSE A deep crack in the surface of a glacier.

CRUST Solid skin of the Earth, 5–50 km (3–32 miles) thick.

CUESTA A ridge created by the erosion of dipping layers of rock, with a steep scarp slope and a gentle back slope.

CUMULUS Fluffy low-level cloud created by convection.

CYCLE OF EROSION The idea that landscapes are worn down in stages – before being "rejuvenated" (uplifted) for the process to begin again.

CYCLONE *See* Depression.

DEFLATION Erosion of sand and soil by wind, hollowing out deserts and beaches.

DENDRITIC DRAINAGE Tree-like pattern of streams.

DENUDATION Gradual wearing down of the landscape.

DEPRESSION A weather system that moves eastwards through the mid-latitudes, bringing stormy weather along warm and cold fronts. Sometimes called a low or a cyclone.

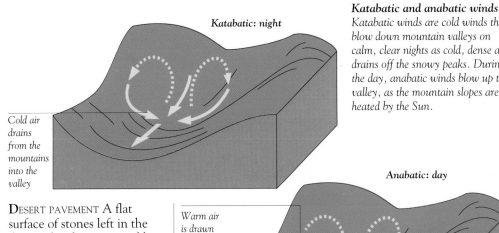

Katabatic: night

Cold air drains from the mountains into the valley

Anabatic: day

Warm air is drawn up the sides of the valley during the day

Katabatic and anabatic winds
Katabatic winds are cold winds that blow down mountain valleys on calm, clear nights as cold, dense air drains off the snowy peaks. During the day, anabatic winds blow up the valley, as the mountain slopes are heated by the Sun.

DESERT PAVEMENT A flat surface of stones left in the desert after finer material has been blown or washed away.

DEW POINT When air cools, it gets steadily nearer its limit for holding water vapour – the dew point. Below that point, the vapour condenses to water.

DIKE A sheet of igneous rock forced into fissures cutting across other layers of rock.

DIP The angle at which layers of rock are tilted.

DISCHARGE The flow of water in a stream, measured in cubic metres (or cu ft) per second.

DRIFT, GLACIAL All material deposited by an ice sheet.

DRIFT, OCEAN A slow current on the surface of oceans, usually driven by wind.

DRUMLIN An egg-shaped hummock of sand and gravel left by an ice sheet.

DRY VALLEY A valley on chalk or limestone in which there is no river or stream.

EARTHQUAKE A shaking and trembling of the ground caused by the sudden movement of rocks in the Earth's crust – and sometimes deeper than the crust.

ELUVIATION The washing out of fine mineral grains from upper layers of soil.

EON The Earth's history is divided by some geologists into three eons: Archaean, Proterozoic, and Phanerozoic.

EQUINOX The two days in the year – usually 21 March and 23 September – when the noon sun is overhead at the equator and when day and night are equally long all over the world.

ERG A region of mobile desert dunes, especially in the Sahara Desert.

EROSION The wearing down of the land surface by running water, waves, moving ice, wind, and weather.

ERRATIC A boulder that has been carried a long distance by a glacier, often into an area of different rock.

ESKER A winding ridge of coarse sand and gravel made by channels of melting water beneath an ice sheet.

EVAPOTRANSPIRATION The combined loss of water from the ground to the air by evaporation from soil and transpiration from plants.

EXHUMATION The uncovering of a geological feature, such as

a batholith, as the material around it is worn away.

EXTRUSION Magma thrust on to the Earth's surface by volcanic eruption.

FAULT The fracture and movement of rock strata.

FETCH The distance winds blow over open water to generate waves.

FIRN Snow compacted into ice by melting and refreezing.

FISSURE VOLCANO A volcano in which runny lava oozes out of a long crack in the Earth's crust, often creating vast basalt plateaux.

FOSSIL The ancient remains of an animal or plant preserved in rock.

FRONT The boundary between two air masses. At a "warm" front, warm air rides up over cold air; at a "cold" front, cold air cuts in under warm.

FROST WEDGING The splitting of rock as water freezes in a crack and expands.

GEOLOGICAL TIME Geologists divide Earth's history into

eons (longest), eras, periods, epochs, ages, and chrons (shortest). Eons typically last billions of years; epochs less than 20 million years.

GLACIATION The moulding of land by a glacier or ice sheet.

GONDWANALAND A super-continent that existed in the southern hemisphere over 200 million years ago. It included Antarctica, Australia, and parts of South America, Africa, and India.

GREENHOUSE EFFECT The way gases in the atmosphere keep the Earth warm by trapping heat from the Sun that would otherwise bounce back into space. Burning fuel is contributing to an increase in the level of these gases, which may cause global warming.

GRIKE A deep groove in a limestone pavement, formed by water dissolving rock along the joints (*see right*).

GROUNDWATER Water that has accumulated underground in the saturated zone.

GUTENBERG DISCONTINUITY The boundary between the mantle and the outer core of the Earth.

GUYOT A flat-topped undersea mountain – which may have been a volcano, with the top eroded by waves.

HADLEY CELL An important circulation of air in the tropics: rising at the equator, flowing polewards, sinking to Earth, and flowing back towards the equator as the trade winds.

HANGING VALLEY A side valley cut off by a glacier in the main valley, leaving it high above the main valley floor.

HOLOCENE The most recent geological epoch, beginning about 10,000 years ago.

HORIZON A distinct soil layer.